P9-CLR-072

THE ANIMAL BOOK

THE ANIMAL BOOK

A visual encyclopedia of life on Earth

DK LONDON
Senior Editor Daniel Mills
Senior Art Editor Vicky Short
US Senior Editor Rebecca Warren
US Editor Margaret Parrish
Jacket Designer Mark Cavanagh
Pre-production Producer Lucy Sims
Production Controller Alice Sykes
Managing Editor Paula Regan
Managing Art Editor Owen Peyton Jones
Publisher Sarah Larter
Art Director Phil Ormerod
Associate Publishing Director Liz Wheeler
Publishing Director Jonathan Metcalf

DK DELHI
Senior Editor Alka Ranjan
Senior Art Editor Mahua Sharma
Editors Susmita Dey, Neha Pande
Art Editors Sanjay Chauhan, Rakesh Khundongbam, Vaibhav Rastogi
Senior DTP Designer Harish Aggarwal
DTP Designer Arvind Kumar
Picture Researcher Ashwin Raju Adimari
Managing Editor Rohan Sinha
Deputy Managing Art Editor Sudakshina Basu
Pre-production Manager Balwant Singh
Production Manager Pankaj Sharma
Picture Research Manager Taiyaba Khatoon

This edition published in 2015
First American edition published in 2013
in the United States by
DK Publishing, 345 Hudson Street
New York, New York 10014

15 16 17 10 9 8 7 6 5 4 3 2 1
019—184809—Nov/15

Copyright © 2013, 2015 Dorling Kindersley Limited
A Penguin Random House Company
All rights reserved

Without limiting the rights under copyright reserved above, no part of this publication may be reproduced, stored in a retrieval system, or transmitted in any form or by any means, electronic, mechanical, photocopying, recording, or otherwise, without the prior written permission of both the copyright owner and the above publisher of this book.
Published in Great Britain by Dorling Kindersley Limited.

A catalog record for this book is available from the Library of Congress.

ISBN: 978-1-4654-5256-6

DK books are available at special discounts when purchased in bulk for sales promotions, premiums, fund-raising, or educational use. For details, contact: DK Publishing Special Markets, 345 Hudson Street, New York, New York 10014 or SpecialSales@dk.com.

Printed in China

A WORLD OF IDEAS:
SEE ALL THERE IS TO KNOW

www.dk.com

This trademark is owned by the Smithsonian Institution and is registered in the United States Patent and Trademark Office.

SMITHSONIAN

Established in 1846, the Smithsonian—the world's largest museum and research complex—includes 19 museums and galleries and the National Zoological Park. The total number of artifacts, works of art, and specimens in the Smithsonian's collection is estimated at 137 million, the bulk of which is contained in the National Museum of Natural History. The National Zoo has more than 4,000 animals in its living collection. The Smithsonian is a renowned research center, dedicated to public education, national service, and scholarship in the arts, sciences, and history.

AUTHOR

David Burnie is a fellow of the Zoological Society of London, and has written and contributed to more than 100 books on the natural world. He was consultant editor of DK's highly successful *Animal* and *The Natural History Book*, and is a former winner of the Aventis Prize for Science Books.

CONTENTS

Foreword   8

Tree of life   10

Microscopic life   12

Bacteria   14
Single-celled life   16
Zooplankton   18
Seaweeds   20

Fungi   22

Mushrooms   24
Sac fungi and lichens   26
Cup fungi   28

Plants   30

Liverworts and mosses   32
Ferns   34
Conifers   36
Flowering plants   38
Venus flytrap   42
Broad-leaved trees   44

Invertebrates   48

Sponges   50
Jellyfish, anemones,
   and corals   52
Pacific sea nettle   54
Worms   56
Mollusks   58
Giant clam   62
Squid, octopuses,
   and cuttlefish   64
Starfish, urchins, and
   sea cucumbers   66
Centipedes
   and millipedes   68
Spiders and relatives   70
Sea spider   74
Crustaceans   76

Nitrobacter

Hare's ear

Scots pine

Red cushion star

Insects 80

Dragonflies and
   damselflies   82

Stick insect   84

Crickets and grasshoppers   86

True bugs and treehoppers   88

Praying mantis   90

Beetles   92

Butterflies and moths   94

Slug moth caterpillar   98

Flies   100

Bees, wasps, and ants   102

Fishes 104

Sharks, rays, and skates   106

Whale shark   110

Saltwater fishes   112

Black-striped salema   118

Deep-sea fishes   120

Freshwater fishes   122

Amphibians 126

Frogs and toads   128

Tree frogs   134

Salamanders and newts   136

Reptiles 138

Turtles and tortoises   140

Lizards   144

Komodo dragon   148

Snakes   150

African bush viper   154

Crocodiles and alligators   156

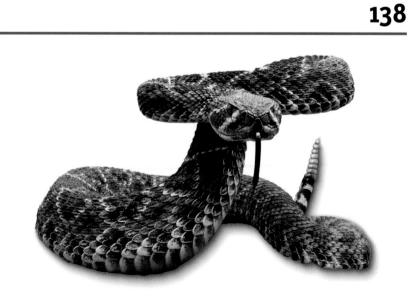

Birds

Ostriches and relatives 160
Game birds 162
Pigeons and doves 164
Parrots and cockatoos 166
Military macaw 168
Cuckoos and turacos 170
Owls 172
Barred owl 174
Hummingbirds and swifts 176
Kingfishers and relatives 178
Toucans and woodpeckers 180
Birds of prey 182

King vulture 186
Ducks, geese, and swans 188
Penguins 190
Emperor penguins 192
Storks, ibises, and herons 194
Pelicans and relatives 196
Flamingos 198
Cranes and relatives 200
Waders, gulls, and auks 202
Albatrosses 206
Perching birds 208
Red-backed shrike 214

Mammals

Mammals with pouches 218
Armadillos, sloths, and anteaters 222
Hedgehogs and moles 224
African elephants 226
Rabbits, hares, and pikas 228
Rodents 230
Bushbabies, lemurs, and tarsiers 234
Gibbons, apes, and humans 236
Orangutans 238
New World monkeys 240
Old World monkeys 242
Bats 244
Honduran white bats 248
Dogs, foxes, and relatives 250
Bears 252

Polar bear 254
Seals and walrus 256
Cats 258
Lions 262
Otters, raccoons, and weasels 264
Mongooses, civets, and genets 266
Meerkats 268
Rhinos and tapirs 270
Horses and relatives 272
Plains zebras 274

Cows, antelope, and sheep 276
Hippopotamuses 280
Pigs, peccaries, and deer 282
Camels, llamas, and giraffes 284
Giraffes 286
Dolphins and porpoises 288
Whales 290
Humpback whale 292

Index

Enterococcus faecalis

Fly agaric

Flame lily

Foreword

For thousands of years, humans have observed nature. Our ancestors watched animals eat plants to learn which were safe to eat. They studied animals to learn where they hid their nests and eggs. Millions of wildlife species benefited our predecessors in many ways and still do today!

A huge diversity, or variety, of species lives on our planet. Animals and plants come in many shapes, sizes, and colors that help them survive in different environments. You can learn more about wildlife diversity if you spend time outdoors in parks, nature centers, zoos, and your own backyard. Even cities are full of wildlife, in gardens, under bridges, in buildings, rivers, and streams.

Scientists organize living things into categories to help understand how they relate to each other.

Plants are in the Plant Kingdom. Animals are in the Animal Kingdom. Animals like humans and tigers have backbones and are called "vertebrates" (vertebrae are the bones in your back). Animals like butterflies have no bones, so are called "invertebrates." Vertebrates are divided into fishes, amphibians, reptiles, birds, and mammals. Mammals have hair, and mother mammals make milk for their young. Tigers are mammals in the cat family. All animals are sorted into unique types called "species." A tiger is a species of animal. You could easily identify a tiger by its large body and orange-and-black stripes, if it were next to a lion, a bobcat, or a house cat.

Around the world, wild animals of all types are kept as pets. Keeping these animals without knowing how to care for them is not right. For example, bad pet-keeping of pythons resulted

Porcupine fish

Cane toad

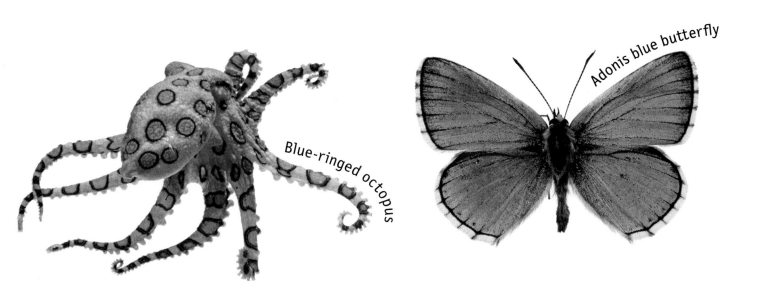

Blue-ringed octopus

Adonis blue butterfly

in these snakes eating native alligators and bobcats in the Everglades. In contrast, the animal care experts at the Smithsonian's National Zoo work to save endangered species. They have bred animals like golden lion tamarins and black-footed ferrets, and released them back into their natural habitats. This is an example of good animal keeping, science, and conservation.

Nature is in trouble. Wildlife conservation needs a next generation of conservationists. Every single person should care about the wonderful life on our planet. All of us, no matter where we live, can make some difference for our future. Wildlife needs us. Be curious. Explore. Have fun. You can help save nature!

Dr. Donald E. Moore III
Smithsonian's National Zoo

Throughout this book you will find scale boxes that show the sizes of living creatures compared to you.

Child = 57 in (145 cm) tall

Hand = 6 in (16 cm) long

Thumb = 1⅓ in (3.5 cm) long

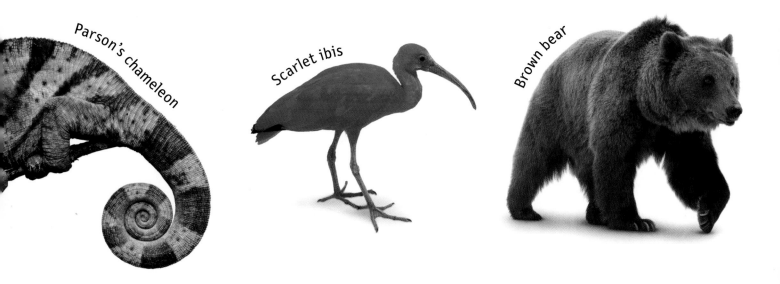

Parson's chameleon

Scarlet ibis

Brown bear

The Tree of Life

Our planet is inhabited by a huge variety of living things. Biologists figure out how different organisms are related by studying their DNA. This helps them to divide all life into kingdoms: animals, plants, fungi, and different types of microorganism. Within each kingdom are smaller groups, linking together similar kinds of creatures. Living beings that can breed together to produce fertile offspring are said to be of the same species. Most of the labels for the pictures in this book are species names.

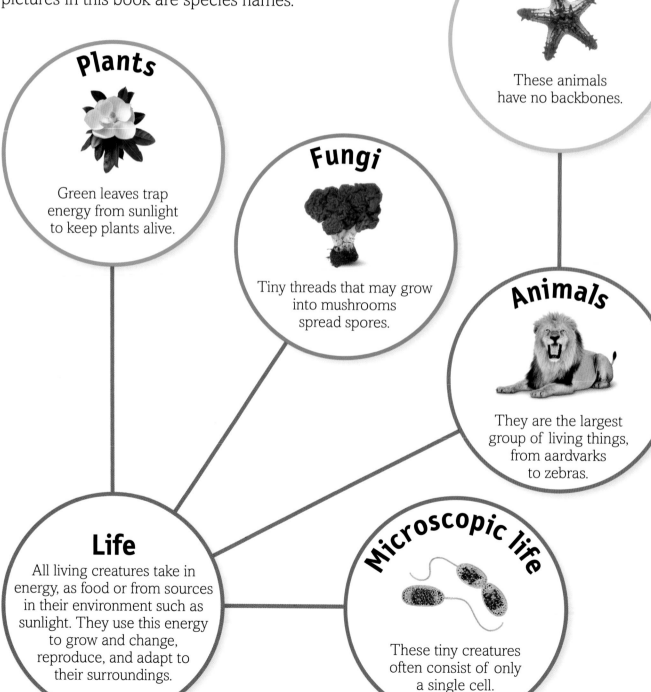

Invertebrates

These animals have no backbones.

Plants

Green leaves trap energy from sunlight to keep plants alive.

Fungi

Tiny threads that may grow into mushrooms spread spores.

Animals

They are the largest group of living things, from aardvarks to zebras.

Life

All living creatures take in energy, as food or from sources in their environment such as sunlight. They use this energy to grow and change, reproduce, and adapt to their surroundings.

Microscopic life

These tiny creatures often consist of only a single cell.

Insects

Insects are the most successful group of invertebrates.

Birds

Feathers make these vertebrates unique.

Mammals

These warm-blooded, furry vertebrates feed their young on milk.

Reptiles

These cold-blooded vertebrates have scaly skin.

Vertebrates

Animals with backbones are called vertebrates.

Amphibians

These vertebrates live partly in water and partly on land.

Fishes

Underwater vertebrates, fishes breathe through gills.

Microscopic life

Tiny micro-organisms were the first living things to evolve. They are too small to be seen with the naked eye: the smallest are less than a micrometer long, or one hundredth of the width of a human hair. Nevertheless, they are the most numerous creatures on Earth, and they play a vital role in supporting all other life-forms.

Giardia lamblia

Cytoplasm › The inside of the cell is made up of a liquid called cytoplasm. Miniature organs, or organelles, float in this liquid. Chemical processes take place in the cytoplasm to keep the organism alive.

Nucleus › This structure contains the cell's DNA, its genetic code. Microorganisms breed by splitting in half to create two clones, each with a copy of the same DNA.

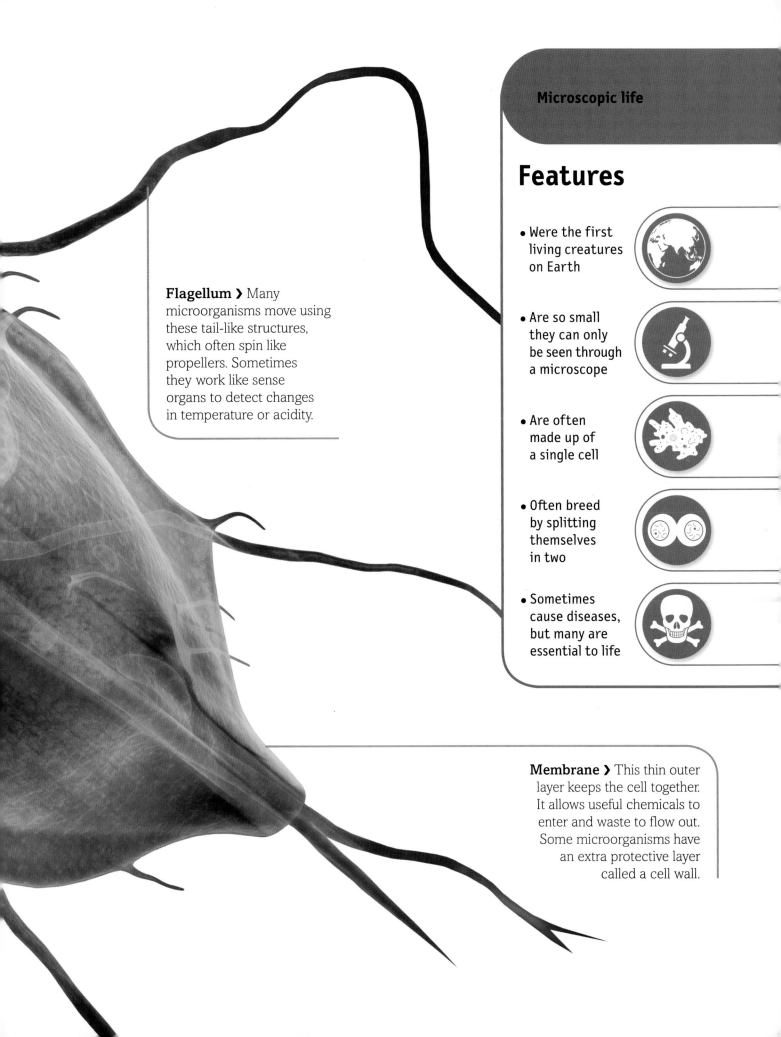

Flagellum > Many microorganisms move using these tail-like structures, which often spin like propellers. Sometimes they work like sense organs to detect changes in temperature or acidity.

Features

- Were the first living creatures on Earth

- Are so small they can only be seen through a microscope

- Are often made up of a single cell

- Often breed by splitting themselves in two

- Sometimes cause diseases, but many are essential to life

Membrane > This thin outer layer keeps the cell together. It allows useful chemicals to enter and waste to flow out. Some microorganisms have an extra protective layer called a cell wall.

Bacteria

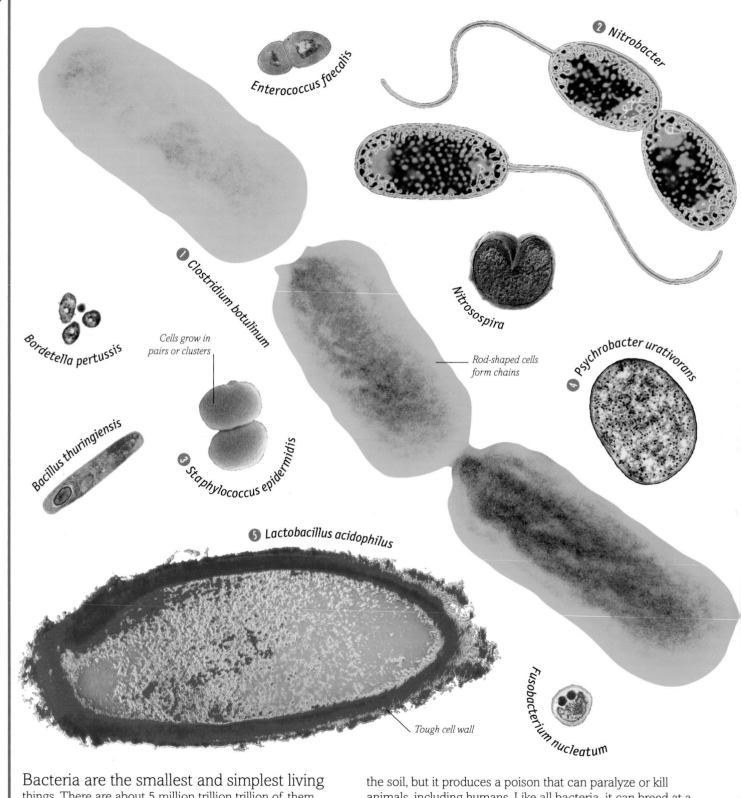

Enterococcus faecalis

2 Nitrobacter

1 Clostridium botulinum

Nitrosospira

Bordetella pertussis

Cells grow in
pairs or clusters

Rod-shaped cells
form chains

4 Psychrobacter urativorans

Bacillus thuringiensis

3 Staphylococcus epidermidis

5 Lactobacillus acidophilus

Tough cell wall

Fusobacterium nucleatum

Bacteria are the smallest and simplest living things. There are about 5 million trillion trillion of them on Earth, each made of a single cell. They live almost everywhere, from hot springs and seabed ooze to animal intestines and plant roots. Many are essential partners for other living things, but some can cause deadly diseases if they get out of control. ***Clostridium botulinum*** **1** normally lives in the soil, but it produces a poison that can paralyze or kill animals, including humans. Like all bacteria, it can breed at a phenomenal rate by repeatedly dividing in two. ***Nitrobacter*** **2** fertilizes soil and water, helping plants and animals to grow. It swims by spinning a long hair, or flagellum, and can move 50 times its own length in a single second. ***Staphylococcus epidermidis*** **3** lives on the surface of human skin. Normally

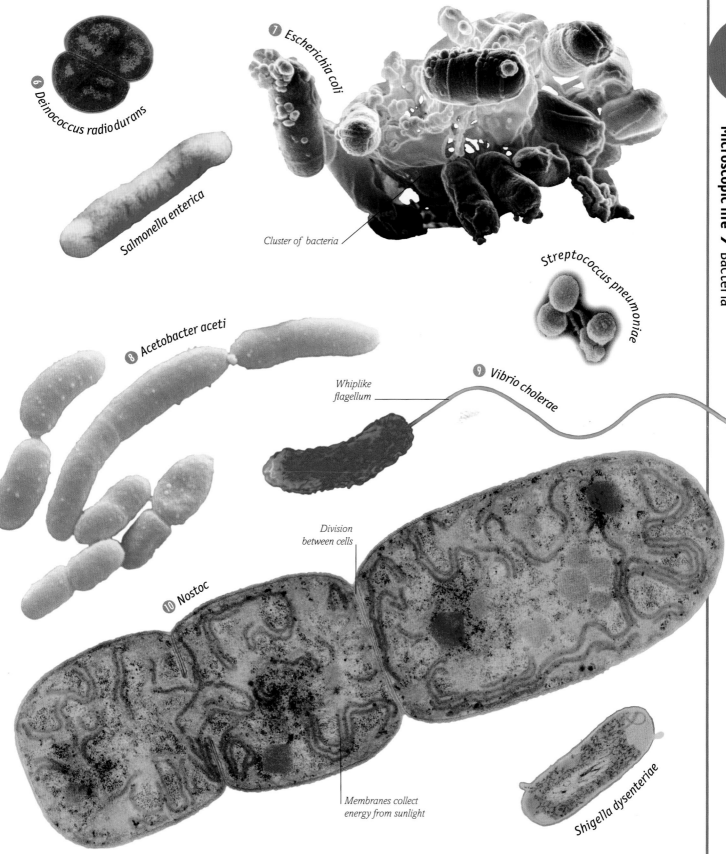

6 Deinococcus radiodurans

7 Escherichia coli

Salmonella enterica

Cluster of bacteria

Streptococcus pneumoniae

8 Acetobacter aceti

Whiplike flagellum

9 Vibrio cholerae

Division between cells

10 Nostoc

Membranes collect energy from sunlight

Shigella dysenteriae

it is harmless, but it can cause life-threatening infections if it gets inside the body. **Psychrobacter urativorans** ❹ contains its own antifreeze and can live in very cold conditions, while **Lactobacillus acidophilus** ❺ grows well in warm milk and is used for making yogurt. **Deinococcus radiodurans** ❻ is one of the world's toughest bacteria. It can survive intense cold, strong acids, and enough radiation to kill a human being 1,000 times over. **Escherichia coli** ❼ is one of the most common bacteria in human intestines. Normally it is harmless, but some strains produce food poisoning. **Acetobacter aceti** ❽ is used to make vinegar, but **Vibrio cholerae** ❾ causes cholera if it contaminates water or food. **Nostoc** ❿ grows in damp places. It forms long chains and lives by collecting the energy in sunlight, just like a plant.

15

Single-celled life

Arcella bathystoma

Jellylike body protected by shell

Green alga swallowed by the cell

② Protacanthamoeba

① Arcella discoides

③ Centropyxis

May have up to 12 short spines

Arcella gibbosa

Shell made of mineral particles

④ Micrasterias

The smallest living creatures on Earth are made up of a single cell. Bacteria are the most numerous, but another group, called protoctists, contains a bewildering variety of life. They are mostly bigger and more complicated than bacteria. Some protoctists are like animals, while others are more like tiny plants. A few are like both at the same time. **Arcella discoides ①** is a protoctist that lives in water,

inside a yellow-brown rounded shell. Its jellylike body reaches out through a hole, trapping any food that drifts by. **Protacanthamoeba ②** also has a shell. Like many single-celled creatures, it can reproduce by dividing in two. **Centropyxis ③** lives in lakes and marshes. Its shell is made up of tiny mineral particles stuck together with a special glue and has short, stubby spines. **Micrasterias ④** is a

16

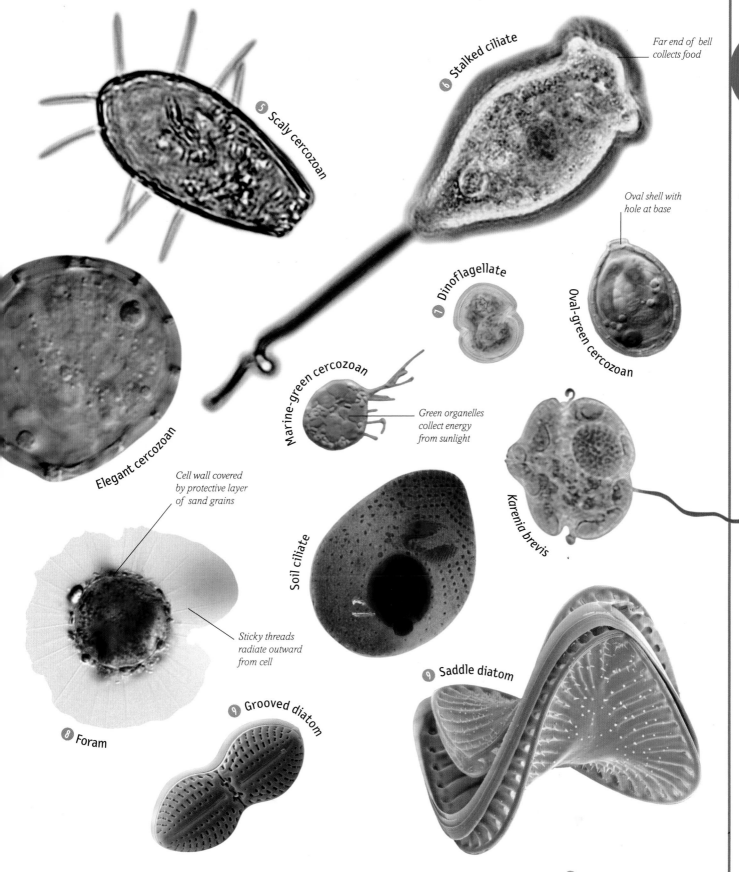

⑤ Scaly cercozoan

⑥ Stalked ciliate

Far end of bell collects food

Oval shell with hole at base

⑦ Dinoflagellate

Oval-green cercozoan

Marine-green cercozoan

Green organelles collect energy from sunlight

Elegant cercozoan

Karenia brevis

Cell wall covered by protective layer of sand grains

Soil ciliate

Sticky threads radiate outward from cell

⑨ Saddle diatom

⑨ Grooved diatom

⑧ Foram

green alga with a cell made of two matching halves. It lives like a plant by collecting the energy in sunlight, and its presence sometimes turns lakes and ponds bright green. **Scaly cercozoa** ⑤ have oval-shaped shells covered with flat silica plates, while the **stalked ciliate** ⑥ has an inverted bell-shaped body on a slender stalk. If its bell is touched, the stalk coils up like a spring, quickly pulling the body out

of harm's way. **Dinoflagellates** ⑦ live mainly in the sea, and many of them are poisonous. Sometimes they explode in numbers, causing "red tides" that kill millions of fish. **Forams** ⑧ have round cells with a starburst of sticky threads. **Diatoms** ⑨ have silica cells and use sunlight to grow. They are the most important part of plankton, the huge mass of life that drifts in freshwater and the oceans.

17

ZOOPLANKTON

Zooplankton are fragile creatures that drift or swim gently through the water. Many species, such as the ones in this picture, are so tiny that they can only be seen through a microscope. Some live as plankton all their lives, while others are the larvae of larger creatures such as fishes and crustaceans. Zooplankton are essential to life in the sea- and freshwater because so many other animals feed on them.

Size > Range from microscopically small up to several yards long. **Habitat >** Oceans, seas, lagoons, lakes, rivers, and other water bodies. **Distribution >** Worldwide **Diet >** Algae, smaller zooplankton, plant plankton, bacteria, and particles of debris. **Breeding >** Most produce eggs. Many tiny species live for only a few weeks. In some species, such as *Daphnia*, the females may release eggs every two to three days. **Predators >** A wide range of water-dwelling animals eat zooplankton, including fishes, crustaceans, mollusks, and corals. Larger kinds are food for seabirds and for animals such as seals, sharks, and whales. **Conservation status >** Vulnerable to warming of the oceans or increased exposure to ultraviolet light from the Sun.

Seaweeds

SCALE

Broad, flat frond

② Broad weed

③ Chondria dasyphylla

⑤ Sea oak

① Toothed wrack

Flat, leathery fronds

④ Irish moss

Air-filled pods or bladders

Seaweeds look like plants, but they are actually simple organisms called algae, with fronds that take in nutrients from seawater. Some are tiny, but the biggest are as tall as a five-story office block. Most seaweeds are firmly attached to rocks, and some are incredibly tough, taking a tremendous battering from the waves. **Toothed wrack ①** is an olive-brown seaweed from the North Atlantic

Ocean. It grows on rocks that are uncovered at low tide. Found in temperate areas, **broad weed ②** looks like a big red leaf. *Chondria dasyphylla* **③** lives along shores worldwide. Like most red seaweeds, it lives below the low-tide mark and sometimes grows on animal shells. **Irish moss ④** is another red seaweed, with flat, branching fronds. It contains a substance called carrageenan, which is used to

20

6 Sea lettuce

Thin, translucent fronds

7 Sea beech

Maerl

Brittle branch

8 Polysiphonia lanosa

Agardhiella subulata

9 Wireweed

Branching, featherlike fronds

10 Coral weed

thicken yogurt and ice cream. A large, dark-brown seaweed, **sea oak 5** has lots of feathery fronds. It often grows in rock pools and has air-filled pods that help it to float. **Sea lettuce 6** is a green seaweed that grows worldwide on mudflats and sheltered rocks. Its crumply fronds are sometimes collected and used as food. **Sea beech 7** has paper-thin red fronds, while *Polysiphonia lanosa* **8**

is a red seaweed shaped like mossy tufts. It grows on other seaweeds instead of on rocks. **Wireweed 9** is a fast-growing brown seaweed that originally comes from Japan. It has accidentally been spread to many other parts of the world. **Coral weed 10** has a crunchy feel. It grows in rock pools and is reinforced with minerals, making it harder for sea animals to eat.

21

Mushroom › Some fungi grow structures, such as mushrooms, above the ground. These develop to spread spores, which are tiny cells that float off and grow into new fungi.

Fungi

Fungi mostly exist as tangles of microscopic threads called hyphae. Some kinds grow into mushrooms to spread their spores. The threads spread into the organic matter on which they grow, breaking them down into food. By doing this, fungi recycle dead plants and animals, turning them into nutrients that other organisms can reuse.

Cap > The top of this mushroom spreads out to give as much area as possible for spores to grow. The red color warns hungry animals that it is poisonous.

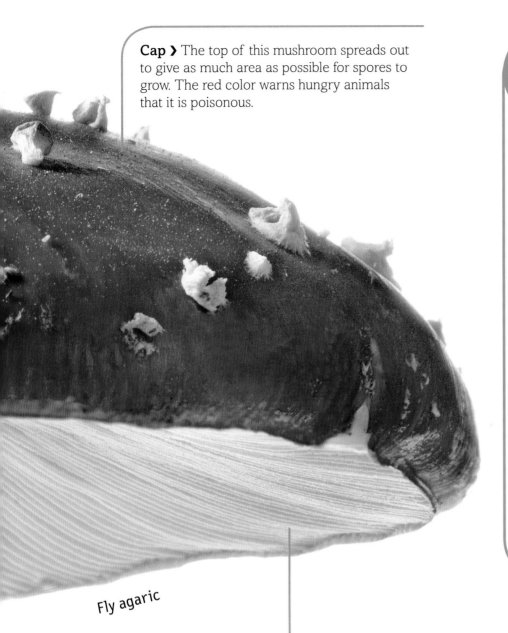

Fly agaric

Features

- Most grow as bundles of tiny threads

- Gain energy by breaking down other living things

- Scatter spores, which can grow into new fungi

- Grow structures such as mushrooms to spread spores

Gills > These thin, fragile membranes are where the spores develop. They fill the space under the cap so that they can produce as many spores as possible.

Stem > The stem of the mushroom connects it to the rest of the fungus, which is a network of fine threads buried underground.

Mushrooms

SCALE

Amethyst deceiver

Bright coloring fades with age

① Violet coral

Petticoat mottlegill

② Pink waxcap

Fleshy, waxy, pink gills

③ Red cage fungus

Cage bursts from "egg"

Lawyer's wig

Earpick fungus

④ Cultivated mushroom

⑤ Velvet bolete

⑥ Fluted bird's nest

Hairy, brown, fluted nests

Jack-o'-lantern

⑦ Sessile earthstar

Most mushrooms grow in damp places, from grassy fields to shady woodlands with lots of fallen leaves. Their purpose is to scatter tiny seedlike spores, so that fungi can spread. Some mushrooms have unusual colors that really stand out. **Violet coral** ① has brightly colored coral-like branches, while the **pink waxcap** ② has a rosy cap on a pale stalk. The unusual **red cage fungus** ③ has

a crimson meshlike structure that hatches from a small whitish "egg." The creamy white **cultivated mushroom** ④ is grown around the world for food. Most mushrooms, including the **velvet bolete** ⑤, make spores that are blown away in the wind. The **fluted bird's nest** ⑥ has a different way of spreading. It makes packets of spores inside tiny cups. If a raindrop lands in one of the cups, the packets

24

⑧ Chanterelle

Oak curtain crust

Silverleaf fungus

Foul-smelling spore mass on cap

Stubble rosegill

⑪ Stinkhorn

Warty scales

Hare's ear

Tall, orange cups

⑩ Fly agaric

Spores grow beneath cap

⑨ Death cap

⑫ Giant puffball

splash out, landing up to 3 ft (1 m) away. The **sessile earthstar** ❼ spreads its spores in a similar way, puffing them out of a papery sac when it is hit by raindrops. While some mushrooms, such as the **chanterelle** ❽, are good to eat, other types are deadly poisonous. The most dangerous of all mushrooms is the **death cap** ❾, since it is highly toxic and looks similar to edible kinds. Some fungi are difficult to mistake because of their size, color, shape, or smell. The poisonous **fly agaric** ❿ is easy to spot with its bright red-and-white cap. The odor of the smelly **stinkhorn** ⓫ carries for long distances. The smell attracts flies, which spread the stinkhorn's spores. The biggest mushroom of all is the **giant puffball** ⓬, which can measure more than 3 ft (1 m) across and weigh as much as 44 lb (20 kg).

25

Sac fungi and lichens

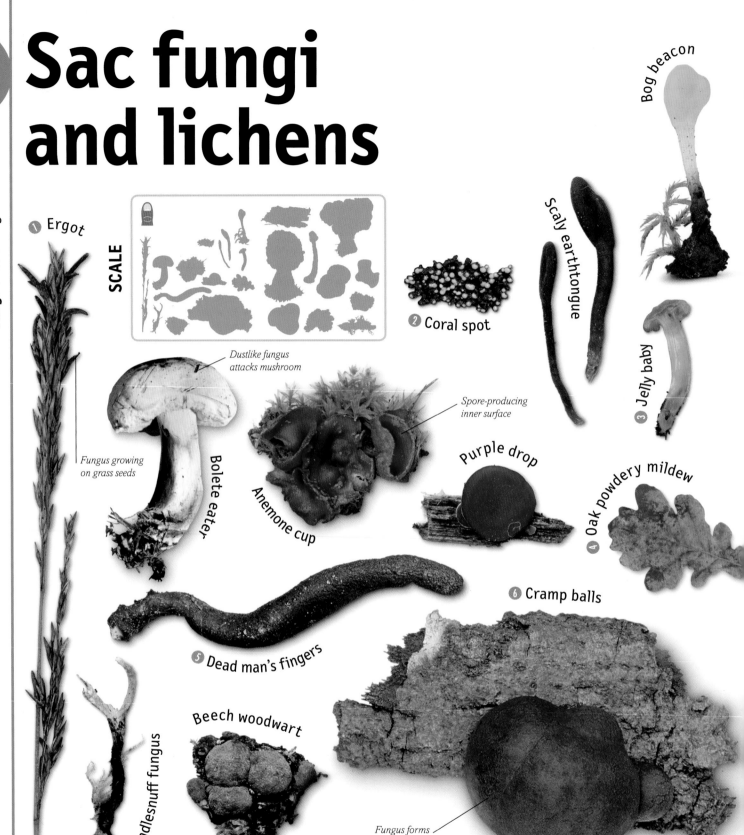

SCALE

① Ergot

② Coral spot

Bog beacon

Scaly earthtongue

③ Jelly baby

Dustlike fungus attacks mushroom

Spore-producing inner surface

Fungus growing on grass seeds

Bolete eater

Anemone cup

Purple drop

④ Oak powdery mildew

⑥ Cramp balls

⑤ Dead man's fingers

Candlesnuff fungus

Beech woodwart

Fungus forms hard balls

Sac fungi make their spores in tiny containers or sacs, which break open when they are ripe. The sacs are much too small to see, but the fungi that produce them have lots of strange and interesting shapes. Many live on dead wood or rotting plants, but **ergot** ① grows on grasses and cereals such as rye and wheat. It produces a powerful poison that can be deadly if it gets into bread. **Coral spot** ② attacks

damp wood, while the **jelly baby fungus** ③ grows in clumps among fallen leaves. Both are harmless, but **oak powdery mildews** ④ are a headache for farmers and gardeners because they attack all kinds of living plants. The first signs of trouble are white spots on the leaves, showing where the fungus is at work. **Dead man's fingers** ⑤ and **cramp balls** ⑥ both feed on dead wood. Unlike most fungi,

Common eyelash

⓻ Morel

False morel

Brown, wrinkly cap

Thimble morel

Honeycomb produces spores

⓼ Périgord truffle

⓽ Orange peel fungus

⓫ Hooded tube-lichen

Fat, blue-gray lobes

Cup faces upward

⓾ Common wall lichen

⓬ Oakmoss lichen

Cellar cup

they are hard to the touch. The **morel** ⓻ looks unappetizing with its spongelike cap, but is valued for its delicious taste. The **Périgord truffle** ⓼ is even more highly prized. It grows underground beneath oak trees and has to be sniffed out by specially trained pigs or dogs. **Orange peel fungus** ⓽ grows on bare ground and has a vivid orange color that makes it easy to spot. Lichens are living partnerships between fungi and algae or bacteria. They grow very slowly but can live to be hundreds of years old. The **common wall lichen** ⓾ is flat and brightly colored and grows on bare rock, particularly near the sea, while the **hooded tube-lichen** ⓫ is common on trees, rocks, and walls. **Oakmoss lichen** ⓬ lives on the bark of oak trees. It has a woody smell and is used for making perfumes.

27

CUP FUNGI
These strange bowls are actually a variety of cup fungus, a group of sac fungi that grow into eye-catching shapes. The cups produce sacs full of spores that are scattered around by wind and rain. In some varieties, these sacs absorb water and swell up until they burst, catapulting the spores out. The biggest cups make an audible pop when this happens, and the spores can sometimes be seen as a faint cloud.

Size ❯ Up to 12 in (30 cm) across **Habitat ❯** Moist, dead wood in tropical or subtropical forest. **Distribution ❯** Tropical and subtropical areas worldwide, from the US, Central and South America, and Africa to Southeast Asia. **Diet ❯** Dead and rotting wood. Like all fungi, they feed by breaking down organic matter in their environment. This can be useful for getting rid of dead plants and animals, but harmful where the fungus grows through living creatures. **Breeding ❯** The fungus consists of a network of threads that mostly grow underground. The cup develops only to spread spores, cells a bit like seeds that grow into new colonies of threads. **Number of species ❯** About 230.

Plants

Plants have the ability to trap energy from sunlight, using it to make food and to grow. By doing this they provide nourishment for themselves and for the animals that feed on them. Plants also absorb carbon dioxide from the atmosphere and release oxygen to replace it, maintaining the balance of gases animals need to survive.

Stargazer lily

Stem > Plant stems can be thin and fragile or thick and woody like tree trunks. They are filled with tiny tubes that carry water from the plant's roots up to the leaves and food from the leaves back down to the roots.

Pollen ❯ Flowers produce a fine dust called pollen, which is spread by wind or animals such as birds and insects. When pollen reaches other flowers of the same species it fertilizes them, causing them to develop seeds.

Flowers ❯ Many types of plant grow flowers to reproduce. They have colorful petals and interesting smells to attract animals, which spread pollen from flower to flower. Some plants offer visitors a meal of sugary nectar.

Features

- Collect energy from sunlight and use it to grow

- Have cells with walls made of microscopic fibers

- Commonly have flowers to produce and fertilize seeds

- Include the longest-living things

- Provide food and oxygen that supports much of life on Earth

Leaves ❯ The green coloring in leaves is a substance called chlorophyll. Plants use it to trap energy from sunlight by a process called photosynthesis. They use this energy to combine carbon dioxide from the air and water from the soil to form sugars, which the plants use as food.

Liverworts and mosses

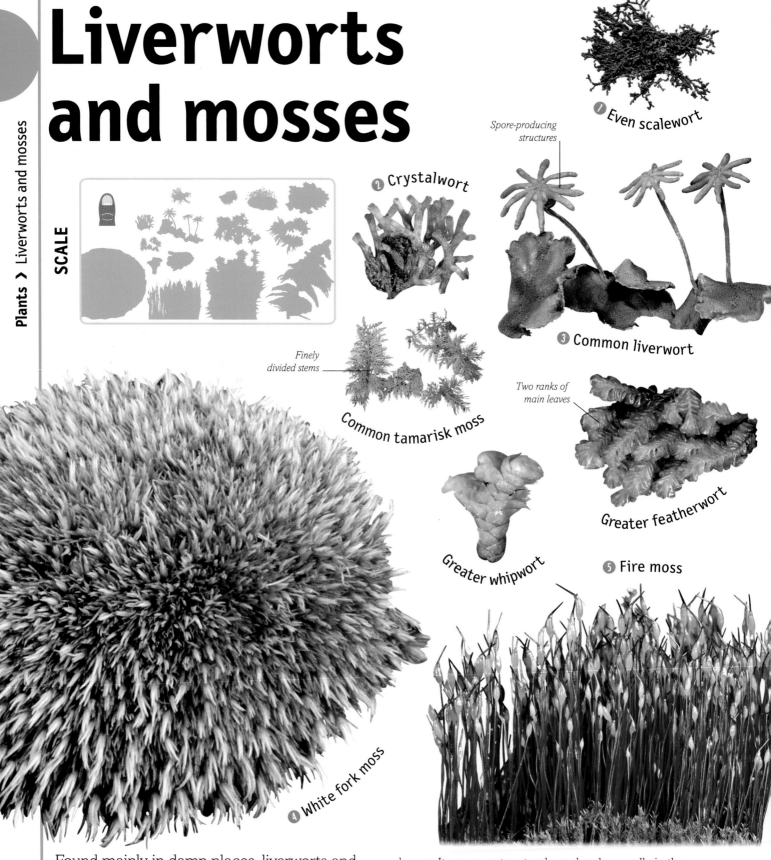

SCALE

Spore-producing structures

① Even scalewort

② Crystalwort

③ Common liverwort

Finely divided stems

Common tamarisk moss

Two ranks of main leaves

Greater featherwort

Greater whipwort

⑤ Fire moss

④ White fork moss

Found mainly in damp places, liverworts and mosses are the world's simplest plants. They don't have roots or flowers, and they spread by making microscopic spores instead of seeds. Some of them could easily sit on a fingernail and even the biggest are only waist-high. Liverworts are often shaped like flat ribbons and keep dividing in two as they grow. Most kinds are green, but **even scalewort** ① is often red or brown. It grows on tree trunks and rocks, usually in the shade. **Crystalwort** ② lives on wet mud or on the surface of ponds. It is sometimes used in aquariums for sheltering newly hatched fish. **Common liverwort** ③ is often seen in lawns and gardens. In the summer it is covered with growths like tiny palm trees, which make and then scatter its spores. Mosses have thin leaves and wiry stems and often grow in clumps.

Cypress-leaved plait moss

Cape thread-moss

Common pocket moss

⑥ Swan's-neck thyme moss

Rosette of small branches

⑦ Blue-leaved bog moss

⑨ Ostrich-plume feather moss

⑧ Common hair-cap moss

Narrow, pointed leaves

Many kinds, including the **white fork moss** ④, turn gray or white if they dry out but become green again within minutes if it rains. **Fire moss** ⑤ makes its spores in capsules shaped like matchsticks. It grows on walls and on burned ground. **Swan's-neck thyme moss** ⑥ is common in woods, while **blue-leaved bog moss** ⑦, or sphagnum, grows in waterlogged places. This moss can hold more than 20 times its own weight in water and slowly forms peat, a brown, soil-like material, when it dies. **Common hair-cap moss** ⑧ is one of the world's tallest mosses, growing in springy tussocks up to 24 in (60 cm) high. Its stems are stiff and unbranched, with narrow painted leaves. **Ostrich-plume feather moss** ⑨ gets its name from its stems, which look like tiny feathers or ferns. It lives in forests in the far north of Europe and Canada.

Ferns

SCALE

Silvery stripes give this fern its name

1 Whisk fern

Silver brake

Black maidenhair fern

2 Horsetail

Branches in rings

3 Ostrich fern

Ladder brake

Glossy, tongue-shaped fronds

4 Hart's-tongue fern

Long before the age of the dinosaurs, ferns and their relatives were the biggest plants on Earth. Today they still include some treelike varieties more than 50 ft (15 m) tall, but most ferns grow much closer to the ground. All these plants spread by making tiny spores instead of seeds, and most of them have feathery fronds that unroll as they grow. The **whisk fern** **1** is a primitive plant with brushlike stems.

It starts life underground, using fungi to help it get food from the soil. **Horsetails** **2** have hollow stems with rings of bright green branches. They contain sharp crystals of silica and were once used for scrubbing pots and pans. The **ostrich fern** **3**, found in the Northern Hemisphere, grows near streams and rivers, while the **hart's-tongue fern** **4** grows on shady banks and old walls. **Common staghorn ferns** **5**

Feathery fronds
absorb sunlight

5 Common
staghorn fern

Antler-shaped
fronds make spores

Toothed, pale
green leaflets

Sensitive fern

Umbrella fern

Fronds like
umbrella spokes

6 Hard fern

Tough,
evergreen fronds

7 Cliff brake

9 Bracken

Squirrel's foot fern

8 Royal fern

live in the forests of the Southern Hemisphere, where they grow on the trunks of trees. Their fronds trap rain and falling leaves, making private compost heaps that help them to grow. **Hard fern** **6** has two types of fronds: feathery ones that catch sunshine, and much narrower ones that spread its spores. Most ferns live in damp places, but **cliff brake** **7** grows in rocky crevices in South Africa and has wiry black

stems that are good at coping with drought. **Royal fern** **8** is an impressive plant with a rosette of spreading fronds. It is sometimes grown in gardens, but **bracken** **9** is a notorious weed. Fast-growing and poisonous to animals, it spreads by underground runners and can form patches more than 1,650 ft (500 m) across. It is found on every continent except Antarctica and on islands far out to sea.

35

Conifers

SCALE

Cedar of Lebanon

Needles grow in dense clusters

Western juniper

Grand fir

Caucasian fir

Needles grow in pairs

European yew

Cones turn red and soft when ripe

Monkey puzzle

❸ **Maritime pine**

Golden larch

Sharp, closely packed leaves

Conifers include the world's tallest, heaviest, and oldest trees. They do not grow flowers, and they make their seeds in cones. Most conifers are evergreen, with tough, waxy leaves that are good at coping with hot summer sunshine as well as freezing winter winds. The **cedar of Lebanon** ❶ comes from the Middle East and is often planted in parks. It has huge branches that spread out

like shelves, and short, needlelike leaves. Common in Europe and the Middle East, the **European yew** ❷ has tiny cones that look like bright red berries. They are poisonous to many animals, but birds feed on them, helping the trees to spread. The **maritime pine** ❸ grows wild in southern Europe. It is full of sticky resin that oozes out if its bark is cut. The **golden larch** ❹ comes from China. It sheds all its leaves

36

California nutmeg

Nutlike seeds

European silver fir

⑥

Monterey cypress

Colorado blue spruce

⑦ Giant sequoia

Round cones produce seeds

Slender, closely packed needles

Stone pine

⑧ Sitka spruce

Cylindrical cones with toothed scales

⑨ Scots pine

Cones open to scatter seeds

in the late fall and sprouts new ones in the spring. The **monkey puzzle** ❺ from South America has sharply pointed leaves and an umbrellalike shape when it is fully grown. The **European silver fir** ❻ has upright cones that disintegrate when they are ripe instead of falling to the ground. **Giant sequoias** ❼ from California are some of the largest living things on Earth. They can weigh more than 2,200 tons (2,000 metric tons) and their fireproof bark is up to 30 in (75 cm) thick. The **sitka spruce** ❽ comes from North America's west coast but is now grown all over the world as a lumber tree. The **Scots pine** ❾ is one of the world's toughest trees and the most widespread conifer. It grows all across Europe and Russia, including places where winter temperatures hit -76°F (-60°C), far colder than a deep freeze.

Flowering plants

① Gorse

Tubular flowers often pollinated by moths

Common jasmine

② Red clover

Flowers protected by thorns

Small flower clusters on long stalks

③ Lilac

Common asphodel

Flowers grow in rounded clusters

Hydrangea

④ Common lavender

⑤ Wild tulip

Flowers come in an incredible variety of shapes. Some are bigger than a large bucket, but the smallest could fit through the eye of a needle with room to spare. Many plants grow flowers to spread their pollen and to scatter their seeds. Like most flowering plants, **gorse** ① attracts insects, which carry its pollen as they wander from plant to plant. It grows its seeds in pods that suddenly snap open when the seeds are ripe. **Red clover** ② is often grown to feed farm animals and to help fertilize the soil. Found on scrubby hillsides in southeastern Europe, **lilac** ③ has strongly scented flowers. An evergreen shrub of dry Mediterranean scrub habitats, **common lavender** ④ is full of fragrant oils. **Wild tulips** ⑤ have yellow flowers that grow from bulbs. Widespread in Europe, they are close

Funnel-shaped flowers with many petals

⑥ Monk's hood cactus

African lily

① Wild carrot

Traps edged with interlocking teeth

Venus flytrap

Stem with eight vertical ribs

Cock's foot grass

⑧ Cock's foot grass

Wild daffodil

Field gladiolus

Wild pansy

⑨ Bee orchid

Spring gentian

SCALE

relatives of cultivated tulips, which are grown as garden flowers. The **monk's hood cactus** ⑥ is adapted for life in very dry conditions. It has spines instead of leaves and a juicy water-storing stem. Like most cacti, it has shallow roots that soak up water during rare periods of rain. **Wild carrot** ⑦ is the ancestor of the carrots that we eat. Grasses are flowering plants, but they use the wind to spread

their pollen, and their flowers are often small. They include wild plants, such as the **cock's foot grass** ⑧, as well as domestic cereals, such as wheat and rice, which are the world's most important foods. The **bee orchid** ⑨ is a little plant from a giant family. Its flowers mimic female insects, such as bumblebees, and spread pollen by attracting male insects looking for a chance to breed.

SCALE

Flowers open at dawn

Morning glory

⑩ Apothecary's rose

Fan of four to five flowers

Strawberry

⑪ Bird-of-paradise plant

⑫ Monkshood

Flowers in tall column

Meadow buttercup

Flowers grow on slender stems

Ring of spines beneath flowerhead

⑬ Milk thistle

⑭ Common poppy

Greater periwinkle

Many flowering plants are grown for their eye-catching blooms. There are more than 100 wild kinds of rose and thousands of cultivated varieties. The **apothecary's rose** ⑩ is one of the oldest. It has been grown in gardens for at least 750 years. The **bird-of-paradise plant** ⑪ from South Africa is also grown for its spectacular flowers. In the wild they are pollinated by

sunbirds, which carry pollen on their feet. Plants are also visited by hungry animals, so some use special defenses to survive. **Monkshood** ⑫ is protected by powerful poisons, while **milk thistle** ⑬ has sharp spines that keep hungry animals at bay. The **common poppy** ⑭ is a frequent weed in fields. Its seeds can survive in the soil for many years, and they start growing as soon as the ground is plowed. The

⑮ Common dandelion

⑯ Daisy

⑰ Foxglove

Top flowers open last

Water hawthorn

Round-headed leek

⑱ Sacred lotus

Royal bluebell

⑳ White water lily

⑲ Common water hyacinth

Gas-filled floats

Floating leaves

common dandelion ⑮ is even more widespread. Its seeds float away on feathery parachutes and take root on roadsides, in fields, and in lawns. The **daisy** ⑯ blooms for most of the year. Like the dandelion, its flowers are made up of lots of mini flowers, or florets, packed together in a single flowerhead. **Foxgloves** ⑰ have tubular flowers that are just the right shape for visiting bumblebees. Flowering

plants are also common in freshwater. The **sacred lotus** ⑱ grows in tropical lakes and has large flowers held above the water, while the **common water hyacinth** ⑲ has air-filled leaf-stalks that make it float. The **white water lily** ⑳ has floating flowers that close up in the late afternoon. They hold pollinating insects overnight and release them the next day.

41

VENUS FLYTRAP
A flesh-eating plant that catches prey in its "jaws" is the stuff of nightmares, but the Venus flytrap is only a threat to flies and spiders. The hinged leaves gape open like a big, red mouth, attracting prey with their bright color. If an insect or a spider lands on "trigger" hairs on the surface, the leaf snaps shut, trapping the prey inside. The plant then releases juices to digest its food.

Size > Up to 12 in (30 cm) tall **Habitat >** Wet, boggy areas of peat or sandy soil. **Distribution >** Coastal areas of North and South Carolina in the southeastern US. **Diet >** Like other plants, the Venus flytrap gets energy from sunlight. It evolved to be carnivorous because it often grows in poor soil and needs the extra nutrients that it can get from insects. **Breeding >** Bears clusters of white flowers from May to June. The small, black seeds may be dispersed in water or picked up by birds. **Life span >** Up to 30 years if cultivated. **Predators >** Slugs, birds, rodents, and tiny insects such as aphids and thrips, which suck the plant's juices. **Conservation status >** At risk due to habitat loss and overcollection for the exotic plant trade.

Broad-leaved trees

① **Common fig**

Fig contains hundreds of tiny flowers

② **Sugar maple**

⑤ **Mango tree**

Paper mulberry

Sandalwood

Yellowhorn

④ **Foxglove tree**

③ **Common ash**

⑥ **Cocoa tree**

Seeds have papery wings

Ribbed, oval fruit

Unlike conifers, broad-leaved trees are flowering plants. There are thousands of different kinds, from mighty giants in wild forests to small, ornamental garden trees. In warm parts of the world, most broad-leaved trees are evergreen. Where winters are cold, they often shed their leaves in the fall and grow a new set in spring. The **common fig** ① is a small broad-leaved tree with tiny flowers hidden inside a special bud. When seeds start to develop, the bud ripens into a fig. The **sugar maple** ② tree from North America is famous for its stunning fall colors. In spring its sweet sticky sap is harvested to make maple syrup. The European **common ash** ③ is a fast-growing tree with winged seeds, while the **foxglove tree** ④ has beautiful mauve flowers that appear before its leaves. **Mango trees** ⑤ come from

⑦ Ylang-ylang

⑧ Common walnut

White poplar

Leaves have white undersides

Bull bay

⑨ Common pear

Chilean fire bush

⑩ Holly

Berries on female trees

Black gum

⑪ Lemon tree

Strawberry tree

Tubular flame-colored flowers

SCALE

South Asia. Like many trees, they hide their seeds in sweet, fleshy fruits. Animals that eat the fruit spread the seeds to new areas. The **cocoa tree** ❻ originally comes from Central and South America. Cocoa is made from its seeds, which grow inside fleshy pods. **Ylang-ylang** ❼ from Southeast Asia has richly scented flowers that are used for making perfumes. **Common walnut** ❽ produces valuable lumber and nutritious nuts, while the **common pear** ❾ from Europe is the ancestor of pears grown to eat. **Holly** ❿ is a small evergreen tree with very prickly leaves. Holly trees are either male or female. In winter, female ones produce bright red berries, which are eaten by birds. **Lemon trees** ⓫ come from Asia. Their fruit contain lots of citric acid, a chemical that gives them their sharp but mouth-watering taste.

45

⑫ **Common laburnum**

⑬ **Quinine tree**

Flowers in hanging clusters

Flowers in catkins

Red alder

⑭ **Silver birch**

⑮ **Pink silk tree**

Leaves are divided into leaflets

Flowers have slender stamens

Broad-leaved trees produce many useful substances as well as some that can be harmful. **Common laburnum** ⑫ contains a deadly poison, while the **quinine tree** ⑬ contains a drug that can be used to treat malaria. It grows in South America, and quinine is extracted from its bark. **Silver birch** ⑭ is a hardy tree, living in very cold climates in northern Europe and Asia. Its flowers grow in catkins, which scatter tiny seeds in the wind. The **pink silk tree** ⑮ has large, feathery leaves and flowers in upright tufts. It is sometimes called the "sleep tree" because its leaves fold up at dusk and open again at dawn. The **Spanish chestnut** ⑯ is a slow-growing tree with edible nuts. These grow inside prickly cases and are often roasted instead of being eaten raw. The **Judas tree** ⑰ has rounded,

Turkish hazel

Flowers in upright catkins

⑲ Spanish chestnut

⑰ Judas tree

American beech

⑱ English oak

Acorns grow in cups

Crape myrtle

⑲ Pomegranate

⑳ Avocado tree

Bay laurel

SCALE

heart-shaped leaves and beautiful purple-pink flowers that appear in spring. These flowers grow in clusters and often sprout directly from the trunk. The **English oak** ⑱ is a long-lived tree with very hard lumber, which was once used to build sailing ships. Like other oaks, it has tiny flowers in trailing catkins, and its seeds are acorns, which grow in scale-covered cups. The **pomegranate** ⑲ is a spiny, shrubby

tree with large, bright-red flowers. It produces tasty fruit that contain hundreds of seeds. **Avocado trees** ⑳ originally come from Mexico and the West Indies, but they are now grown in warm places around the world. They have small creamy flowers and pear-shaped fruit with a single, very large pit. In the wild, avocados fall off the tree when they are still hard and ripen on the ground.

Invertebrates

The largest group of animal, invertebrates range from sponges and jellyfish to shellfish, crabs, spiders, and insects. They mostly hatch out from eggs. Some start life as larvae—tiny creatures which look very different from their parents. Others hatch as miniature versions of adults, growing bigger as they mature.

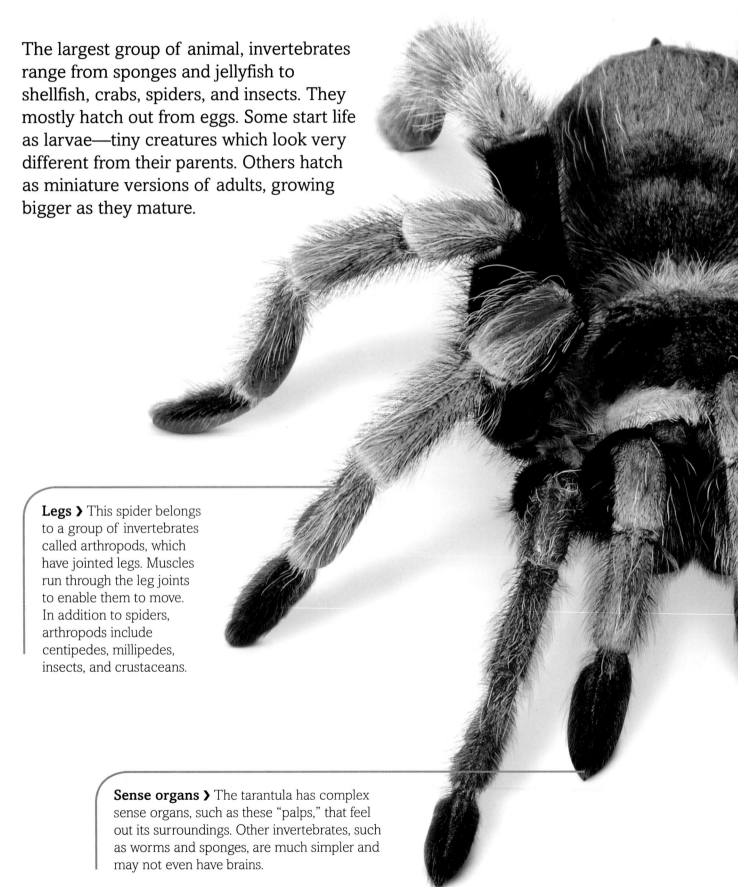

Legs ❯ This spider belongs to a group of invertebrates called arthropods, which have jointed legs. Muscles run through the leg joints to enable them to move. In addition to spiders, arthropods include centipedes, millipedes, insects, and crustaceans.

Sense organs ❯ The tarantula has complex sense organs, such as these "palps," that feel out its surroundings. Other invertebrates, such as worms and sponges, are much simpler and may not even have brains.

Features

- Do not have backbones or a bony skeleton

- Often have a hard outer coating (exoskeleton)

- Often hatch from eggs

- Often hatch as larvae, changing shape to become adults

Exoskeleton ❯ Many invertebrates have a hard outer casing called an exoskeleton. It supports their internal organs, helps them to move around, and provides protection. The exoskeleton does not stretch, so the creature has to shed its skin as it grows.

Mexican red-kneed tarantula

Spiny hairs ❯ Small animals such as invertebrates make tasty morsels for larger predators, so many have evolved defense systems. This tarantula can release stinging hairs from its legs that stick into its attacker's skin, causing pain and itching.

Sponges

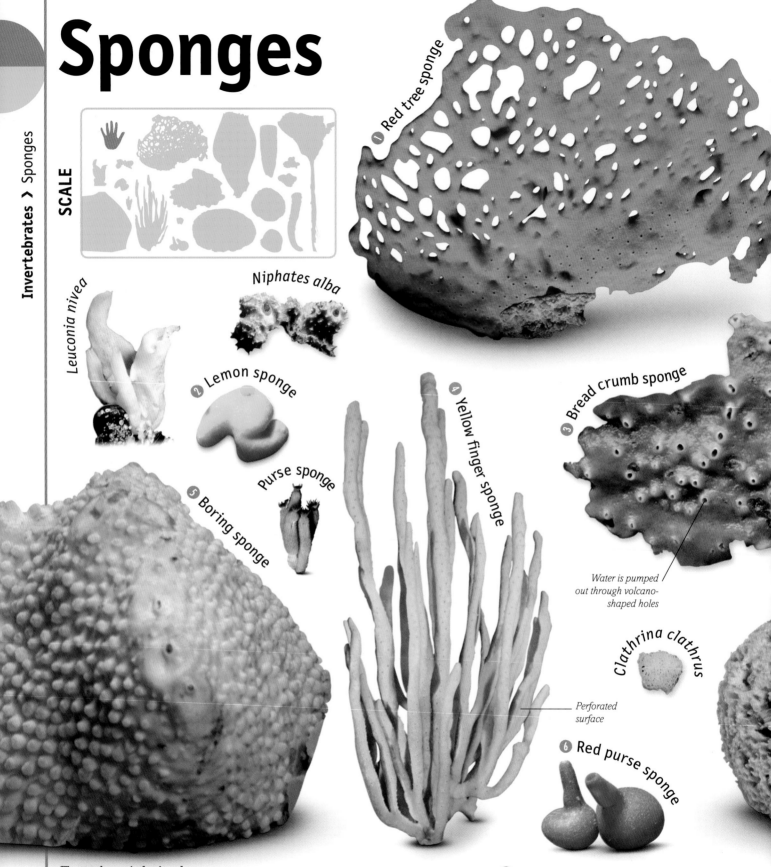

SCALE

Red tree sponge ①

Leuconia nivea

Niphates alba

② Lemon sponge

④ Yellow finger sponge

③ Bread crumb sponge

Purse sponge

⑤ Boring sponge

Water is pumped out through volcano-shaped holes

Clathrina clathrus

Perforated surface

⑥ Red purse sponge

Found mainly in the sea, sponges are some of the world's simplest animals. They don't have heads, tails, eyes, or even mouths. Instead of moving around, they pump water through pores in their bodies and filter out tiny particles of food. Sponges don't have bones, but their bodies are often reinforced by mineral crystals and fibers, which give them a crunchy or spongy feel. Some sponges, such as the

red tree sponge ①, grow upward like underwater plants. Others, such as the **lemon sponge** ②, are almost spherical, while some, such as the **bread crumb sponge** ③, grow as a crust on rocks. The **yellow finger sponge** ④ grows in upright columns, peppered with pores. The European **boring sponge** ⑤ uses acids to tunnel through shells and solid rock. Growing on shallow reefs in Malaysia and Indonesia, the

50

Ridged surface

❽ Pink vase sponge

Elk horn sponge

Long, thin stalk

⓫ Deep-sea glass sponge

❶ Azure vase sponge

Elephant hide sponge

❾ Mediterranean bath sponge

Orange puffball sponge

Golf ball sponge

❿ Venus's flower basket

red purse sponge ❻ resembles a miniature balloon. Water flows in through its sides and out through the narrow opening at the top. Vase sponges work in the same way, but are much larger. The **azure vase sponge ❼** and **pink vase sponge ❽**, both from the Caribbean, can be up to 1½ ft (45 cm) high, but the world's tallest vase sponges grow bigger than a refrigerator and are known to live for more than 100 years. The **Mediterranean bath sponge ❾** lives on the shallow seabed. Its extra-springy skeleton makes it perfect for washing with, once it has been cleaned. Most sponges grow near the surface of the sea, but **Venus's flower basket ❿** lives deep down. Like the **deep-sea glass sponge ⓫**, it has an intricate skeleton made of silica, which lasts long after the sponge has died.

Jellyfish, anemones, and corals

SCALE

Flexible stalks appear like underwater bushes

Blue jellyfish

1 White-spotted jellyfish

2 Sea wasp

Box-shaped body

Hula skirt siphonophore

Purple lace "coral" hydroid

3 Moon jellyfish

Upside-down jellyfish

Gas-filled float blown along by the wind

Sea strawberry

4 Portuguese man-of-war

Long, transparent tentacles

Kidney sea pen

Armed with stinging tentacles, jellyfish and their relatives catch and kill prey. All of them are soft-bodied, although many corals protect themselves by building hard cases or tubes. Most kinds, including the **white-spotted jellyfish 1**, have mild venom, but the deadly **sea wasp 2** from Australia and Southeast Asia can kill humans who brush against its tentacles. The poison acts within seconds, and stings continue to work even when the tentacles are pulled away. The **moon jellyfish 3** lives close to coasts all over the world. It is fairly compact, but the **Portuguese man-of-war 4** has tentacles up to 165 ft (50 m) long, almost the length of four buses. Its powerful venom makes it nearly as dangerous as the sea wasp. The **red coral 5** has a brightly colored skeleton, which is sometimes made into jewelry.

5 Red coral

Tentacles armed with stings

6 Magnificent sea anemone

Mushroom coral

Snakelocks anemone

7 Red sea whip

Common dead-man's fingers

8 Common sea fan

Common tube anemone

Parallel chalky tubes

9 Orange sea pen

10 Organ pipe coral

Carnation coral

Flat mesh of branches

Sea anemones have extra-thick tentacles, with stings that work like harpoons. The **magnificent sea anemone** **6** is one of the biggest, growing up to 3 ft (1 m) wide. It lives on coral reefs and its tentacles often shelter brightly colored clownfish, which are immune to its stings. The **red sea whip** **7** has thin stalks that bend in the current, while the **common sea fan** **8** has large flaps held at right angles to the current. This maximizes water flow toward the sea fan and allows it to get the most food. The **orange sea pen** **9** has two food-collecting lobes and a swollen "root" that anchors it in the seabed. When touched, it vanishes into a burrow in the sand. The **organ pipe coral** **10** gets its name from its bright red, pipe-shaped tubes. It is found in shallow waters in the Indian and Pacific Oceans.

53

PACIFIC SEA NETTLE
With their soft, golden bells and fine, trailing tentacles, these jellyfish look harmless. But they are carnivores. Their tentacles are equipped with millions of tiny barbs that inject poison into anything they touch. The venom paralyzes prey, which is fed into a mouth under the sea nettle's bell. Although it can give humans a painful sting, this jellyfish is rarely dangerous to us.

Size › Bell up to 18 in (45 cm) across; tentacles and arms up to 15 ft (4.6 m) long **Habitat ›** Surface waters of the Pacific Ocean in the fall and winter, deeper waters in the spring and summer. **Distribution ›** West coast of Canada, the US, and Mexico. Also found around Japan. **Diet ›** Small fishes, crustaceans, and other jellyfish.

Breeding › Eggs hatch into larvae. These grow into stationary structures called polyps, from which new jellyfish grow. **Life span ›** Up to a year in the wild and up to 18 months in captivity. **Predators ›** Sea turtles and fishes. **Conservation status ›** The species is not under threat. In fact, in some areas they swarm in large numbers.

Worms

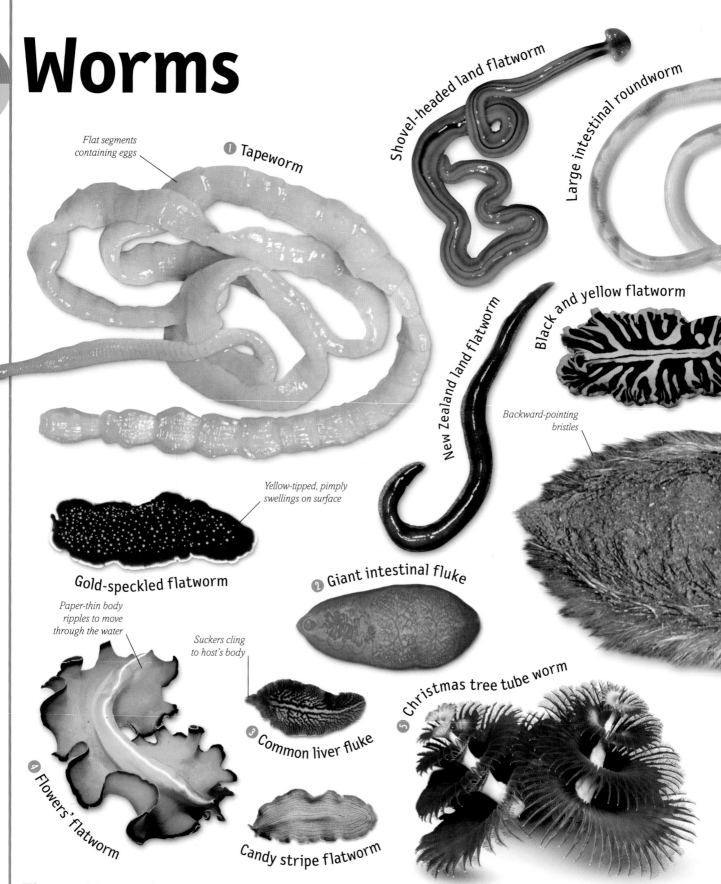

Flat segments containing eggs

❶ Tapeworm

Shovel-headed land flatworm

Large intestinal roundworm

Black and yellow flatworm

New Zealand land flatworm

Backward-pointing bristles

Yellow-tipped, pimply swellings on surface

Gold-speckled flatworm

Paper-thin body ripples to move through the water

Suckers cling to host's body

❷ Giant intestinal fluke

❺ Christmas tree tube worm

❹ Flowers' flatworm

❸ Common liver fluke

Candy stripe flatworm

The word "worms" describes many different kinds of creature. Most of them have flat or round bodies with a head and tail. While some are smaller than a period, worms also include the world's longest and skinniest animals, stretching farther than an Olympic-sized swimming pool. Worms usually live in water or wet places, but many are parasites of other creatures. **Tapeworms** ❶ feed inside the intestines of animals such as cats, pigs, and humans, and can grow to many yards in length. Several leaf-shaped flatworms, such as the **giant intestinal fluke** ❷ and **liver fluke** ❸, also infect people, sometimes causing serious diseases and even death. Fortunately, most other worms are harmless, although their bright colors warn predators that they have a nasty taste. **Flowers' flatworm** ❹ lives on coral reefs and ripples

SCALE

⑥ Southern African velvet worm

⑦ Caribbean velvet worm

Sea cucumber scale worm

Tiger worm

Food-collecting tentacles

Pacific feather-duster worm

⑧ Lugworm

Stream flatworm

Segmented body

⑨ Sea mouse

⑩ Common earthworm

⑪ Fire worm

⑫ King ragworm

Bristly legs

Poisonous bristles used for defense and movement

its body as it swims. The **Christmas tree tube worm** ⑤ stays in the safety of a burrow. It collects food with a spiral tuft of tentacles, which instantly fold up and disappear if a predator comes nearby. **Southern African velvet worms** ⑥ and **Caribbean velvet worms** ⑦ have short, stumpy legs. They creep along the forest floor and capture their prey by spraying it with sticky threads. **Lugworms** ⑧ live in burrows on beaches and mudflats. The **sea mouse** ⑨ has a bristly body for digging through sand. Best known of all worms, the **common earthworm** ⑩ helps to make the soil fertile by burrowing through it and eating dead leaves and other waste. The **fire worm** ⑪ has poisonous bristles that help it to crawl over rocks and coral reefs. The **king ragworm** ⑫ eats seaweed and carrion using its two pincerlike teeth.

Mollusks

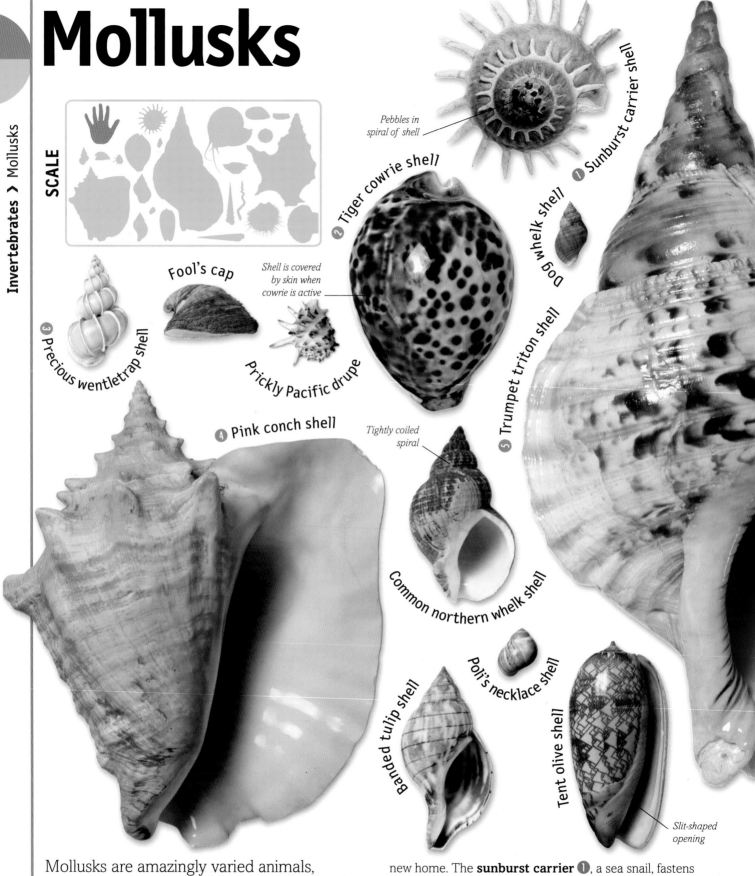

SCALE

Pebbles in spiral of shell

① Sunburst carrier shell

② Tiger cowrie shell

Dog whelk shell

Shell is covered by skin when cowrie is active

Fool's cap

③ Precious wentletrap shell

Prickly Pacific drupe

Trumpet triton shell **⑤**

④ Pink conch shell

Tightly coiled spiral

Common northern whelk shell

Banded tulip shell

Poli's necklace shell

Tent olive shell

Slit-shaped opening

Mollusks are amazingly varied animals, ranging from fast-moving squid, to clams, slugs, and snails. Most of them live in water and have shells. Clams and their relatives have two-part shells joined by a hinge. If danger strikes, the shell snaps shut, protecting the animal inside. Snails and their relatives have spiral shells. Like clam shells, they keep growing, so their owners never have to move to a new home. The **sunburst carrier ①**, a sea snail, fastens pebbles to its shell, using them as camouflage. The **tiger cowrie ②** has an egg-shaped shell with a beautiful pattern and glossy sheen. The **precious wentletrap ③** has a ribbed shell. It preys on anemones and corals, using cutting jaws. Found in tropical oceans, the **pink conch ④** and **trumpet triton ⑤** are two of the largest sea snails. The pink conch

❻ Channelled apple snail

❼ Common mussel

Noah's ark

European bittersweet

❽ Common pelican's foot shell

Long tentacles

❾ Edible oyster shell

Great screw shell

West Indian worm shell

Cat's tongue oyster shell

Spired shell

Subulate auger shell

Shell covered in spines

❿ Great scallop shell

grazes on seagrass and seaweed, while the triton is a predator, attacking starfish and other slow-moving prey. It hunts at night and paralyzes its victims with poisonous saliva before beginning to feed. Like most apple snails, the **channeled apple snail** ❻ has gills and lives in freshwater. The **common mussel** ❼ lives just below the waterline on rocky shores, using its gills to filter out small particles of food.

The **common pelican's foot** ❽ creeps across mud and sand on the seabed. Its shell has extensions that resemble webbed feet. The **edible oyster** ❾ and the **great scallop** ❿ are often harvested to eat. Mussels and oysters glue themselves to rocks using sticky threads. Scallops lie on the seabed. If a predator tries to creep up on them, they swim away by clapping their shells open and shut.

59

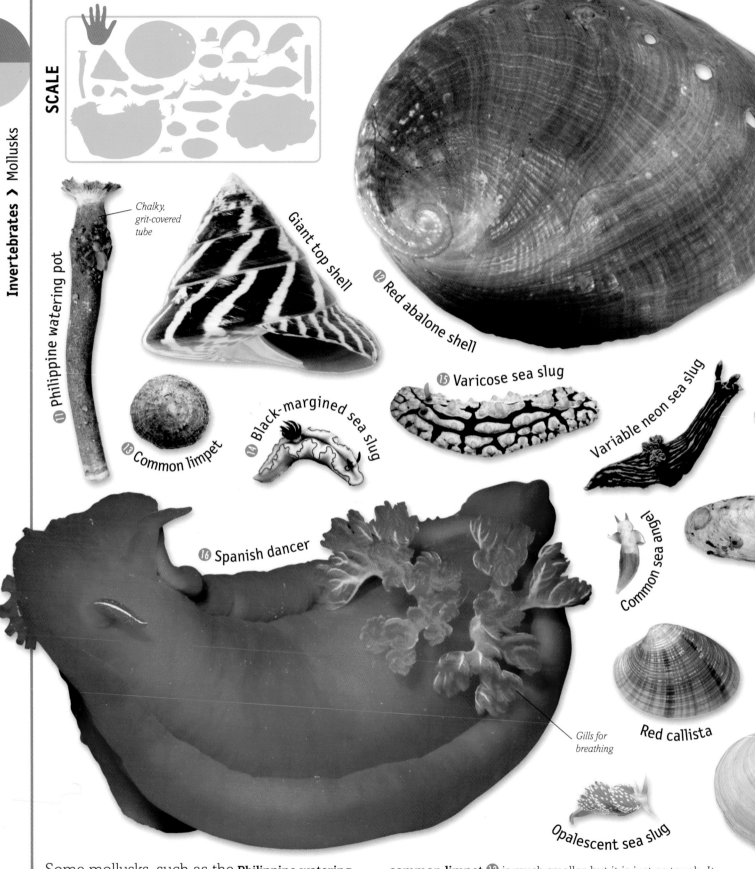

SCALE

Philippine watering pot ⑪

Chalky, grit-covered tube

⑫ Red abalone shell

Giant top shell

⑬ Common limpet

⑭ Black-margined sea slug

⑮ Varicose sea slug

Variable neon sea slug

Common sea angel

⑯ Spanish dancer

Gills for breathing

Red callista

Opalescent sea slug

Some mollusks, such as the **Philippine watering pot** ⑪, do not need to move, because they strain their food out of the water. But many others, including the **red abalone** ⑫, creep around on a muscle-packed sucker that works like a foot. The red abalone grazes on algae, and its grip is incredibly strong. When threatened, it clamps its shell to the rock and is almost impossible to dislodge. The

common limpet ⑬ is much smaller, but it is just as tough. It clings to wave-battered rocks and can withstand the fiercest winter storms. Sea slugs, or nudibranchs, have a foot but no shell. They are famous for their brilliant colors. Many kinds, such as the **black-margined sea slug** ⑭, have a tuft of gills on their backs and a pair of tentacles that look like miniature horns. The black-margined sea slug feeds on sponges. So do

Great ramshorn snail

Pacific banana slug ⑰

European black slug ⑱

This species has black or orange skin

West African tellin

Brown garden snail

Silver mouth turban shell

Giant African snail ⑲

Sword razor clam shell

Spotted sea hare

Royal comb venus

Common piddock

Growth rings

⑳ Swan mussel

Soft shell clam

㉑ Fluted giant clam

the **varicose sea slug** ⑮ and the **Spanish dancer** ⑯, a giant sea slug that swims by rippling its body, making it look like a dancer wearing a skirt. Mollusks are also common on land, particularly in damp areas. The **Pacific banana slug** ⑰ and the **European black slug** ⑱ live in cool climates, but the **giant African snail** ⑲ is a tropical species that has become a major pest in warm parts of the world because of its large appetite and fast breeding. Back in the water, clams are mollusks with hinged shells. A few, such as the **swan mussel** ⑳, grow in rivers and streams, but most, including the **fluted giant clam** ㉑, live in the sea. Like its big brother the giant clam, it contains microscopic algae that live in its flesh. These algae produce nutrients, which contribute to the clam's food supply.

61

GIANT CLAM
The giant clam is the world's heaviest shelled animal, and possibly the largest species that has ever lived. It has a huge, thick shell formed of two parts, with a deeply folded edge. The edges of the inner body, or mantle, are often a beautiful iridescent blue-green or gold, and they can be seen when the shell opens to feed. It is a myth that a giant clam can catch and swallow people, because a clam will only close, slowly, if it is attacked.

Size > Shell up to 5 ft (1.5 m) long **Weight >** Up to 440 lb (200 kg) **Habitat >** The clams anchor themselves on sand or coral rubble in reefs or in lagoons. **Distribution >** Tropical areas of the Indian and western Pacific oceans and South China Sea. **Diet >** Giant clams filter plankton out of the sea using their gills. They also get nutrients from the plantlike algae called zooxanthellae that live inside their mantle tissues. **Breeding >** Giant clams expel sperm and eggs into the ocean. The eggs develop into larvae called veligers, which swim freely and hunt for food. **Predators >** Sea stars, snails, some fishes, and humans. **Conservation status >** Vulnerable due to harvesting for food and the aquarium trade.

Squid, octopuses, and cuttlefish

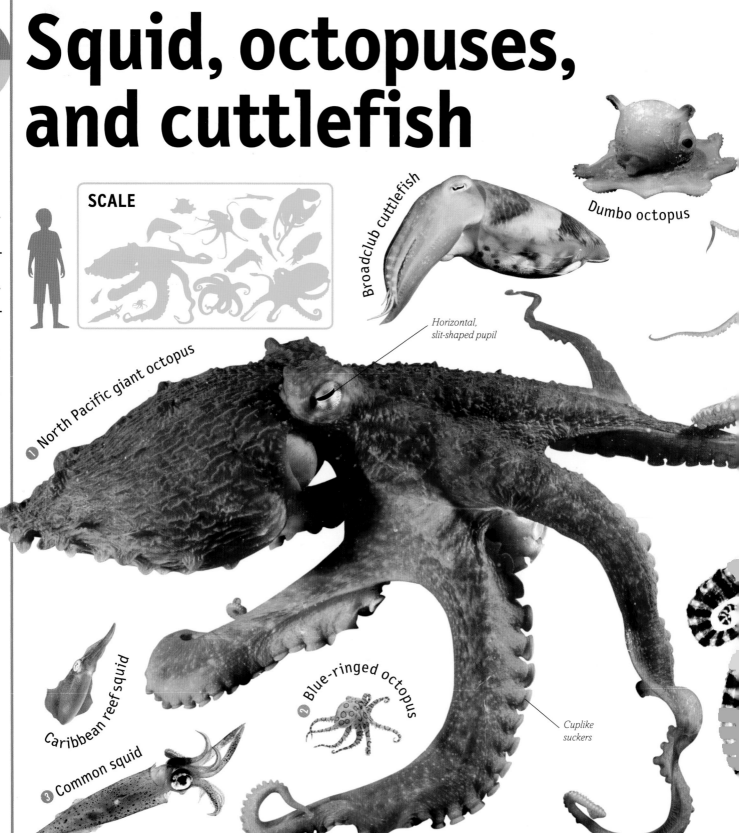

SCALE

Dumbo octopus

Broadclub cuttlefish

Horizontal, slit-shaped pupil

① North Pacific giant octopus

Caribbean reef squid

② Blue-ringed octopus

Cuplike suckers

③ Common squid

Unlike other mollusks, squid and their relatives are fast-moving hunters with keen senses and big brains. Octopuses have eight arms covered in suckers. Squid and cuttlefish also have eight arms, plus two long tentacles that shoot out to catch their prey. Many of these animals can change color in seconds, helping them to hide. The **North Pacific giant octopus** ① hunts on the seabed. Like many octopuses, it can squirt clouds of black pigment into the water to confuse predators. Fully spread out, its legs can measure over 13 ft (4 m) from tip to tip. Far smaller, but much more dangerous, the **blue-ringed octopus** ② has a highly toxic bite. It can kill humans, although it usually swims away. The **common squid** ③ has a streamlined body with prominent side fins, and it lives in the open sea. Like other squid, it zooms

Prey-snatching
tentacles

4 **Whip-lash squid**

6 *Atlantic octopus*

5 **Chambered nautilus**

Day octopus

Bigfin reef squid

8 *Common cuttlefish*

7 *Australian giant cuttlefish*

9 **Mimic octopus**

Long,
muscular arms

Common octopus

backward by sucking in water and squirting it out in a jet. Jet propulsion is also important for octopuses when they need to make a quick getaway. The **whip-lash squid** 4 hovers in deep water, waiting for prey with its long tentacles extended. The **chambered nautilus** 5 has a spiral shell and about 90 tentacles which tightly grip its prey. Mostly found in shallow waters, the **Atlantic octopus** 6 spends the daytime in rocky lairs and hunts after dark. The **Australian giant cuttlefish** 7 and **common cuttlefish** 8 cruise over the shallow seabed looking for crabs and other prey. The extraordinary **mimic octopus** 9 is one of the few octopuses that hunts while the sun is up. In addition to changing color, it can disguise itself to resemble more than a dozen different animals, making it look more dangerous than it really is.

65

Starfish, urchins, and sea cucumbers

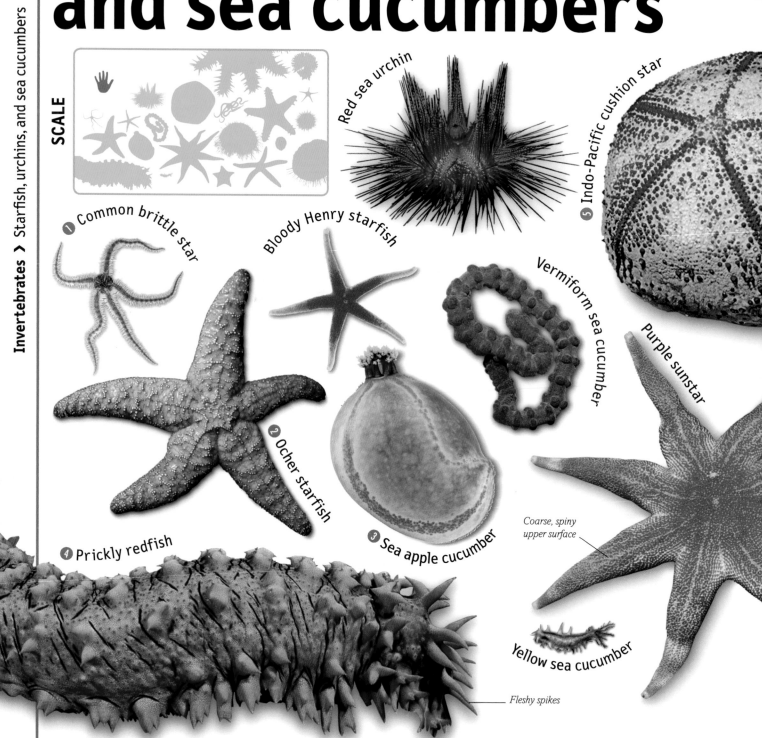

SCALE

Red sea urchin

⑤ Indo-Pacific cushion star

① Common brittle star

Bloody Henry starfish

Vermiform sea cucumber

Purple sunstar

② Ocher starfish

③ Sea apple cucumber

Coarse, spiny upper surface

④ Prickly redfish

Yellow sea cucumber

Fleshy spikes

Found only in salt water, starfish and their relatives are unique in many ways. Most of these slow-moving creatures have five arms branching out from the center of their bodies. They have skeletons or cases made of hard, chalky plates. The **common brittle star** ❶ moves by snaking its arms, but most animals in this group move around using hundreds of little tubes, which act as feet.

The **ocher starfish** ❷ feeds on mussels and other mollusks, using the tubes to grip its prey. Sea cucumbers collect food using a ring of tentacles around their mouths. The **sea apple cucumber** ❸ is a highly poisonous reef-dweller. It has bright colors warning predators not to attack. Other species, such as the sausage-shaped **prickly redfish** ❹, are colored to match the sand. The **Indo-Pacific cushion star** ❺ becomes

⑥ Crown of thorns starfish

Yellow feather star

Rows of red tubercles

Short-spined brittle star

Venomous spines for protection

Red general starfish

Icon starfish

⑦ Edible sea urchin

⑧ Purple urchin

Fire urchin

⑨ Sea potato

Red cushion star

Smooth, spineless surface

⑩ Blue starfish

Short, venomous spines can deliver painful sting

short-armed as it gets bigger, eventually maturing into a dumpy pillow shape. It often grazes on coral. The notorious **crown of thorns starfish** ⑥ is a large species with venomous, thorny arms. It can devastate reefs with its voracious appetite for coral. Sea urchins creep over rocks and reefs, scraping up food with their downward-pointing mouths. The **edible sea urchin** ⑦ has short spines and a rounded case, while the **purple urchin** ⑧ has extra-long spines that break off easily. The **sea potato** ⑨ burrows into seabed mud, and has bristly spines and a streamlined shape. Sea urchins use their spines for self-defense, while sea cucumbers squirt out a mass of sticky threads. The **blue starfish** ⑩ and its relatives have a different kind of protection: if any of their legs are bitten off, they slowly grow back.

Centipedes and millipedes

Eastern flat-backed millipede

SCALE

① Yellow earth centipede

② Tiger giant centipede

Brown stone centipede

③ American giant millipede

Megarian banded centipede

Banded stone centipede

American short-headed millipede

④ Black giant pill millipede

Brown snake millipede

Sonoran tiger centipede

Tanzanian flat-backed millipede

Flat body can fit under stones

Centipedes and millipedes belong to a group of animals called arthropods, which have legs with joints and a hard body case. Millipedes are slow-moving vegetarians, but centipedes are agile predators, with keen senses and poisonous fangs. **Yellow earth centipedes** ① hunt underground. With their flexible bodies and short legs, they squeeze between particles of soil. If they are dug up, they quickly wriggle away. The Indian **tiger giant centipede** ② is one of the biggest, growing up to 10 in (25 cm) long. It can easily kill small rodents and can give humans an extremely painful bite. Centipedes have two legs on each segment of their bodies, but millipedes have four. The **American giant millipede** ③ can have more than 200 legs. Like other millipedes, it grows extra pairs every time

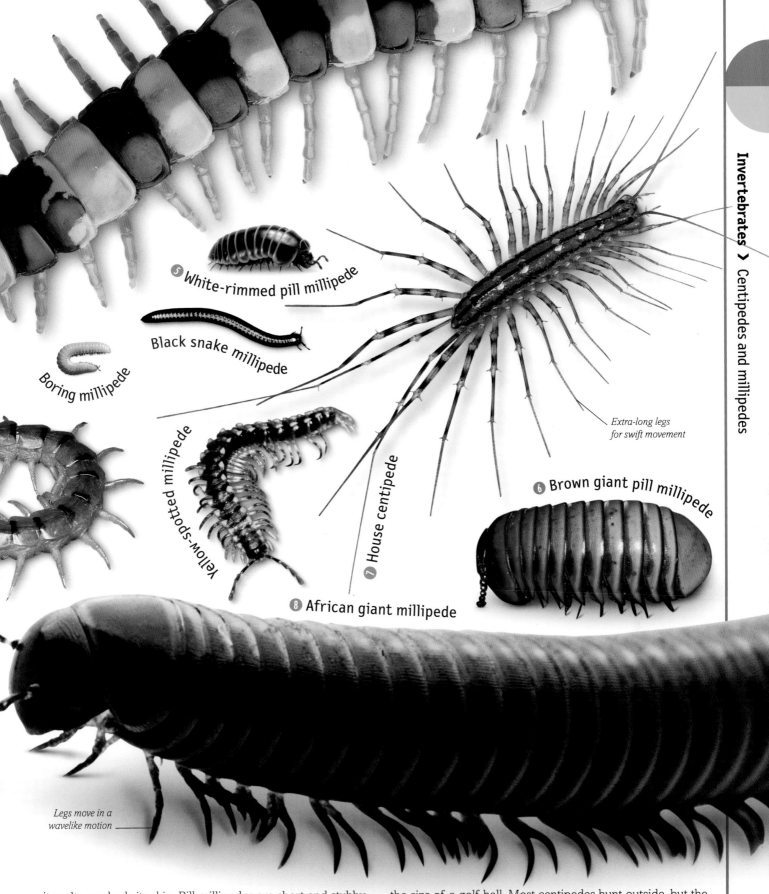

⑤ White-rimmed pill millipede

Black snake millipede

Boring millipede

Yellow-spotted millipede

Extra-long legs for swift movement

⑦ House centipede

⑥ Brown giant pill millipede

⑧ African giant millipede

Legs move in a wavelike motion

it molts, or sheds its skin. Pill millipedes are short and stubby, and often have 50 legs or fewer. They get their name because they can tuck in their legs and roll up into a ball. The **black giant pill millipede ④** comes from Madagascar, while the **white-rimmed pill millipede ⑤** is found in Europe. The **brown giant pill millipede ⑥** from the forests of Borneo is one of the biggest pill millipedes. Fully rolled up, it is about

the size of a golf ball. Most centipedes hunt outside, but the **house centipede ⑦** often comes indoors. With its long legs, it is an amazingly fast sprinter, scuttling up walls and ceilings to catch spiders and other prey. With over 300 legs, the **African giant millipede ⑧** is one of the largest millipedes. If threatened by predators, it releases a foul-smelling liquid to persuade them it is not nice to eat.

Spiders and relatives

American sun spider

Domestic huntsman spider

Horned harvestman

Stinging hairs can be fired at enemies

① Chaco tarantula

② Marbled orb weaver

③ Goldenrod crab spider

④ Audouin's trapdoor spider

European wolf spider

Say's harvestman

Pear-shaped body and small head

Ladybug spider

Whip spider

Long front legs used as feelers

SCALE

Many people are scared of spiders, but the world would be very different without them. These eight-legged animals are superefficient hunters. Out of many thousands, scientists have found only one kind that feeds on plants. Close relatives of spiders include sun spiders, whip spiders, and harvestmen, as well as ticks, mites, and scorpions. The **chaco tarantula** ① lives in a burrow by day and comes out to feed after dark. Like all spiders, it kills its prey by injecting venom through a pair of fangs. The **marbled orb weaver** ② catches flying insects by spinning wheel-shaped webs, but the **goldenrod crab spider** ③ sits on top of flowers where it ambushes bees and butterflies. **Audouin's trapdoor spider** ④ lurks in a silk-lined burrow, equipped with trip lines and a camouflaged lid. If anything

Legs end in retractable claws

⑤ Mexican red-kneed tarantula

⑥ Northern black widow

⑦ Daddy longlegs spider

European garden spider

St. Andrews cross spider

⑧ Giant house spider

Jumping spider

Eight small eyes

⑨ Raft spider

Elegant jumping spider

⑩ Goliath tarantula

Brown jumping spider

touches a trip line, the spider flings open the lid and grabs its prey. The **Mexican red-kneed tarantula** ⑤ is a forest-dwelling spider, and a popular pet. It grows slowly and can live for more than 20 years. The **northern black widow** ⑥ from North America is far smaller but more dangerous. Females are much bigger than males, and they can give people a fatal bite. The **daddy longlegs spider** ⑦ often lives indoors, and so does the **giant house spider** ⑧, a species that spins funnel-shaped webs. **Raft spiders** ⑨ lie in wait by the edges of ponds and pools, where they catch tadpoles and small fish. The enormous **goliath tarantula** ⑩ from South America eats insects, rodents, frogs, and even bats. It is one of the biggest spiders in the world, with a leg span as big as a dinner plate.

SCALE

Brazilian wandering spider ⑪

Crablike spiny orb weaver

⑫ Sydney funnel-web spider

Sac spider

Eight walking legs

Silk egg sac carried by female

⑬ Woodlouse spider

⑭ Nursery web spider

Four pairs of eyes

Lone star tick

⑮ Cave spider

⑯ American golden silk orb weaver

Pincerlike mouthparts

Whip scorpion

Walnut orb weaver

Tufts of hair on legs

All spiders make silk, but only some species spin webs to catch their prey. Many other kinds hunt on the ground. The **Brazilian wandering spider** ⑪ is one of the most dangerous of these prowling predators. It roams through forests after dark, and sometimes wanders into urban areas, where it clambers over people as they sleep. The **Sydney funnel-web spider** ⑫ from Australia is also hazardous to humans. Females live in burrows, but males sometimes stray into backyards, and will bite humans if they feel threatened. The **woodlouse spider** ⑬ is much smaller, but it has extrastrong fangs for biting into the hard body cases of woodlice. **Nursery web spiders** ⑭ and **cave spiders** ⑮ make silk sacs to carry their eggs, while the **American golden silk orb weaver** ⑯ uses its silk to build some of the world's

Giant desert hairy scorpion ⑰

Chilean burrowing scorpion

Sting raised to threaten enemies

Yellow thick-tail scorpion ⑱

Imperial scorpion ⑳

Pincers grip prey

Gold scorpion ⑲

Pincers covered with sensitive hairs

Common European scorpion

Red velvet mite

biggest webs. Shaped like cartwheels and more than 3 ft (1 m) across, the webs are strong enough to catch hummingbirds and even frogs. Like spiders, scorpions have eight legs, but they also have a pair of pincers and a poisonous sting in their tails. The **giant desert hairy scorpion** ⑰ is the largest kind in North America. Like other scorpions, it uses its pincers to tear apart its prey, while its sting is mainly for self-defense. The **yellow thick-tail scorpion** ⑱ is smaller, but its venom is much more powerful. It comes from the Sahara Desert and the Middle East. **Gold scorpions** ⑲ also live in the same part of the world, but the **imperial scorpion** ⑳ is a forest species from tropical Africa. It is one of the biggest scorpions, measuring up to 10 in (25 cm) long. Although it looks menacing, its sting is not much stronger than that of a wasp.

SEA SPIDER
Sea spiders belong to a group of marine animals called Pantopoda, meaning "all legs." Their legs are so long compared to their tiny bodies that they have to keep some of their internal organs inside them. This strikingly colored yellow-kneed sea spider comes from the coral reefs off the coast of Australia. It is only a few centimeters across, but larger specimens can grow up to 35 in (90 cm) from tip to tip.

Size ❯ ¹⁄₁₆ in–35 in (1 mm–90 cm) **Habitat ❯** Seabed; smaller species live in shallow water, while larger sea spiders live in the deep waters of the Antarctic Ocean. **Distribution ❯** Seas and oceans worldwide **Diet ❯** Soft-bodied animals such as sea sponges, anemones, and coral polyps. The sea spider uses its sucking mouthpart, or proboscis, to extract fluids from the prey, or breaks off pieces and puts them in its mouth. **Breeding ❯** The eggs hatch into larvae. In most species the larvae float around freely as they grow. In some they live on their father's front legs, while in others the larvae live as parasites in animals such as coral polyps or clams.

Crustaceans

① Edible crab

Thick carapace

② Red reef hermit crab

③ White-spotted hermit crab

Abdomen hidden inside shell

④ Blue swimming crab

Wide, flattened carapace

Pincers used for catching prey

Freshwater crab

Anemone porcelain crab

Velvet swimming crab

⑥ Christmas Island red crab

⑤ Warty box crab

Painted pebble crab

Legs with a single claw

Crustaceans are not common on land, but they flourish in freshwater and in the sea. They include lobsters, shrimp, and also hundreds of different kinds of crabs. Some crustaceans swim in gigantic swarms, but crabs usually roam the seabed or scuttle over the shore. The **edible crab ①** has an extra-tough shield, or carapace. Its powerful pincers can crack open mollusk shells, and crush human fingers, too.

The **red reef hermit crab ②** and **white-spotted hermit crab ③** have small pincers and live in shells borrowed from other animals. Like other hermit crabs, they change shells as they grow. Each time these crabs move to a new home, they carefully check their new shell to make sure that it is exactly the right fit. **Blue swimming crabs ④** have back legs that work like paddles. These crabs like spending time on sandy

SCALE

Sponge crab

Short hind legs

Spotted coral crab

Pear-shaped body

7 Orange fiddler crab

8 Panamic arrow crab

9 Japanese spider crab

Heavily armored legs and body

or muddy coastlines. **Warty box crabs** 5 burrow in seabed sand. They shield their faces with their claws, giving them the alternative name, the shame-faced crab. **Christmas Island red crabs** 6 live in tropical forests, surrounded by the Indian Ocean. During the breeding season, millions of them emerge from the forest and march to the coast, where they mate and lay their eggs. **Orange fiddler crabs** 7 make burrows in mangrove swamps. Males have a tiny claw for feeding and a giant one for signaling to females across the mud. The **Panamic arrow crab** 8 lives on reefs, while the **Japanese spider crab** 9 prowls the seabed. Measuring up to 13 ft (4 m) across, this amazingly leggy animal is the world's biggest crustacean, with a life span of up to 100 years.

10 Norway lobster

Two pairs of antennae, or feelers

Red, threadlike antennae

11 Blue-striped squat lobster

Flexible body ending in a broad tail fan

White-clawed crayfish

Long pincers

12 Reef lobster

Aesop shrimp

13 Striped-leg spiny lobster

Black "tiger" stripes

Tiger prawn

15 Sculptured slipper lobster

Paddles at end of abdomen

14 Antarctic krill

Regal slipper lobster

Giant acorn barnacle

Lobsters, shrimp, and prawns are crustaceans with long bodies and lots of legs. The **Norway lobster** **10** lives in a burrow and feeds at night on live animals and carrion. **Blue-striped squat lobsters** **11** are close relatives of crabs. Like other squat lobsters, they have 10 legs, but the last leg pair is small, and tucked away underneath their tails. **Reef lobsters** **12** are brightly colored, which makes them popular aquarium pets. The **striped-leg spiny lobster** **13** has extra-long antennae that can make a creaky, clicking sound to scare predators away. If it is cornered, it swims backward at high speed. **Antarctic krill** **14** live in the icy Southern Ocean in swarms that can stretch for miles in every direction. These finger-sized crustaceans are a vital food for penguins, seals, and whales, including the blue whale, which can swallow

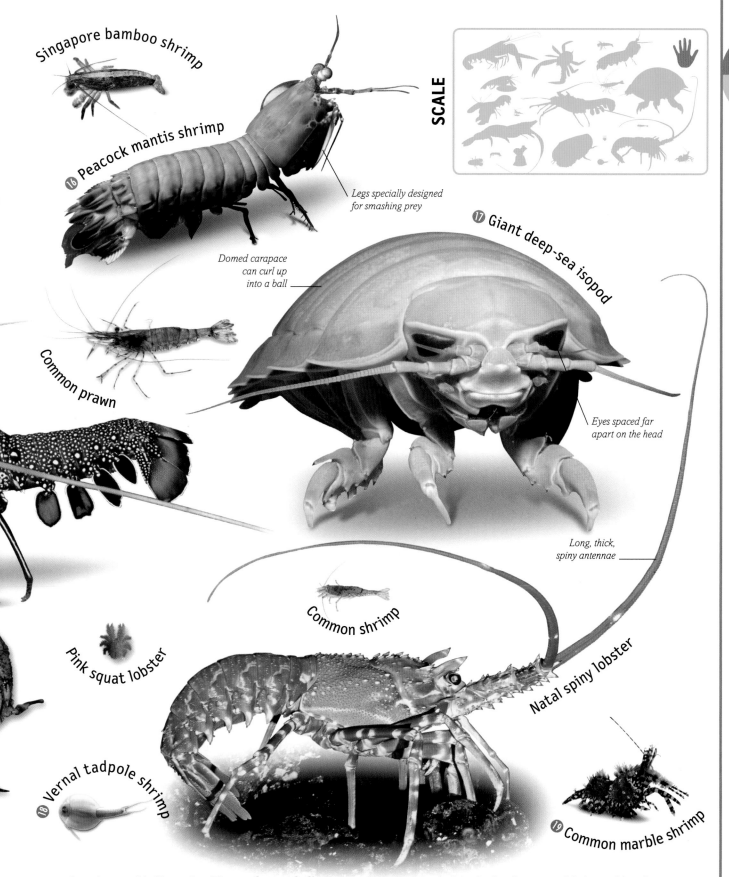

Singapore bamboo shrimp

⑯ Peacock mantis shrimp

Legs specially designed
for smashing prey

⑰ Giant deep-sea isopod

Domed carapace
can curl up
into a ball

Common prawn

Eyes spaced far
apart on the head

Long, thick,
spiny antennae

Common shrimp

Pink squat lobster

Natal spiny lobster

⑱ Vernal tadpole shrimp

⑲ Common marble shrimp

more than 4 tons of krill per day. The **sculptured slipper lobster** ⑮ has a rounded shape and blends in against seabed sand. The **peacock mantis shrimp** ⑯ is a predator with a knockout punch. Using its front legs, it smashes open snail shells and crabs, and can even shatter the glass of aquariums. The **giant deep-sea isopod** ⑰ scavenges food on the seafloor, occasionally feeding on live prey. Since light is extremely faint in the deep sea, this isopod has large antennae to help it feel its way around. **Vernal tadpole shrimp** ⑱ from California breed in short-lived freshwater pools. The adult shrimp die when the pools dry up, but their eggs can survive for up to 10 years, hatching when it rains. The **common marble shrimp** ⑲ is brown with green spots during the day, but turns red at night.

Insects

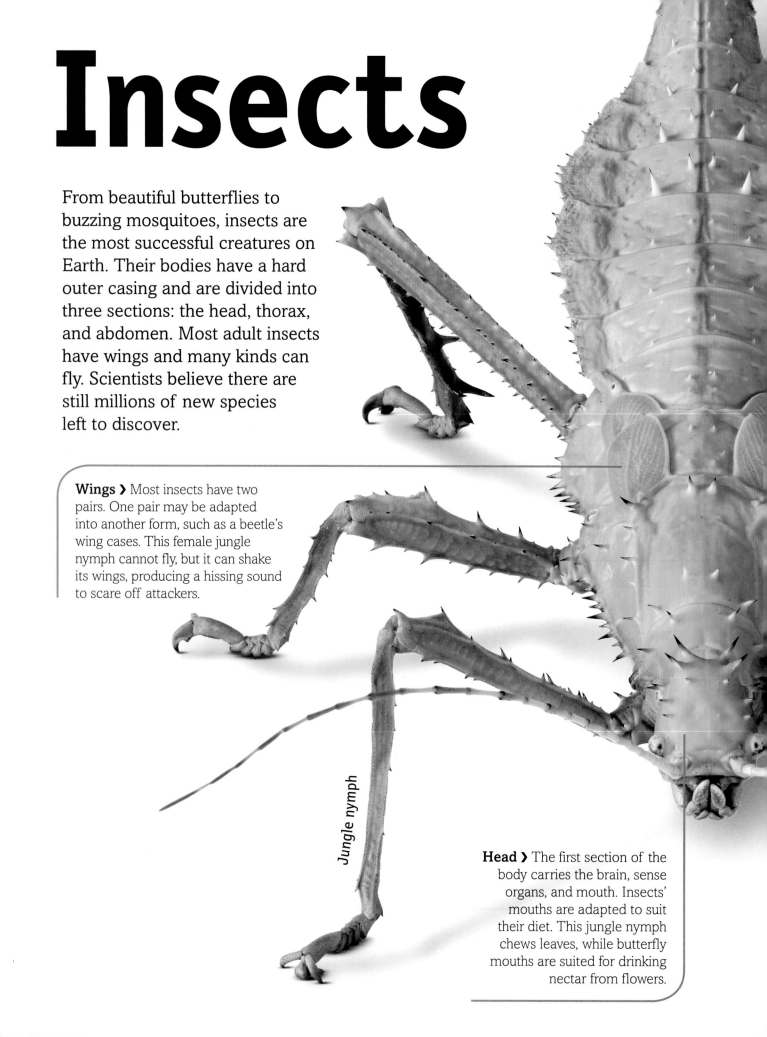

From beautiful butterflies to buzzing mosquitoes, insects are the most successful creatures on Earth. Their bodies have a hard outer casing and are divided into three sections: the head, thorax, and abdomen. Most adult insects have wings and many kinds can fly. Scientists believe there are still millions of new species left to discover.

Wings ❯ Most insects have two pairs. One pair may be adapted into another form, such as a beetle's wing cases. This female jungle nymph cannot fly, but it can shake its wings, producing a hissing sound to scare off attackers.

Jungle nymph

Head ❯ The first section of the body carries the brain, sense organs, and mouth. Insects' mouths are adapted to suit their diet. This jungle nymph chews leaves, while butterfly mouths are suited for drinking nectar from flowers.

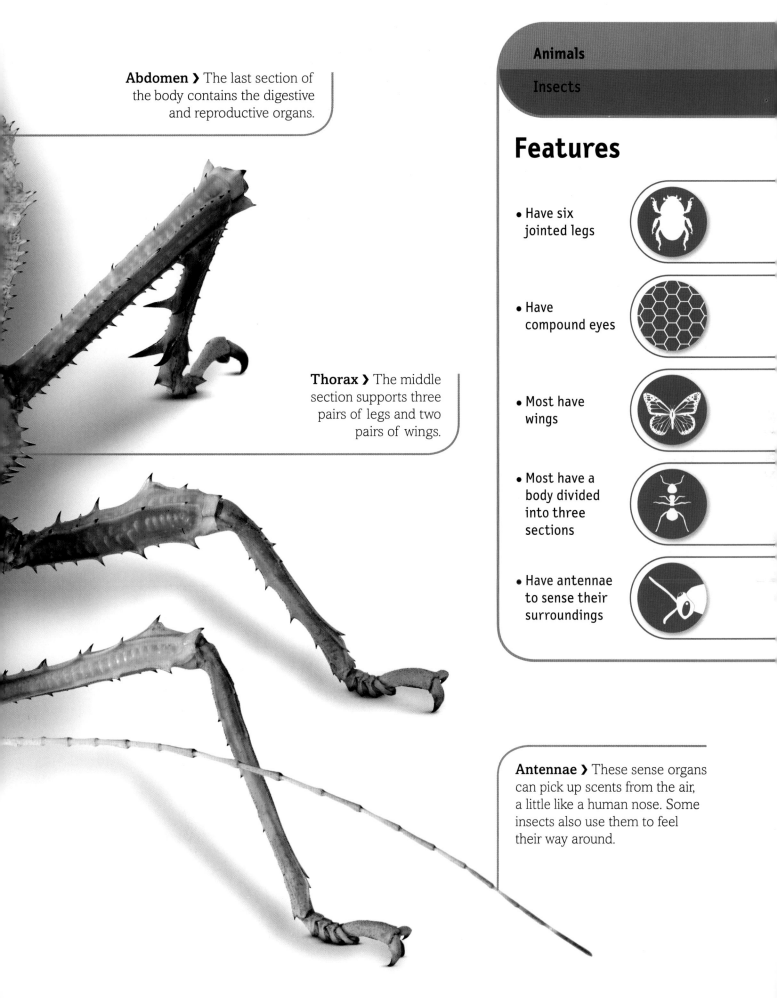

Abdomen ❯ The last section of the body contains the digestive and reproductive organs.

Thorax ❯ The middle section supports three pairs of legs and two pairs of wings.

Features

- Have six jointed legs

- Have compound eyes

- Most have wings

- Most have a body divided into three sections

- Have antennae to sense their surroundings

Antennae ❯ These sense organs can pick up scents from the air, a little like a human nose. Some insects also use them to feel their way around.

Dragonflies and damselflies

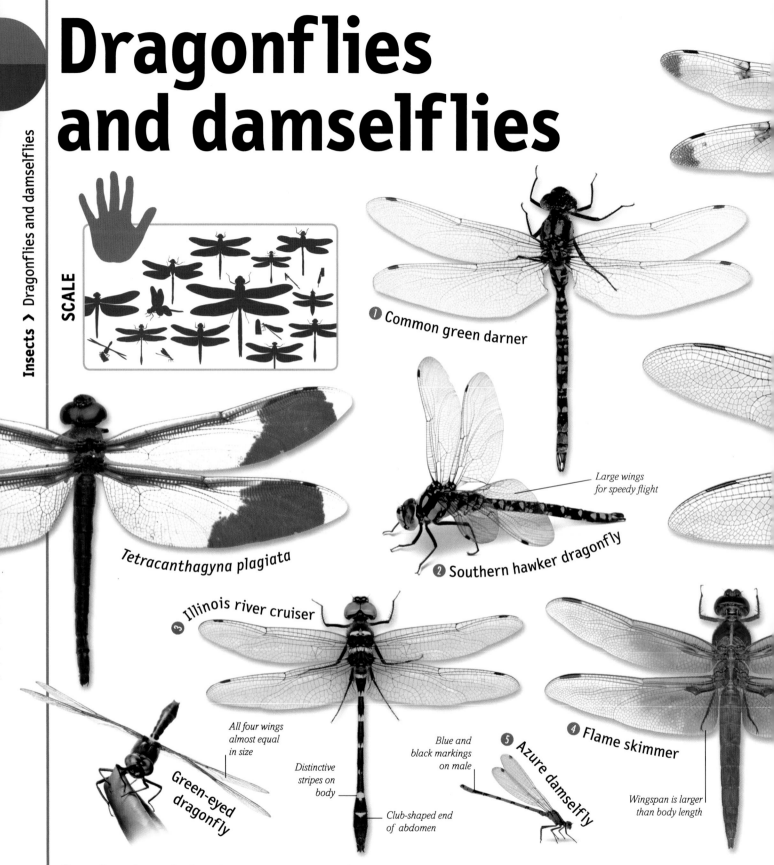

SCALE

① Common green darner

Tetracanthagyna plagiata

Large wings for speedy flight

② Southern hawker dragonfly

③ Illinois river cruiser

All four wings almost equal in size

Distinctive stripes on body

Green-eyed dragonfly

Club-shaped end of abdomen

Blue and black markings on male

⑤ Azure damselfly

④ Flame skimmer

Wingspan is larger than body length

Speeding through the air on transparent wings, dragonflies and damselflies chase insects for food. Dragonflies are robust with rounded heads, whereas damselflies are more slender with broader heads. Both have extra-large eyes for spotting anything that moves and can zoom sideways and even backward as they close in for a kill. Their young, known as nymphs, are also hunters. They grow up underwater, and use stealth and camouflage to catch their prey. The **common green darner** ① flies over streams in North America. Its stiff wings stick out sideways when it rests. The **southern hawker dragonfly** ②, from Europe, breeds in small ponds. It hunts away from water and approaches people that come nearby. The **Illinois river cruiser** ③ patrols rocky streams and rivers, while the **flame skimmer** ④ prefers warm water, sometimes

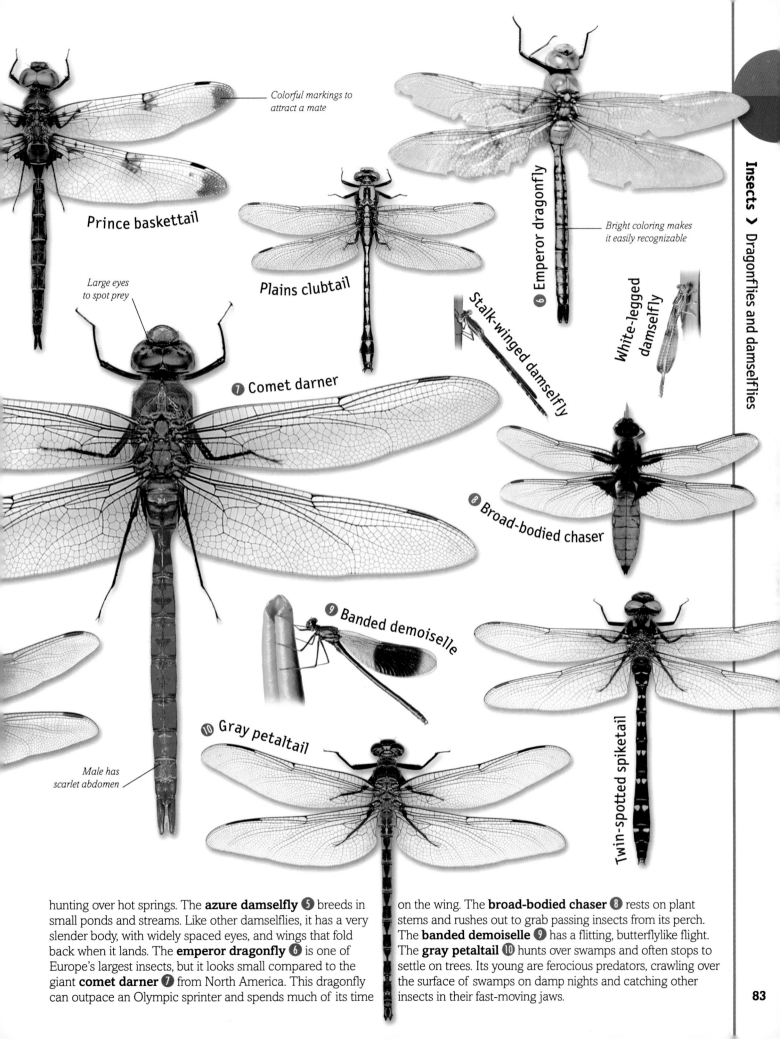

Colorful markings to attract a mate

Prince baskettail

Large eyes to spot prey

Plains clubtail

Emperor dragonfly 6

Bright coloring makes it easily recognizable

Stalk-winged damselfly

White-legged damselfly

7 Comet darner

8 Broad-bodied chaser

9 Banded demoiselle

10 Gray petaltail

Twin-spotted spiketail

Male has scarlet abdomen

hunting over hot springs. The **azure damselfly** ❺ breeds in small ponds and streams. Like other damselflies, it has a very slender body, with widely spaced eyes, and wings that fold back when it lands. The **emperor dragonfly** ❻ is one of Europe's largest insects, but it looks small compared to the giant **comet darner** ❼ from North America. This dragonfly can outpace an Olympic sprinter and spends much of its time on the wing. The **broad-bodied chaser** ❽ rests on plant stems and rushes out to grab passing insects from its perch. The **banded demoiselle** ❾ has a flitting, butterflylike flight. The **gray petaltail** ❿ hunts over swamps and often stops to settle on trees. Its young are ferocious predators, crawling over the surface of swamps on damp nights and catching other insects in their fast-moving jaws.

STICK INSECT
Masters of disguise, stick insects sit quietly on tree branches, looking exactly like dead twigs or green shoots so that predators don't notice them. There are thought to be more than 3,000 species across the world, ranging from tiny leaf and twig shapes up to "branches" 22 in (55 cm) long. This stick insect from Madagascar resembles a thorny bramble shoot, a very unappetizing prospect for predators.

Size ❯ 1–22 in (2.5–55 cm) **Weight** ❯ Up to 2¼ oz (65 grams)
Habitat ❯ Rain forests and jungles. **Distribution** ❯ Tropical
and subtropical areas of Southeast Asia and Australia, also
Madagascar, South and Central America, and Southern US.
Some species also found in mainland Europe as well as the
British Isles. **Diet** ❯ Leaves of trees and shrubs and berries.

Breeding ❯ Females lay live eggs on their own or by mating
with males. The eggs hatch into nymphs, which molt several
times as they grow into adults. **Life span** ❯ From a few months
to a few years. **Predators** ❯ Birds, small reptiles, and rodents.
Defenses include camouflage, sharp spines, flashing wings,
hissing, or spraying bad-smelling or burning liquid.

Crickets and grasshoppers

❶ Green milkweed locust

Antennae longer than body

Speckled bush cricket

Large eyes

❷ Desert locust

Pygmy locust

House cricket

Calliptamus italicus

❸ Foaming grasshopper

Common macrotona grasshopper

With their powerful back legs, crickets and grasshoppers are some of the best jumpers in the insect world. They are also some of the loudest, rubbing their legs or wings to make high-pitched sounds. Many live on their own, but locusts are famous for migrating in enormous swarms. The African **green milkweed locust** ❶ is one of the biggest of these insect travelers, while the **desert locust** ❷ holds the record for numbers. Some of its swarms contain more than 30 billion insects, which is four times the number of people on Earth. Most grasshoppers rely on camouflage for protection. The **foaming grasshopper** ❸, however, oozes poisonous froth from behind its head, while its day-glow colors warn that it is dangerous to eat. Adult grasshoppers usually have two pairs of wings, but some

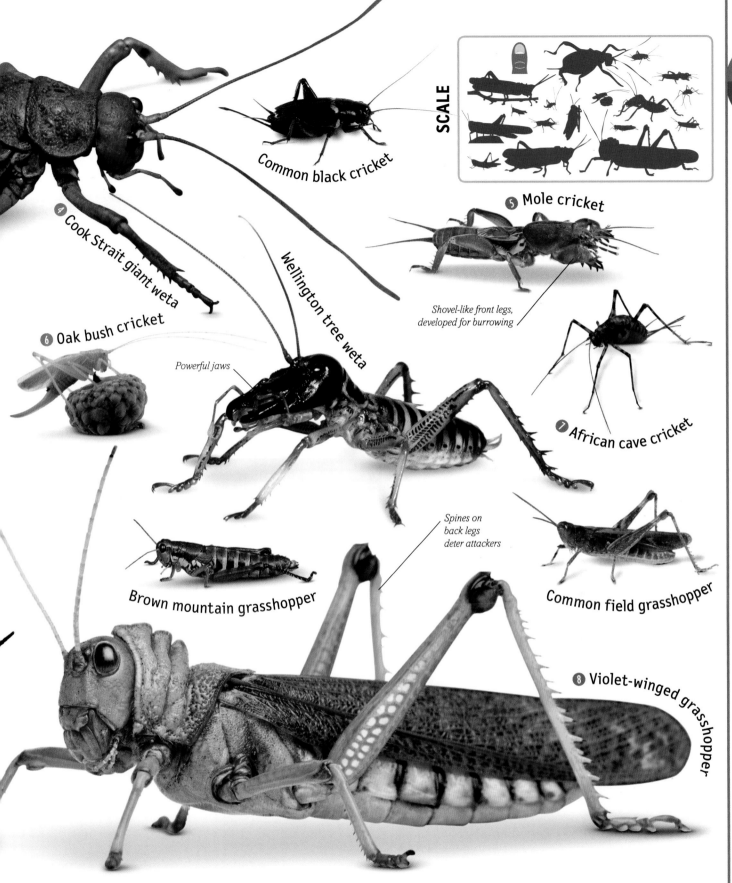

④ Cook Strait giant weta

Common black cricket

SCALE

⑤ Mole cricket

Shovel-like front legs, developed for burrowing

⑥ Oak bush cricket

Wellington tree weta

Powerful jaws

⑦ African cave cricket

Spines on back legs deter attackers

Brown mountain grasshopper

Common field grasshopper

⑧ Violet-winged grasshopper

crickets are wingless and cannot fly. The biggest of these include wetas from New Zealand. The **Cook Strait giant weta** ④ is almost as large as a mouse. If it is threatened, it raises its spiny back legs over its head, making it look ready for a fight. Most crickets and grasshoppers feed on plants, but some species are predators and scavengers. Some others even feed on their own kind. The **mole cricket** ⑤ spends its life in underground burrows, feeding on worms, roots, and grasses. Like real moles, it has massive front legs that work as shovels. The **oak bush cricket** ⑥ is a hunter, while the **African cave cricket** ⑦ feeds on almost anything, from bat droppings to carrion. The huge **violet-winged grasshopper** ⑧ comes from South America. Measuring up to 5 in (12 cm) long, it is even bigger than some birds.

True bugs and treehoppers

Toad bug

Thorn bug

Water scorpion

Wart-headed bug

Nut-shaped head

Common green shield bug

Water measurer

Spittle bug

Peanut-headed bug

Common green capsid

Brightly colored hind wings

Large eye spots to keep away predators

Bedbug

True bugs are a special group of insect that live in freshwater as well as on land. They have sharp mouthparts for sucking up liquids. Some feed on plant sap, while others eat blood or fluids from their partly digested prey. Sapsucking bugs feed in the open and often use camouflage to hide. The **thorn bug** ❶ has an amazingly realistic spike that looks just like a thorn. Tropical species, such as the **wart-headed bug** ❷, can be bigger than some butterflies. This bug has brightly colored hind wings to startle enemies that get too close. The green color of the **common green shield bug** ❸ helps it to blend in among leaves. Young **spittle bugs** ❹ shelter inside nests of foam, which protect them from hungry birds. The **peanut-headed bug** ❺, another tropical species, has large eye spots on its hind

Hawthorn shield bug

7 White-spotted assassin bug

Strong claws to overpower large prey

Common flower bug

8 Common pond skater

Leaf-footed bug

Fire bug

9 Giant water bug

European tortoise bug

10 Himalayan cicada

Birch bark bug

SCALE

89

wings to confuse predators. The **bedbug** **6** is a flightless parasite that emerges after dark to suck human blood. Many predatory bugs ambush their prey. On land they include the **white-spotted assassin bug** **7** and its many relatives. In freshwater, predatory bugs are even more common. Some, such as the **common pond skater** **8**, live on the water's surface, attacking other insects that

crash-land. A strong swimmer, the **giant water bug** **9** is big enough to prey on frogs and fish. It can even give humans a painful bite. Most bugs are silent, but some make amazingly loud sounds. Male **Himalayan cicadas** **10** attract females by making a deafening courtship song. Like other cicadas, they sing when they are adult, but the rest of their lives are spent feeding on roots underground.

PRAYING MANTIS
With strange angular features and triangular heads, praying mantises look almost like creatures from another planet. They are instantly recognizable by their long, folded front legs, held up together as if in prayer. These can lash out with astonishing speed to catch hold of live prey. Some species, such as this Thai boxer praying mantis, are brightly colored, but most blend in with their surroundings.

Size > ½–⅔ in (1.2–15 cm) **Weight >** up to ⅓ oz (10 g)
Habitat > Rain forests and jungles. **Distribution >** Tropical areas, especially Africa, Southeast Asia, and Australia. Also South and Central America and Southern US. Some species are also found in Europe, Central Asia, and Japan. **Diet >** Flying insects such as moths, grasshoppers, flies, and other mantises. Females eat males after, or even during, mating. **Breeding >** Females lay hundreds of eggs in an egg case stuck to a plant or buried in the ground. Eggs hatch into nymphs. **Life span >** 10–12 months. **Predators >** Large birds, frogs, chameleons, snakes, bats, and monkeys. Mantises protect themselves by camouflage.

Beetles

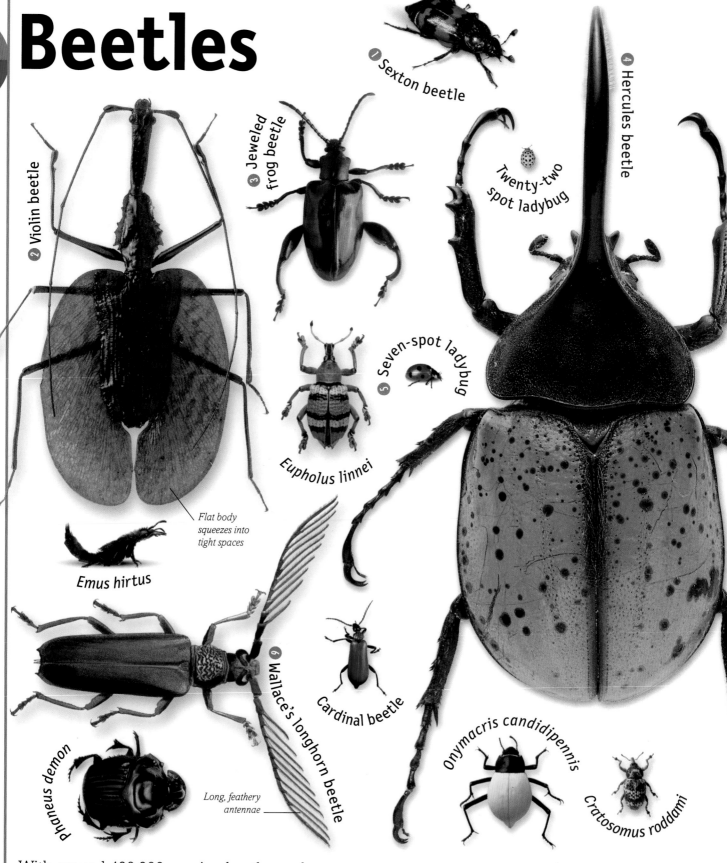

① Sexton beetle

④ Hercules beetle

③ Jeweled frog beetle

② Violin beetle

Twenty-two spot ladybug

⑤ Seven-spot ladybug

Eupholus linnei

Flat body squeezes into tight spaces

Emus hirtus

⑥ Wallace's longhorn beetle

Long, feathery antennae

Cardinal beetle

Phaneus demon

Onymacris candidipennis

Cratosomus roddami

With around 400,000 species, beetles make up by far the largest group of insect. They start life as larvae, also known as grubs. Adults usually have two pairs of wings. Their front wings, called elytra, are specially hardened and fit over the hind wings like a case. Beetles eat a huge range of different foods. The **sexton beetle** ❶ buries the dead bodies of small birds and rodents such as mice. The female lays eggs in these remains, so her grubs have their own private food supply. The **violin beetle** ❷ squeezes its flat body under tree bark, where it feeds on other insects and snails. The grubs of the **jeweled frog beetle** ❸ grow up inside plant stems. Beetles vary greatly in size. While the smallest could easily fit on the head of a pin, the biggest kinds, such as the **Hercules beetle** ❹, can be more than

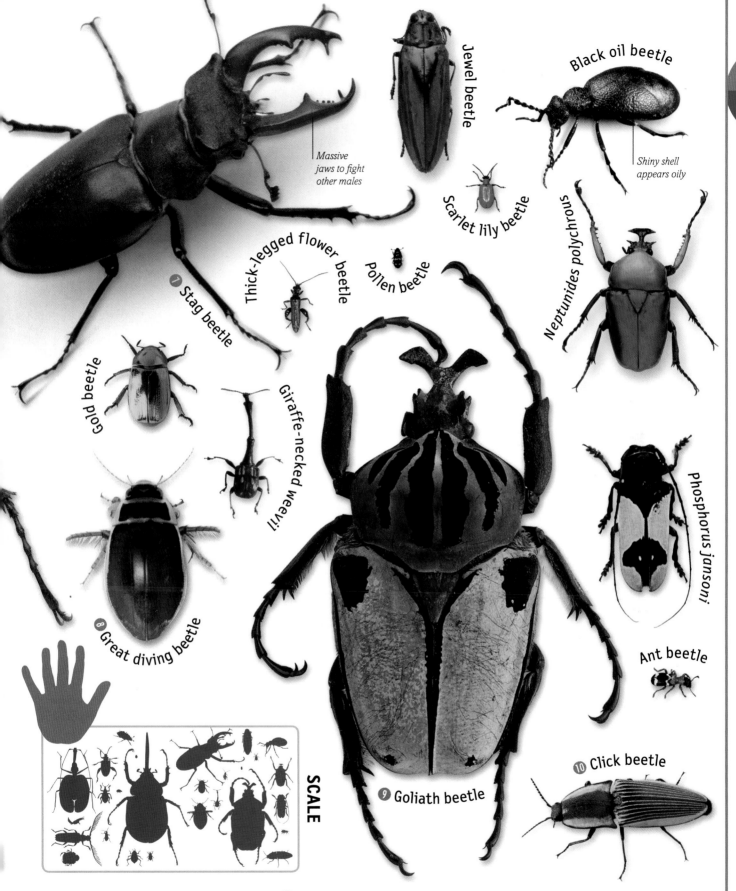

Massive jaws to fight other males

Jewel beetle

Black oil beetle

Shiny shell appears oily

Scarlet lily beetle

Neptunides polychrous

Thick-legged flower beetle

Pollen beetle

7 Stag beetle

Gold beetle

Giraffe-necked weevil

Phosphorus jansoni

8 Great diving beetle

Ant beetle

SCALE

10 Click beetle

9 Goliath beetle

6 in (15 cm) long. The **seven-spot ladybug** 5 feeds on aphids, making it a useful ally for farmers and gardeners. **Wallace's longhorn beetle** 6 grubs bore into living trees, while **stag beetle** 7 grubs live in rotting wood. They stay hidden for up to six years before turning into adults. Adult males fight with their antler-shaped jaws and the winner gets a chance to mate. The **great diving beetle** 8 is found in ponds and streams, where it swims with back legs that work like a pair of oars. It eats tadpoles and even small fish. Measuring up to 4 in (10 cm) long, the **goliath beetle** 9 is the heaviest insect in the world. Its grubs can weigh up to 3½ oz (100 g). Beneath the soil's surface, **click beetle** 10 grubs, known as wireworms, chew their way through roots. They can cause serious damage to crops.

Butterflies and moths

① Wallich's owl moth

② Queen cracker

Regent skipper

Adonis blue

Garden tiger

Snout moth

Diva moth

Male has feathery antennae

Australian magpie moth

③ Apollo

Oak eggar

Blue triangle

Blue tharops

Blue band on upper side of each wing

④ Madagascan sunset moth

Six-spot burnet

Coppery dysphania

⑤ Hercules moth

White plume moth

Cleopatra

Unlike other insects, butterflies and moths are covered with thousands of tiny scales that create vivid patterns. Butterflies are often brightly colored, while moths are usually drab. Most moths, including **Wallich's owl moth** ①, fly by night and use their camouflaged markings to hide during the day, but some fly by day and have eye-catching wings. Male **queen cracker** ② butterflies click their wings when they fly as a way of marking their territory. **Apollo** ③ butterflies often live in cold climates on mountains, but far more butterflies and moths come from warm parts of the world. Often mistaken for a butterfly, the beautiful **Madagascan sunset moth** ④ is a daytime flyer. The **Hercules moth** ⑤ is one of the largest species, measuring up to 13 in (34 cm) across. From Papua New Guinea,

Purple emperor

Green dragontail

Hornet coloring deters predators

Hornet moth

Queen Alexandra's birdwing ❻

⑦ Monarch butterfly

Guava skipper

Tiger pierid

Clara's satin moth

Small postman

⑧ Indian leaf butterfly

Big greasy butterfly

False eyes frighten attackers

Polyphemus moth

❾ Silk moth

Narrow tail mimics leaf stalk

Rajah Brooke's birdwing

Small copper

⑩ American moon moth

Duke of Burgundy fritillary

Long hind wing tail

Queen Alexandra's birdwing ❻ is the world's biggest butterfly with a wingspan of up to 12 in (31 cm). It flies high up, and in the past collectors used shotguns to knock it out of the trees. The North American **monarch butterfly** ❼ is the greatest traveler, flying 2,800 miles (4,500 km) from Mexico as far north as Canada to breed. When winter comes, it flies all the way back again to escape the cold. **Indian leaf**

butterflies ❽ are easy to spot with their wings open, but look just like dead leaves with them closed. **Silk moths** ❾ have been bred in captivity for thousands of years. Silk is made by unwinding the cocoons that shelter their caterpillars. The **American moon moth** ❿ lives for less than a week as an adult. Like many other moths, it only eats as a caterpillar. Adults do not have working mouths.

⑪ Purple mort bleu

Blue night butterfly

Silver-spotted ghost moth

White admiral

Large emerald

Bent-wing ghost moth

SCALE

⑫ Acacia carpenter moth

⑬ Tiger swallowtail

Drinker moth

Narrow tail on hind wing

Ilia underwing

Cramer's mesene

⑭ Zebra swallowtail

Cairns birdwing

Elephant hawk moth

⑮ Swallowtail

California dog-face

⑯ Scarce swallowtail

Black-veined white

Butterflies and moths live their lives in four stages: egg, caterpillar, pupa, and adult. The caterpillar stage is the main feeding period, and butterflies and moths are often very choosy about their food. The **purple mort bleu** ⑪, from Central and South America, grows up on bamboo leaves, while in Australia caterpillars of the **acacia carpenter moth** ⑫ bore their way into wattle or acacia trees.

The **tiger swallowtail** ⑬ from North America lays its eggs on many kinds of plants, but the **zebra swallowtail** ⑭ always picks out pawpaw trees. The **swallowtail** ⑮ and **scarce swallowtail** ⑯ have caterpillars with inflatable colored "horns." The horns suddenly appear if the caterpillar is touched, and they have a repulsive smell that helps to keep predators away. The **common morpho** ⑰, from Central

Brown hairstreak

Lappet moth

Buff-tip

⑱ Atlas moth

Metallic blue upperwings

Transparent "windows" on all four wings

Argent and sable

⑰ Common morpho

⑲ Verdant sphinx

Long, oval-shaped forewings

Small white

⑳ Owl butterfly

Orange-barred sulphur

pine-tree lappet

Spanish festoon

⑳ Giant Agrippa

Forewings much longer than hind wings

Sonoran blue

False eyes on hind wings

Red patches on forewings scare off predators

Schulze's agrias

Orange tip

Giant leopard moth

and South America, has striking, bright blue wings. The butterfly was once collected for use in jewelry because its blue color does not fade even after it has died. The huge **Atlas moth** ⑱, found in Southeast Asia, has the largest wing area of any butterfly or moth. At over 62 sq in (400 cm²), it is the size of a dinner plate. The **verdant sphinx** ⑲ and its relatives are some of the fastest fliers. Narrow wings and streamlined abdomens help these moths to attain top speeds of more than 22 mph (35 kph). The **owl butterfly** ⑳ gets its name from the huge eyespots on its hind wings. They give it a scary "face," making birds think twice before risking an attack. The **giant Agrippa** ㉑ has the biggest wingspan of any insect. The largest giant Agrippa moth on record measured 14 in (36 cm) from tip to tip.

SLUG MOTH CATERPILLAR
Butterflies and moths begin life as wingless larvae called caterpillars. Some of these are hard to spot, but others, such as this slug moth caterpillar from Papua New Guinea, are brightly colored and bizarrely shaped. You might expect such a colorful creature to develop into an equally striking adult, but fully developed slug moths are often dull in color.

Size › Variable, but small **Habitat ›** Lowland forest, swamps, and mangroves. **Distribution ›** Tropical, subtropical, and some temperate areas, including the eastern US, sub-Saharan Africa, South and Southeast Asia, and Australasia. **Diet ›** In many species adults have no mouthparts. They do all their eating as caterpillars, devouring the leaves of plants such as figs. Some species are seen as pests because they eat crops. **Breeding ›** Caterpillars retreat into hard, round cocoons, from which they emerge as adult moths. Adults mate and lay eggs that will hatch into new caterpillars. **Predators ›** Parasitic flies and wasps. Pest species may be killed by humans. **Number of species ›** About 1,000 slug moth species.

Flies

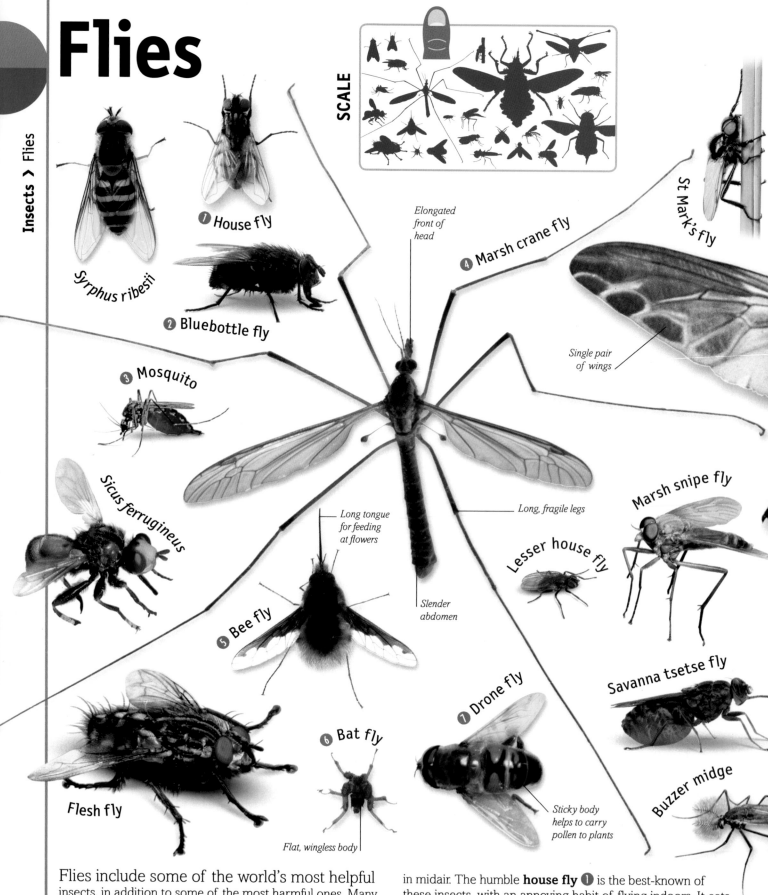

SCALE

1 House fly

Syrphus ribesii

2 Bluebottle fly

3 Mosquito

Elongated front of head

4 Marsh crane fly

St Mark's fly

Single pair of wings

Sicus ferrugineus

Long tongue for feeding at flowers

Long, fragile legs

Marsh snipe fly

Lesser house fly

Slender abdomen

5 Bee fly

6 Bat fly

7 Drone fly

Savanna tsetse fly

Flesh fly

Flat, wingless body

Sticky body helps to carry pollen to plants

Buzzer midge

Flies include some of the world's most helpful insects, in addition to some of the most harmful ones. Many of them have bristly bodies, and most have just one pair of wings. In place of the rear wings, they have a pair of tiny knobs. These work like an aircraft's gyroscopes, keeping the fly stable in the air so it can perform extreme aerobatics. These include landing upside down and hovering steadily in midair. The humble **house fly 1** is the best-known of these insects, with an annoying habit of flying indoors. It eats anything sweet and spreads germs as it feeds. The **bluebottle fly 2** lays its eggs on meat and carrion, which its maggots burrow into, eating as they go. **Mosquitoes 3** have sharp mouthparts and drink blood by piercing the skin of other animals. In some parts of the world they carry parasites

Long, flexible snout for stabbing and sucking prey

8 Giant blue robber fly

9 Stalk-eyed fly

Cabbage root fly

10 Banded brown horsefly

Forest fly

Legs with strong claws

Moth fly

Platyura marginata

11 Timber fly

Dark cloud on wing

Leucozona leucorum

Marmalade hoverfly

Dumpy abdomen

that can cause malaria and other killer diseases. The **marsh crane fly** **4** has extra-long legs that break off if it is touched. **Bee flies** **5** do a useful job by pollinating flowers. The **bat fly** **6** has no wings. It does not need them because it spends its adult life in the fur of bats. **Drone flies** **7** are very good at mimicking honey bees. Like bee flies, they are effective pollinators. The awesome-looking **giant blue robber fly** **8** from Australia grabs other insects on the wing and flies with a distinctive buzzing sound. Male **stalk-eyed flies** **9** have bizarre heads with eyes set far apart. In the breeding season, males stand head to head, and the one with the widest eyes wins. The **banded brown horsefly** **10** bites horses, and sometimes humans, too, but **timber flies** **11** are harmless and do not feed at all as adults.

Bees, wasps, and ants

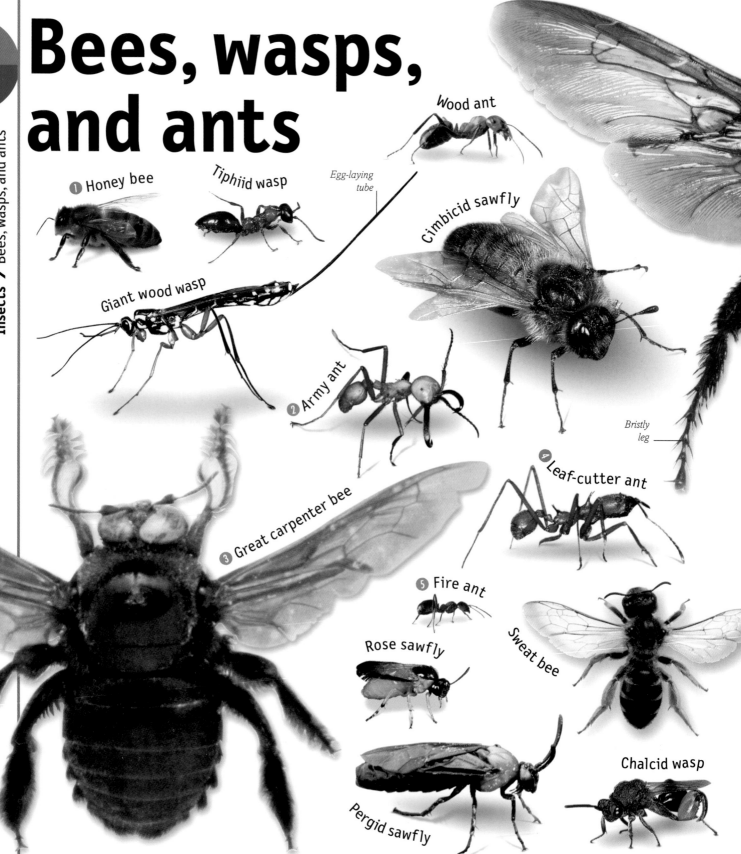

① Honey bee

Tiphiid wasp

Giant wood wasp

Wood ant

Egg-laying tube

Cimbicid sawfly

Bristly leg

② Army ant

④ Leaf-cutter ant

③ Great carpenter bee

⑤ Fire ant

Rose sawfly

Sweat bee

Chalcid wasp

Pergid sawfly

Bees and their relatives are very useful insects. Although many of them pack a painful sting, they help farmers by pollinating crops and killing pests. Except for sawflies, they all have slender waists and most have two pairs of transparent wings. **Honey bees ①** live in nests containing thousands of workers ruled by a single queen. The queen lays the eggs, while the worker bees build the nest, collect food, and care for the young. **Army ants ②** also live together but do not make a permanent home. Instead, millions of them rush across the rain-forest floor, grabbing small animals with their powerful jaws. The **great carpenter bee ③** feeds on nectar from flowers, and lays its eggs in tunnels in dead wood. Like other bees, it uses its sting only if attacked. **Leaf-cutter ants ④** make giant nests underground, and feed on a special

Mammoth wasp 6

Orchid bee

Extra-long tongue

Slender waist

Splendid emerald wasp

Oak apple gall wasp

Common wasp 7

Long antennae

Plasterer bee 8

Pteromalid wasp

Horntail 10

SCALE

Furlike bristles

Egg-laying tube

Buff-tailed bumblebee 9

fungus that they grow on chewed-up leaves. These ants are harmless, but some others are not. Tropical **fire ants** 5 have a vicious sting that feels worse than a burn. The **mammoth wasp** 6 is a predator. It paralyzes the grubs of scarab beetles and lays eggs on their bodies, so its young have a private food supply. **Common wasps** 7 make papery nests and help to get rid of pests by hunting insects to feed their

young. **Plasterer bees** 8 and **buff-tailed bumblebees** 9 nest in the ground. Plasterer bees waterproof the walls of their nests with a fluid from their bodies. Bumblebees have furry insulation that lets them fly in the cold days of early spring. They are good crop pollinators. The **horntail** 10 looks dangerous but cannot sting. Females lay their eggs in pine trees, and their grubs feed by chewing through wood.

Fishes

Fishes were the first vertebrates to evolve. They live underwater and their streamlined bodies are adapted for speedy swimming. They breathe by absorbing oxygen from the water through their gills. Fishes have a special extra sense, using organs along their sides to detect vibrations in the water.

Tail › Most fishes use their tails to power themselves through the water. This lionfish can use its tail to stay steady in the water, so it can hang motionless, ready to ambush passing prey.

Fins › Fish fins consist of bony spines linked by membranes. The fish uses them to steer its body through the water. In some species they are adapted for other purposes, such as burrowing into mud or sand to hide. This lionfish can inject venom through spines in some of its fins.

Red lionfish

Features

- Most lay eggs to reproduce

- Live underwater

- Absorb oxygen from the water using gills

- Swim with the help of fins and a tail

- Most are cold-blooded

Gills › Like all animals, fishes need oxygen to survive, which they absorb from the water using gills. As the fish swims, water constantly flows across a stack of fine membranes inside the gills, through which oxygen passes into the fish's bloodstream.

Sharks, rays, and skates

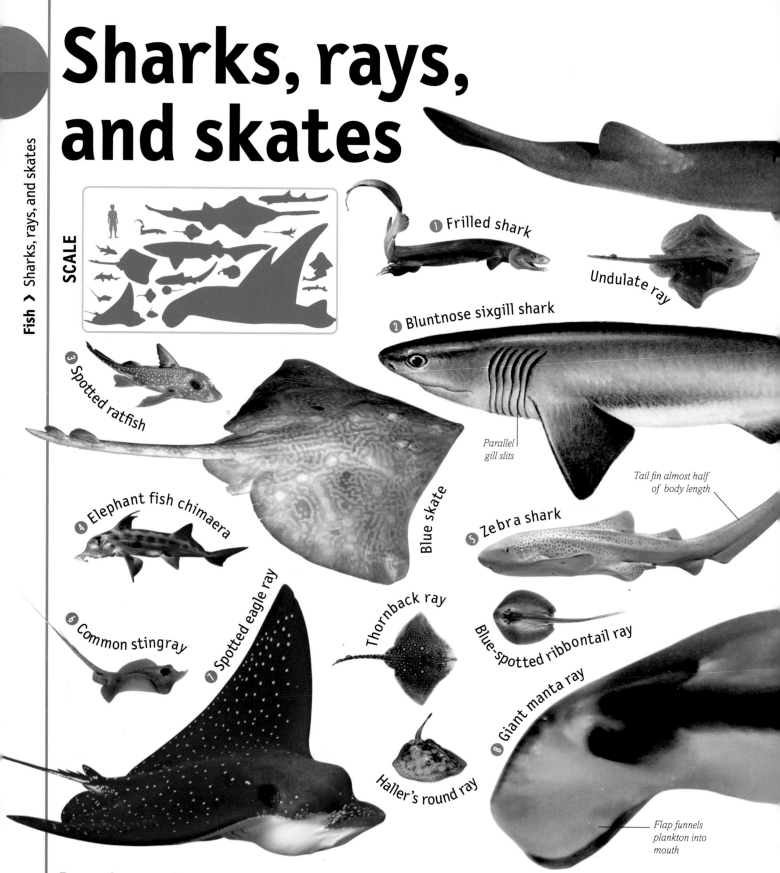

SCALE

① Frilled shark

Undulate ray

② Bluntnose sixgill shark

③ Spotted ratfish

Parallel gill slits

Tail fin almost half of body length

④ Elephant fish chimaera

Blue skate

⑤ Zebra shark

⑥ Common stingray

⑦ Spotted eagle ray

Thornback ray

Blue-spotted ribbontail ray

Giant manta ray

Haller's round ray

Flap funnels plankton into mouth

Razor-sharp teeth and powerful jaws make sharks the most fearsome hunters in the seas. Like skates and rays, they have skeletons made of cartilage or gristle. **Frilled sharks ①** and **bluntnose sixgill sharks ②** live in deep water, but many other sharks live near the surface, in open water or close to the shore. Most sharks have a streamlined body and several rows of sharp teeth that are constantly replaced throughout their lives. Their relatives chimaeras, a group of blunt-headed fish, have teeth that last the whole of their lives. The **spotted ratfish ③** and **elephant fish chimaera ④** use their flat teeth for crushing mollusks and crabs. Some sharks have to swim nonstop to breathe, but **zebra sharks ⑤** spend the day resting on the seabed, waking up to hunt after dark. Skates and rays have winglike front fins

⑨ Smalltooth sawfish

Nurse shark

Snout can sense prey buried in seabed

⑩ Longnose sawshark

Sensory barbels used to detect vibrations

Winglike front fins

Sand devil

Brownish gray color acts as camouflage on the ocean floor

Marbled electric ray

Epaulette catshark

and mouths on their undersides. Some kinds, including the **common stingray** ⑥, have a venomous spine in their tails. Accidentally stepping on these fish can be very dangerous. In some cases, a single jab from a spine can kill a person. Rays swim by beating their front fins like a bird's wings. The **spotted eagle ray** ⑦ feeds on seabed animals, while the **giant manta ray** ⑧ scoops up plankton as it "flies" through the open sea.

Measuring up to 30 ft (9 m) across, this colossal but harmless fish is the largest ray in the world, with an exceptionally big brain. The **smalltooth sawfish** ⑨ is a rare and unusual ray with a toothed snout like a saw. It uses this to dig up animals in the seabed and to slash at other fish that come nearby. The **longnose sawshark** ⑩ looks similar, but is much smaller, with two barbels, or feelers, attached to its snout.

107

⑪ Shortfin mako

⑫ Great white shark

Piked dogfish

Large, sawlike teeth for ripping apart prey

Blacknose shark

Kitefin shark

Large dorsal fin

Starry smooth-hound

⑬ Blue shark

Sharply pointed snout

⑮ Smooth hammerhead

SCALE

⑭ Small-spotted catshark

Pectoral fins act as stabilizers

Some of the world's biggest sharks roam the open seas. The **shortfin mako** ⑪ is one of the fastest of these tireless hunters. In short bursts, it can swim up to 45 mph (70 kph). Makos feed mainly on fast-swimming fish and squid, but the **great white shark** ⑫ has a taste for seals, dolphins, and occasionally humans, too. Growing up to 24 ft (7 m) in length and weighing as much as 2 tons, this gigantic and much-feared predator typically attacks from below, and it sometimes bursts out of the water as it slams into its prey. The beautifully streamlined **blue shark** ⑬ travels thousands of miles a year, between the places where it feeds and the places where it breeds. Like most large sharks, it gives birth to live young. **Small-spotted catsharks** ⑭ and their relatives lay eggs with leathery cases. Called

16 Port Jackson shark

Highly flexible tail used to stun prey

17 Horn shark

18 Thresher shark

Light and dark shading hides shark from above and below

Sharpnose sevengill shark

Tail with two equal-sized blades

19 Blacktip reef shark

20 Whitetip reef shark

21 Bull shark

"mermaid's purses," these can take over a year to hatch. The **smooth hammerhead 15** belongs to a family of shark with strange T-shaped heads. Its eyes are at each end of the head, enabling it to see all around as it swims. **Port Jackson sharks 16** and **horn sharks 17** live on the seabed. They have downward-facing mouths and flat back teeth that crunch up mollusks and other hard-bodied animals. The **thresher shark 18** is an open-water predator. Its extra-long tail works like a whip, stunning other fish and making them easy to catch. **Blacktip reef sharks 19** and **whitetip reef sharks 20** rarely harm humans, but the **bull shark 21** is a notorious man-eater, with a habit of swimming up rivers and cruising close to the shore. Despite its size—up to 11 ft (3.4 m) long—it can hunt in water just 3 ft (1 m) deep.

109

WHALE SHARK
By far the largest fish in the world, the whale shark has a huge mouth that stretches almost as wide as its whole body and is armed with up to 300 rows of tiny teeth. Despite its fearsome appearance, however, this gentle giant feeds on plankton. In fact, it is often followed by schools of smaller fish that keep the shark clean by eating bacteria and debris from its mouth.

Size > 23–40 ft (7–12 m). Some may grow even larger. **Weight >** Up to 20 tons (18½ metric tons) **Habitat >** Tropical and warm temperate seas. They migrate thousands of miles every year. **Distribution >** Pacific, South Atlantic, and Indian oceans. **Diet >** Plankton, small fishes, and crustaceans. Whale sharks feed by taking in water then pushing it through their gills to filter out the food. **Breeding >** The female carries up to 300 embryos and gives birth to live young. **Life span >** Unknown, but thought to be up to 150 years. **Predators >** Adults have no enemies except humans. Other sharks, sailfishes, and killer whales may attack the young. **Conservation status >** Vulnerable due to hunting.

Saltwater fishes

① Spotted boxfish

White-spotted puffer

Warty frogfish

Body swollen with water

② Long-spine porcupine fish

Spiny front fins can grip seaweed

③ Clown triggerfish

④ Sargassum fish

Large mouth has blunt teeth adapted for crushing prey

⑤ Zebra moray

Spotted garden eel

Tail burrows into sand as anchor

Saltwater fishes come in a mind-boggling variety of shapes, sizes, and colors, and scientists discover many new kinds every year. Rays and sharks have rubbery (cartilaginous) skeletons, but most saltwater fishes have bony skeletons and are covered in scales. The **spotted boxfish's** ① scales fit together like armor plating, while the **long-spine porcupine fish** ② has scales with sharp spines. If it feels threatened, this fish swallows lots of water and turns into a prickly ball. The **clown triggerfish** ③ lives in the Indian and Pacific oceans and jams itself in coral reefs if danger comes its way. It feeds by crunching up sea urchins and other hard-shelled animals. The **sargassum fish** ④ lives in floating seaweed around the world. Even in broad daylight, its incredible camouflage makes it almost impossible to see. The **zebra moray** ⑤

⑥ Needlefish

Variegated lizard fish

Striped eel catfish

Pineapple fish

Longspined bullhead

Crowned squirrelfish

⑦ Red lionfish

Flying gurnard

Camouflage imitates rock

Upturned mouth sucks in smaller fish

⑨ Yellow seahorse

⑧ Stonefish

Weedy seadragon

Smallscale scorpionfish

Tail winds around solid objects

⑩ Coral toadfish

Extra-large fins for gliding over seabed

Trumpet fish

SCALE

comes out to feed at night. To grip its prey firmly, it has a second set of jaws in its throat that can spring forward into its mouth. **Needlefish** ⑥ live near the surface of the water. Large specimens have been known to spear people by jumping on to boats. The **red lionfish's** ⑦ striped colors warn predators that this fish is venomous. It defends itself by spreading out its poison-tipped fins. The **stonefish** ⑧

can give humans a lethal jab with its venomous spines. The **yellow seahorse** ⑨ swims with its body upright. Like other seahorses, it is one of the world's slowest fishes, with a maximum speed of just a few yards an hour. Male **coral toadfish** ⑩ make strange grunting or whistling sounds to attract females. After the females have laid their eggs, the males guard them until the young fishes hatch and swim away.

113

SCALE

⑪ Emperor angelfish

⑫ Banded archerfish

Royal gramma

Royal angelfish

Long dorsal fin raised like a sail

Butterfly blenny

Ocher-striped cardinal fish

Brown meagre

⑬ Blue-spotted sea bream

⑭ Powder-blue surgeonfish

Longnose hawkfish

⑮ Clown anemonefish

Slender body fits in burrow

Red mullet

Fleshy barbels help detect buried prey

More fishes live on coasts and coral reefs than anywhere else in the seas. The **emperor angelfish** ⑪ and its relatives are some of the most colorful reef-dwellers, with vivid markings that change as they mature. **Banded archerfish** ⑫ live in estuaries in Southeast Asia. They look for insects on overhanging branches and knock them off by squirting a jet of water from their mouths. The **blue-spotted sea bream** ⑬ eats animals on the seabed, while the beautiful **powder-blue surgeonfish** ⑭ feeds mainly on algae and underwater plants. Surgeonfish look harmless, but when attacked they fight back using two sharp blades on both sides of their tails. The **clown anemonefish** ⑮ hides in the tentacles of sea anemones. Unlike other fish, it is not harmed by their stings. **Common bluestripe snappers** ⑯

Harlequin sweetlips

Bold pattern camouflages eyes

16 Common bluestripe snapper

17 Harlequin tuskfish

Bluefish

18 Mediterranean parrot fish

19 Atlantic mudskipper

Foxface rabbitfish

Red bandfish

20 Albacore tuna

live on coral reefs. They move in fast-swimming schools by day, dispersing at night to feed. The **harlequin tuskfish 17** flips over stones with its teeth to get at small animals hiding underneath. The **Mediterranean parrot fish 18** crunches up food with its beak-shaped mouth. Like many other parrot fishes, it starts out life as female, but may change into a male as it grows older. **Atlantic mudskippers 19** live in mangrove swamps, where they climb up roots or hop across the mud. Their front fins work like stubby legs, and they can survive out of the water by breathing air through their skin. The **albacore tuna 20** belongs to a family of high-speed swimmers with muscle-packed bodies and long, razorlike fins. Unlike most fishes, tunas are warm-blooded, and they can hurtle through water at up to 50 mph (80 kph).

SCALE

㉑ Shore rockling

Snakelike body

Three fins on back

Slippery body without scales

Gunnel

㉓ Turbot

Upper side camouflaged against seabed

㉒ Atlantic mackerel

㉔ Lesser weever fish

Small sandeel

Sea fishes thrive in cold water because it is often full of food. **Shore rocklings ㉑** search for shrimp and crabs in rock pools using sensitive whiskers or barbels. **Atlantic mackerels ㉒** live in the open sea. Like tunas, they have muscle-packed bodies and a streamlined shape for speeding through the water. They have to keep swimming, as they rely on the flow of water to breathe. **Turbot ㉓** and other flatfishes live on the seabed. Very young flatfishes look like other fishes. As they grow up, one eye moves around their heads until, as adults, they swim on one side with both eyes facing up. The **lesser weever fish ㉔** also lives on the bottom, with its body half-buried near the shore. This venomous fish has spines on its back, which it raises to defend itself against predators. It can even give humans a painful sting. **Sockeye salmon ㉕** spend

116

㉕ Sockeye salmon

㉖ John Dory

Large eyes give good vision

Jaws extend to catch prey

㉗ Atlantic cod

Fleshy barbel on chin

Peruvian anchoveta

㉘ Atlantic herring

Allis shad

European plaice ㉙

Lemon sole ㉚

Both eyes on right-hand side, which always faces upward

their adult lives in the northern Pacific Ocean but return to freshwater to breed. In some rivers, thousands of sockeyes fight their way upstream, creating a feast for fish-eating eagles and bears. The **John Dory** ㉖ looks big when seen from the side, but it is good at sneaking up on other fish because its body is as thin as a human hand. The **Atlantic cod** ㉗ and **Atlantic herring** ㉘ are often fished for food. Cod can produce 5 million eggs every time they breed, but their numbers have plummeted due to overfishing. Herrings are some of the most common fishes in the seas. A single school can contain more than a billion members, attracting predators such as seals, whales, and larger fishes. The **European plaice** ㉙ and **lemon sole** ㉚ are two flatfishes that are highly prized as food. Both of them often hide on the seabed by covering themselves with sand.

BLACK-STRIPED SALEMA

These tropical fish are found in waters around the Galápagos Islands. They form huge schools of hundreds or thousands. When a predator approaches, the school bunches into a tight cluster known as a bait ball. By swarming together, splitting, and changing direction in a flash, these fish try to confuse predators, making it difficult for them to attack.

Size ❯ Up to 12 in (30 cm) long **Habitat ❯** Reefs and rocky areas in shallow waters. They gather in large schools during the day, but disperse at night. **Distribution ❯** Eastern Pacific Ocean, only around the Galápagos Islands. **Diet ❯** Plankton and fish larvae **Breeding ❯** The female releases eggs that float freely in the ocean. These eggs hatch into tiny larvae without scales or fins, which slowly develop into young fishes. **Predators ❯** Dolphins, seals, penguins, and sharks. **Conservation status ❯** Vulnerable due to changes in its environment. Recently, a weather system called El Niño has disrupted the oceans around the Galápagos, increasing water temperatures, which may affect fishes like these.

Deep-sea fishes

① Tripodfish

② Common fangtooth

Bristlemouth

Pacific hatchetfish

Elongated rays form a tripod

③ Orange roughy

Lure can be held in front of mouth

④ Football fish

Northern stoplight loosejaw

Giant super-flexible jaws

Tiny lights or photophores on both sides

Viperfish

The deep sea is dark, silent, and bitterly cold. The fishes that live here have evolved strange shapes to survive. Food is hard to find here, so deep-sea fishes cannot waste any chance to catch a meal. The **tripodfish** ① perches above the seabed, propped up by three long rays that stick out from its fins. It faces into the current and catches small animals that drift by. The **common fangtooth** ② lives at depths of up to 16,500 ft (5,000 m). It feeds on smaller fishes, grabbing them with its needlelike fangs and swallowing them whole. The **orange roughy** ③ gathers over ocean ridges and underwater mountains. It grows very slowly and can live to be 150 years old. The **football fish** ④ attracts its prey using luminous lures that dangle in front of its mouth. If other fishes come near to investigate, they are instantly

5 Pacific grenadier

6 Black swallower

Luminous lanternfish

Spotted lanternfish

Narrownecked oceanic eel

Prickly lanternfish

Slender fins held above body

Sense organs on the sides detect vibrations in the water

7 Feelerfish

Pearlfish

Pink frogmouth

Long, whiplike tail

Flabby whalefish

Stretchy stomach can contain large prey

9 Pelican eel

SCALE

8 Dragonfish

Glowing lure attracts prey

sucked inside. Female football fishes really are as big as footballs, but the males are tiny and often fasten themselves to the females as parasites. The **Pacific grenadier 5** cruises over the ocean floor, gently rippling its long, ratlike tail, while the **black swallower 6** has a super-stretchy stomach and can gulp down prey larger than itself. The **feelerfish 7** stays close to the ocean floor. Its front fins are thin and whiskery and work like antennae for sensing food. The **dragonfish 8** is a ferocious predator. Like many deep-sea fish, it has organs called photophores which glow in the dark, to attract prey or signal to mates. The **pelican eel 9** has enormous jaws but tiny teeth. It uses its mouth like a scoop to catch its prey. Like the black swallower, it has an expandable stomach to deal with oversized meals.

Freshwater fishes

1 Goldfish

Green sunfish

Clown loach

Extra-large decorative scales

2 Koi carp

3 Glass catfish

Brown bullhead

Tench

4 Tiger shovelnose catfish

5 Chain pickerel

Giant whiptail catfish

Sensitive barbels to probe for food

Fishes live in a huge variety of freshwater habitats, from lakes and rivers to streams and ponds. They can be found in hot springs, where the water temperature is a steamy 104°F (40°C), and in chilly caves hundreds of feet underground. The smallest fishes, even the fully grown ones, are not much bigger than a grain of rice, while the biggest are as long as a family car. Some freshwater fishes, including the **goldfish** 1 and **koi carp** 2, have been raised in captivity for hundreds of years. There are many varieties of both of these fishes, and the rarest koi carp can be worth more than $1 million. Catfish are common freshwater fishes, particularly where the water is murky or the current is slow. The **glass catfish** 3 from Southeast Asia has a transparent body. The South American **tiger shovelnose catfish** 4 has

Longsnout distichodus

This cave-dwelling species has no eyes

Mexican tetra

6 Red piranha

7 American paddlefish

Mudminnow

8 Tigerfish

Prominent jaw with sharp teeth

River hatchetfish

Striped anostomus

9 European eel

Large rear fins help the fish to hover in one spot

SCALE

long barbels that probe the riverbed for food. The **chain pickerel** 5 is an ambush hunter. It lurks in the shallows and lunges at other fish with a powerful flick of its tail. The **red piranha** 6 from South America usually eats fishes, worms, and crustaceans, but a large group of red piranhas can attack big mammals, stripping away chunks of flesh with their razor-sharp teeth. The **American paddlefish** 7 looks ferocious, but it feeds only on tiny animals filtered out by its gills. The **tigerfish** 8 is a fierce predator from Africa's rivers. It is famous for putting up a tremendous fight if hooked. The **European eel** 9 is a long-distance migrant. It spawns in the Sargasso Sea, in the North Atlantic Ocean, and its tiny young travel all the way back to Europe's rivers, an epic journey of up to 3,700 miles (6,000 km).

SCALE

⑩ **Elephantnose fish**

Long lower jaw used to probe for food

Chipokae

Clown knifefish

⑪ **Electric eel**

Mouth can gulp air in stagnant water

⑫ **Four-eyed fish**

Slippery skin without scales

Burbot

Spotted ctenopoma

Large mouth with strong jaws

⑬ Siamese fighting fish

Thin, rounded tail

Zebrafish

⑭ **Arctic char**

Many freshwater fishes have special skills that help them to survive. The **elephantnose fish** ⑩ from tropical Africa lives in murky rivers. It finds its way by giving off weak electric signals and probes for food using its long lower jaw. The **electric eel** ⑪ from South America uses electricity to find and kill prey. It can give a jolt of up to 650 volts, enough to shock a person standing in nearby water. The **four-eyed fish** ⑫ has eyes that are divided into two, letting it see clearly above and below the waterline. **Siamese fighting fish** ⑬ are small but famously aggressive. When two males clash, they sometimes fight to the death. Far away from the tropics, the **Arctic char** ⑭ lives in icy rivers and cold lakes. It is one of the world's most northerly freshwater fishes, surviving as close as 500 miles (800 km)

⑮ European perch

⑯ Nile tilapia

⑰ African lungfish

Blade-shaped tail

⑱ Rainbow trout

Threadlike front fins

⑲ Longnose gar

to the North Pole. The **European perch** ⑮ is a patient predator, lying in wait for its prey. It lays eggs in long ribbons and fastens them to underwater plants. A distant relative of the European perch, the African **Nile tilapia** ⑯ breeds in a very different way. The female scoops up her eggs, up to 2,000 at a time, and holds them in her mouth until they hatch and her young swim away. The **African lungfish** ⑰ lives in lakes and swamps that can dry out for months at a time. It seals itself up in a cocoon of mud and survives by breathing air. The **rainbow trout** ⑱ originally came from North America but has been introduced into lakes and rivers in many other parts of the world for food and sport. Another American fish, the **longnose gar** ⑲ bursts out of hiding to stab other fish with its needle-sharp teeth.

Amphibians

Amphibians spend part of their lives in the water and part on land. Some kinds undergo metamorphosis, like many invertebrates, starting out as water-based tadpoles with gills and evolving into air-breathing adults. They need freshwater to survive, and many species are threatened with extinction due to pollution, disease, and destruction of their habitats.

Yellow banded poison-dart frog

Skin › Amphibians have permeable skin, so water can pass outward and evaporate. Becuase of this, they mostly live in water or in damp areas to keep their bodies from drying out.

Poison glands > Many species of amphibian secrete a poisonous slime from glands in their skin. This helps to keep them moist and deter predators. Some amphibians simply taste nasty, while others, like this yellow banded poison-dart frog, can be deadly to some predators.

Features

- Usually lay eggs to reproduce

- Have moist skin and may die if they dry out

- Often spend much of their lives in water

- Some hatch as tadpoles and change shape to become adults

- Are cold-blooded

Legs > Some amphibians only have legs as adults. These kinds hatch out from eggs as tadpoles, tiny swimming creatures with tails. As the tadpoles mature, legs grow out of their bodies and their tails shrink and disappear.

Frogs and toads

Tongue flips out to catch prey

A grub makes a tasty morsel

① Lemur frog

② Giant broad-headed treefrog

③ Australian green treefrog

Loose skin soaks up water for use in dry conditions

Fringe-limbed treefrog

Suckers on all toes

④ Amazon milk frog

Orange-legged leaf frog

Yucatan casque-headed treefrog

⑤ Paradoxical frog

⑥ Solomon Islands horned frog

SCALE

Frogs and toads look very different from other amphibians, with their stubby bodies and long back legs. Frogs are usually sleek and slippery, but most toads have dry, warty skin. Nearly all of these animals start life as tadpoles, changing shape as they grow up. The **lemur frog** ① from Central America hunts insects by night and hides under leaves during the day. Like other treefrogs, it is an expert climber with slender, sucker-tipped toes. The **giant broad-headed treefrog** ② lives in South American forests. It clings to tree trunks and branches, while the **Australian green treefrog** ③ sometimes climbs into houses, where it makes itself at home in water tanks and kitchen sinks. The **Amazon milk frog** ④ lays its eggs in rain-filled tree-holes. It lives high in the treetops and hardly ever comes to the

European common toad ⑦

Golden mantella ⑧

Elegant Madagascan frog

Guyanan stubfoot toad

Malayan tree toad ⑨

Eyes with slit-shaped pupils detect small, moving prey

Cane toad ⑩

Raucous toad

Warts on male's skin develop dark, sharp spines in the breeding season

Natterjack toad

ground. The South American **paradoxical frog** ❺ spends its life in lakes and pools. It gets its name from its monster tadpoles, which are up to four times the adult's length. The **Solomon Islands horned frog** ❻ has a pointed snout and hornlike projections above its eyes, camouflaging it perfectly among fallen leaves. The **European common toad** ❼ hunts all kinds of small animals, including beetles, snails, and slugs.

The rare **golden mantella** ❽ frog from Madagascar is brilliantly colored, warning predators that it has poison-covered skin. The **Malayan tree toad** ❾ is one of the few true toads that lives off the ground. The enormous **cane toad** ❿ gulps down mice and even snakes. Originally from Central America, this ravenous predator has become a major pest in Australia and other parts of the world.

Common parsley frog

⑪ European common frog

⑫ Golden poison-dart frog

⑬ Granular poison-dart frog

Brazil-nut poison-dart frog

Yellow-banded poison-dart frog

Dyeing poison-dart frog

⑭ Edible frog

Three-striped poison-dart frog

Circular eardrums behind eyes

⑯ American bullfrog

⑮ Wood frog

SCALE

Tungara frog

Toads usually move by crawling, but frogs often hop and jump. In emergencies, the **European common frog** ⑪ can leap more than seven times its own length, equivalent to a human athlete clearing a school bus without a run-up. In Central and South America, tiny poison-dart frogs climb up trees or hop over the rain-forest floor. Their bright colors are a warning to predators to stay away. The **golden poison-dart frog** ⑫ is the deadliest, with enough poison to kill two African elephants, while the **granular poison-dart frog** ⑬ is one of the smallest and could easily fit inside a matchbox. In the past, Native Americans used these frogs to make poison hunting darts, which is how they got their names. In the breeding season, frogs and toads often make loud calls. Male **edible frogs** ⑭

17 Asian horned frog

18 Indian bullfrog

Bolifamba reed frog

Giant stump-toed frog

Common skittering frog

19 Painted toad

Rajamally wart frog

Couch's spadefoot

Sticky, bright red skin to ward off predators

Foulassi banana frog

21 Tinker reed frog

20 Tomato frog

and **wood frogs** **15** sound like quacking ducks, while the male **American bullfrog** **16** sounds more like a mooing cow. This massive frog swallows almost anything it can cram into its mouth, including smaller frogs, young turtles, and small water birds. The "horns" and the brown color of the **Asian horned frog** **17** help it blend in among fallen leaves. The **Indian bullfrog** **18** leaps into water if it is disturbed.

It usually climbs out after a few minutes, but can stay underwater for several hours. **Painted toads** **19** and **tomato frogs** **20** live on land and come out to feed at night. Their skin is covered with a gluelike substance, which helps to protect them from attack. **Tinker reed frogs** **21** from Africa lay their eggs on waterside plants. Their tadpoles wriggle down into the water after hatching.

22 Mexican burrowing toad

Spotted-thighed poison-dart frog

SCALE

Oriental fire-bellied toad

Horned marsupial frog 23

Eggs wrapped around male's hind legs

painted frog

25 Fleischmann's glass frog

24 Midwife toad

26 Ornate horned frog

Mouth as wide as head

Mascarene ridged frog

Big-headed rain frog

Frogs and toads have lots of different shapes and varied lifestyles that help them to survive. If threatened, the **Mexican burrowing toad** 22 can blow itself up to resemble a small balloon. It lives underground and feeds on ants, coming to the surface only when it breeds. The **horned marsupial frog** 23 has a strange way of breeding that lets it stay high up in trees. The female carries her eggs in a pouch on her back. Instead of producing tadpoles, they hatch directly into baby frogs. The **midwife toad** 24 was so named because the male carries the female's eggs. When the eggs are ready to hatch, he takes them to water so that the tadpoles can swim away. **Fleischmann's glass frog** 25 lives in trees. On its underside, its tiny beating heart can be seen through its transparent skin. The **ornate horned frog** 26 is a sit-and-

132

African foam-nest treefrog

Darwin's frog

Webbed feet work like parachutes

Coromandel New Zealand frog

27 Desert rain frog

Mossy frog

Southern whipping frog

Wallace's flying frog

28 Wallace's flying frog

African treefrog

West Cameroon forest treefrog

Puerto Rican coqui

Brown-striped marsh frog

29 Fraser's clawed frog

Limon robber frog

31 Common spadefoot toad

30 African bullfrog

wait hunter from the grasslands of Argentina. Camouflaged by its green and brown markings, it lurks in muddy ground and grabs anything edible that comes nearby. The **desert rain frog 27** lives and breeds among Namibian sand dunes, hiding beneath the surface during the day. **Wallace's flying frog 28** glides through the forests of Southeast Asia on its webbed feet. **Fraser's clawed frog 29** from Africa

stays in water all its life. It has a flat body, sensitive fingers, and upward-facing eyes. The **African bullfrog 30** lives in grassland and savanna. Big and aggressive, it sometimes eats its own kind. It spends the dry season underground. Males of this species defend their eggs fiercely until they hatch. The **common spadefoot toad 31** digs burrows with its back legs and spends half the year hidden away.

TREE FROGS

There are more than 900 known species of tree frog, most of which live high up in the branches of tropical rain forests. These red-eyed tree frogs are easy to recognize, thanks to their startling coloring. Their bright eyes are thought to surprise predators and discourage them from attacking. However, during the day they often keep their eyes shut, relying on their green skin to camouflage them among forest leaves.

Size > Up to 2¾ in (7 cm) **Habitat >** Trees and shrubs near water in warm, tropical forests and jungles. **Distribution >** Central America **Diet >** Insects such as crickets, flies, and moths; also worms and spiders. **Breeding >** Females lay a batch of 50 eggs on a leaf over water. This process is repeated several times. The eggs hatch after about five days and tadpoles fall into the water. **Life span >** Up to five years. **Predators >** Many climbing and flying birds, reptiles, and mammals, including snakes and monkeys. Fishes may prey on tadpoles. **Conservation status >** Numbers of some species are declining where their forest habitats are being cut down.

Salamanders and newts

SCALE

① Fire salamander

Lorestan newt

② Tiger salamander

③ Crocodile newt

Black-spotted stout newt

Sensors in skin detect prey by vibrations

④ Japanese giant salamander

Blue markings attract a mate

Oita salamander

Splayed legs

With their slender bodies and long tails, salamanders and newts look very different from frogs and toads. Many are well camouflaged, but others, including the **fire salamander** ① and **tiger salamander** ②, have bright warning colors. This shows other animals that they are poisonous and best left alone. Some species spend all their lives on land, but most return to water to mate and lay their eggs. The Asian **crocodile newt** ③ heads for ponds at the beginning of the monsoon, while the **Japanese giant salamander** ④ is fully aquatic and never leaves its watery home. Measuring up to 5 ft (1.5 m) long, this huge, wrinkly-skinned amphibian feeds on fish and freshwater insects and hunts after dark. Young salamanders and newts breathe using feathery gills. Some salamander species, such as the

⑤ Axolotl

Feathery gills

⑥ Olm

Three-lined salamander

Sardinian brook salamander

Italian cave salamander

⑦ Great crested newt

⑧ California newt

Sharp-ribbed salamander

Bones can poke through sides for defence

California giant salamander

Alpine newt

⑨ Ensatina salamander

Spectacled salamander

⑩ Three-toed amphiuma

Four-toed salamander

axolotl ⑤ and **olm ⑥**, keep their gills throughout their lives. If the axolotl loses a body part, it can regrow the entire part within months. The olm lives in dark, flooded caves. Extremely slender and totally blind, it finds its food by smell and touch. **Great crested newts ⑦** breed in ponds and have elaborate courtship displays. The male grows his impressive crest in spring and uses it to attract females waiting to lay their eggs.

On land, salamanders and newts live in damp woodlands and rocky places, and they hunt mainly after dark. During the summer, many species, such as the **California newt ⑧** and **Ensatina salamander ⑨**, keep moist by hiding under rotting logs. The **three-toed amphiuma ⑩** buries itself in mud and makes a waterproof cocoon. This slimy, snakelike amphibian has tiny legs but a powerful bite.

Reptiles

Millions of years ago reptiles ruled the Earth in the form of dinosaurs. Modern reptiles are mostly smaller, although they still include fearsome predators such as the Komodo dragon, giant snakes, and ferocious crocodiles, which can attack and kill human beings. However, they also include gentle vegetarians, such as giant tortoises and the green sea turtle.

Cold-blooded ❯ Unlike birds and mammals, reptiles cannot keep their bodies warm by burning food. Instead, they rely on sources of heat in their environment to stay warm.

Scaly skin > In addition to skin, reptiles have an outer layer of protective armor. Lizards and snakes are covered in scales. Turtles, tortoises, crocodiles, and alligators have scutes, which are horny layers of skin backed by bony plates.

Features

Panther chameleon

- Most lay eggs to reproduce

- Have dry, scaly skin

- Most are meat-eaters

- Most live in warmer climates

- Are cold-blooded

Lungs > Reptiles have lungs and must breathe air to survive. Even turtles that live underwater usually return to the surface to breathe.

Legs > Most reptiles have four legs. Some groups, such as snakes, have no legs at all. They move by pushing against the ground with their flexible bodies.

Turtles and tortoises

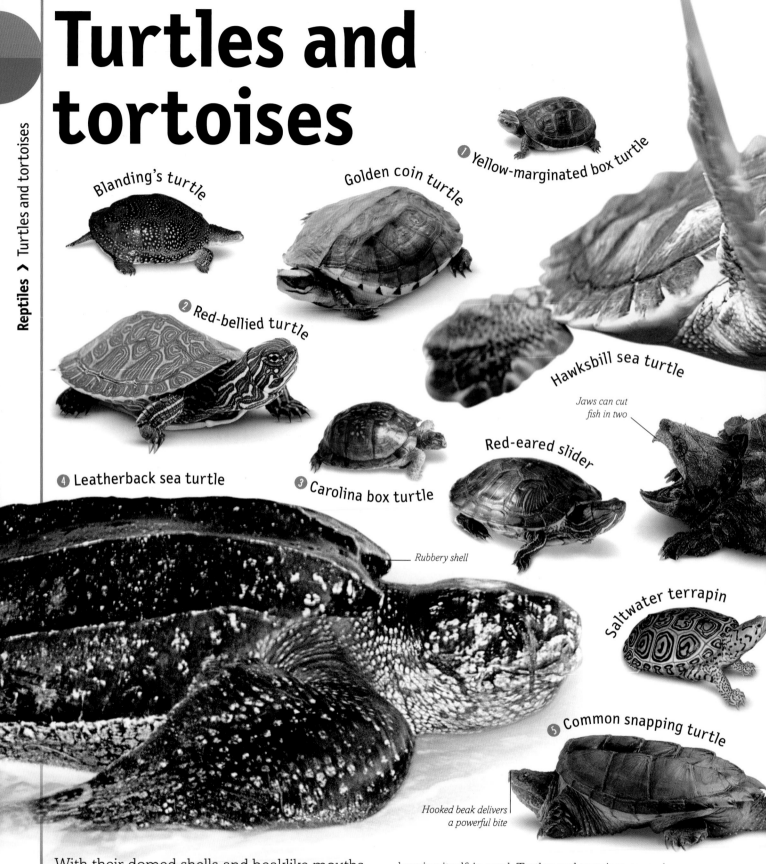

Blanding's turtle

Golden coin turtle

① Yellow-marginated box turtle

② Red-bellied turtle

Hawksbill sea turtle

Jaws can cut fish in two

Red-eared slider

④ Leatherback sea turtle

③ Carolina box turtle

Rubbery shell

Saltwater terrapin

⑤ Common snapping turtle

Hooked beak delivers a powerful bite

With their domed shells and beaklike mouths, turtles and tortoises are easy to recognize. The **yellow-marginated box turtle** ① has a hinge on the underside of its shell. If danger strikes, it quickly pulls in its head and legs and shuts itself away. The American **red-bellied turtle** ② likes sunning itself near the shore, while the **Carolina box turtle** ③ escapes the heat by retreating into cover or by burying itself in mud. Turtles and tortoises come in many sizes. The smallest ones are not much bigger than a baseball, but the record-breaking **leatherback sea turtle** ④ can weigh as much as a small car. It is one of the greatest travelers in the animal world, swimming vast distances with its large flippers. Sea turtles live mainly in tropical oceans, but freshwater turtles live in rivers and lakes, where they eat

140

Big-headed turtle

6 Chinese soft-shelled turtle

7 Painted turtle

European pond turtle

Matamata

False map turtle

Common snake-necked turtle

Asian leaf turtle

Mississippi mud turtle

8 Alligator snapping turtle

Common musk turtle

Ornate box turtle

9 Loggerhead sea turtle

Paddlelike limb

Yellow slider

SCALE

plants or animal prey. The **common snapping turtle** **5**, from North America, is one of the world's biggest freshwater turtles. It lurks in the mud at the bottom of rivers and lakes. The **Chinese soft-shelled turtle** **6** has a nose like a snorkel, and it spends most of its time in the water. Turtles and tortoises breed by laying eggs. Freshwater kinds, such as the **painted turtle** **7**, lay theirs in holes not far from the water's edge. The

female **alligator snapping turtle** **8** leaves the water in the spring to lay eggs, whereas the male spends most of his time at the bottom of rivers or lakes. Sea turtles, including the **loggerhead** **9**, dig nests in sandy beaches. After hatching, the young turtles dig their way to the surface and then scuttle toward the sea. It is a dangerous time, and many are caught by predators before they reach the water's edge.

SCALE

Saddle shape allows tortoise to raise its head

⑪ **Hermann's tortoise**

Sharp jaw for cutting through food

⑩ **Red-footed tortoise**

⑬ **Pancake tortoise**

⑫ **Aldabra giant tortoise**

Scales on shell show growth rings

Bowsprit tortoise

Tortoises are close relatives of turtles, but they have stronger legs and spend all their lives on land. Like turtles, tortoises breed by laying eggs. Most of them are vegetarian, although some, including the South American **red-footed tortoise** ⑩, also eat small animals and dead remains. Tortoises are famous for being slow, but to make up for this, they can be amazingly long-lived. The

Hermann's tortoise ⑪, for example, has a life span of 50 years, while the **Aldabra giant tortoise** ⑫ from coral islands in the Indian Ocean can survive for more than two centuries. One recently died in captivity at the astonishing age of 255. Most tortoises have high shells, which predators find hard to break. The African **pancake tortoise** ⑬ is almost flat, which allows it to hide in rocky cracks to avoid

142

⑭ Galápagos tortoise

⑮ Radiated tortoise

Shell with vertical streaks

Elongated tortoise

⑯ Indian starred tortoise

Bumpy shell

Serrated hinge-back tortoise

Wood turtle

⑰ Spur-thighed tortoise

Leopard tortoise

⑱ Desert tortoise

predators. It has the tiniest families, since it lays just one egg at a time, although it usually breeds several times each year. **Galápagos tortoises** ⑭ live on islands in the Pacific Ocean. They are as large as the Aldabra giant tortoise and often have shells with a saddle-shaped front. This lets them stretch their necks high up to munch prickly cacti, their primary food. **Radiated tortoises** ⑮, from Madagascar,

have shells with raised knobs, but the lumpiest shell belongs to the **Indian starred tortoise** ⑯, which has starlike markings that hide it in dry grass. The **spur-thighed tortoise** ⑰ from Europe and North Africa has bony projections on its hind legs. It lays up to 20 eggs at a time, while the **desert tortoise** ⑱, found in small burrows in the deserts of North America, lays as few as four eggs.

143

Lizards

SCALE

① Emerald skink

Slender toes for climbing trees

Green anole

Cape girdled lizard

Shiny, beadlike scales

② Gila monster

Desert horned lizard

③ Asian water monitor

④ Madagascar day gecko

Toes with sharp claws for climbing

There are more than 4,000 lizard species in the world, more than all other reptiles put together. Most of them hunt small animals, and most lay eggs, although some give birth to live young. The **emerald skink** ① preys on insects. It spends most of its time on tree trunks, while the heavy-bodied **Gila monster** ② stays on the ground. Found in North American deserts, the Gila monster is one of the few lizards with a poisonous bite. Fortunately, it is a slow mover, so attacks on people are very rare. The fierce **Asian water monitor** ③ grows up to 6½ ft (2 m) long. A good swimmer, it hunts all kinds of animals, from fishes and frogs to crabs. The **Madagascar day gecko** ④ is mostly found on trees and belongs to a family of lizard famous for its "sticky" toes. Like other geckos, it can cling to almost any

⑤ Frilled lizard

⑥ Sandfish skink

Frill opens like
an umbrella

Strong back legs
built for speed

Long, flattened tail
used in swimming

⑦ Green basilisk

Knight anole

Large psammodromus

Spiky crest

⑧ Marine iguana

Rough-scaled plated lizard

Viviparous lizard

Wonder gecko

surface, and can even hunt upside down. When faced with danger, many lizards shed their tails. This distracts their enemies while they run away. The Australian **frilled lizard** ⑤ uses a different technique to protect itself. It stands its ground and opens up its frill, making it look much more threatening than it really is. The North African **sandfish skink** ⑥ dives for safety, disappearing into the desert sand by "swimming" through it. The **green basilisk** ⑦ from Central America has the most impressive escape trick of all. Standing on its back legs, it runs over the surface of lakes and streams, before swimming away from the predator. Found in the Galápagos Islands, the **marine iguana** ⑧ is the only lizard that feeds in the sea. It uses its blunt jaws to tear seaweed from underwater rocks.

9 Common leopard gecko

10 Slow worm

Solomon Islands skink

11 Common scaly foot

Berber skink

Mediterranean gecko

12 Green iguana

Italian wall lizard

Moorish gecko

13 Parson's chameleon

Tail can wrap around branches

Colorado desert fringe-toed lizard

SCALE

Fringe-toed lizard

Geckos are widespread in warm parts of the world, where there are plenty of insects for them to hunt. One of the most popular reptile pets, the **common leopard gecko** 9 from South Asia is easy to care for. This small gecko has an amazingly loud call for an animal just 8 in (20 cm) long. The **slow worm** 10, from Europe, has no legs at all, while the **common scaly foot** 11, from Australia,

looks like a snake with tiny leg flaps, Both of these lizards hunt insects and spiders, finding their prey on the ground. The Central American **green iguana** 12 is a much bigger reptile, with a spiked crest. Although it looks dangerous, it feeds mainly on plants and often climbs high up in trees. Chameleons are even better climbers and hardly ever come to the ground. **Parson's chameleon** 13 from Madagascar

Western banded gecko

14 Tokay gecko

Yellow-spotted night lizard

Green-striped tree dragon

15 African fat-tailed gecko

Body fat in tail used as a food reserve

16 Jackson's chameleon

17 Red tegu

is the largest chameleon. It creeps along branches using its feet and its tail and catches insects by shooting out its unbelievably long, sticky tongue. Like other chameleons, its eyes swivel in all directions, and it can change color to match its background or to show its mood. The **tokay gecko** 14 gets its name from its harsh "to-kay" call. This large gecko from Southeast Asia lives in houses and often hunts indoors. **African fat-tailed geckos** 15 live in deserts. Unlike other geckos, they do not have sticky toes, and they rarely climb. **Jackson's chameleon** 16 lives in East Africa. The males of this species are identified by the three horns on their snouts. The **red tegu** 17 is one of the biggest lizards in South America. A predator and a scavenger, it sometimes steals chickens from farms.

147

KOMODO DRAGON

Like a creature out of a horror movie, the Komodo dragon lurches over the ground in search of carrion and live prey. The world's largest lizard, it has a poisonous bite and can smell food more than 3 miles (5 km) away by flicking out its forked tongue. It can swallow small prey whole and knock down bigger animals with a swipe of its powerful tail, killing them with a bite to the throat.

Size > Up to 10 ft (3.1 m) long **Weight >** Males up to 200 lb (90 kg); females weigh about half as much. **Habitat >** Tropical forest and scrub. Adults live on the ground, but young dragons are more agile and live in trees to stay safe. **Distribution >** Indonesian islands of Komodo, Rinca, Padar, and western Flores. **Diet >** All kinds of carrion and live prey, including wild pigs, water buffalo, snakes, and lizards. **Lifespan >** About 30 years **Top speed >** 12 mph (20 kph), but only in short bursts. **Predators >** Adults have no natural enemies. Young dragons may be eaten by snakes, birds of prey, and even other dragons. **Conservation status >** Komodo dragons are threatened by hunting and by forest and scrub clearance.

Snakes

SCALE

Prairie rattlesnake

① Gaboon viper

Malayan pit viper

Asp viper

② Mole viper

Red spitting cobra

Red color darkens with age

③ Desert death adder

④ Boa constrictor

Sunbeam snake

Wide scales on underside

Ceylonese pipesnake

East African sand boa

⑤ King cobra

Neck widens into "hood" to scare off predators

⑥ Monocled cobra

Rainbow boa

With their sleek, shiny bodies and needle-sharp fangs, snakes often trigger panic and fear. Most kinds are harmless to humans, but venomous ones kill more than 20,000 people a year. All snakes are legless, and nearly all eat live prey. Their amazingly flexible jaws and stomachs let them swallow animals much wider than themselves. The African **Gaboon viper ①** waits to ambush its prey with record-breaking fangs

up to 2 in (5 cm) long. In a single bite, it can inject enough venom to kill a baboon or an antelope. The African **mole viper ②** catches small animals underground, while the extremely venomous **desert death adder ③** from Australia attracts food by using the thin, wormlike tip of its tail as a lure. The **boa constrictor ④** from Central America is nonvenomous and kills by muscle power alone. Like other

Western diamond-backed rattlesnake ❼

"Rattle" made of dry skin

Desert horned viper

Dusty color provides camouflage

❽ Green anaconda

Central American coral snake

❾ Eurasian blindsnake

Rosy boa

❿ Yellow-lipped seakrait

constrictors, it coils around its prey, tightening its grip while the victim slowly suffocates. Boas feed mainly on mammals and birds, but the Asian **king cobra** ❺ is an expert at eating other snakes. At 16 ft (5 m) long, it is the biggest venomous snake on Earth. The **monocled cobra** ❻ expands its neck into a "hood" when threatened, while the North American **western diamond-backed rattlesnake** ❼ makes a rattling sound with its tail to warn off enemies. The mighty **green anaconda** ❽ is one of the world's longest and heaviest snakes, weighing more than 220 lb (100 kg). At the other extreme, the **Eurasian blindsnake** ❾ is often less than 12 in (30 cm) long. It feeds on ants, spiders, and centipedes. Most snakes are good swimmers. The **yellow-lipped seakrait** ❿ spends its life in tropical waters, coming to land only when it is time to breed.

151

⑪ Blood python

Long-nosed snake

Banded flying snake ⑬

⑫ Green tree python

⑭ Burmese python

Balkan racer

Heat sensors in front of eyes to detect prey

Smooth snake

⑮ California mountain kingsnake

Some snakes give birth to live young, but most breed by laying eggs. Female **blood pythons** ⑪ from Southeast Asia coil around their eggs to keep them warm. The mother stays with her eggs for up to three months and does not eat until her young have hatched. The **green tree python** ⑫ from Australasia is a superb climber, but the Asian **banded flying snake** ⑬ is even better at moving around in trees. It jumps from tree to tree, gliding up to 330 ft (100 m) by stretching out its body and flattening its underside. The **Burmese python** ⑭ is one of the longest snakes in the world, measuring up to 23 ft (7 m) from head to tail. Like all pythons and rattlesnakes, it has heat sensors on its head, letting it "see" warm-blooded prey even when it is completely dark. The brightly patterned **California**

Spotted python

Pointed snout adapted for burrowing

⑯ Pine snake

⑰ Grass snake

Distinctive yellow collar

Giant Malagasy hognose snake

Brown treesnake

Ruthven's kingsnake

⑱ False water cobra

Broad black streak behind eyes

Red-tailed green ratsnake

⑲ Garter snake

Tail used as an anchor while climbing

SCALE

mountain kingsnake ⑮ looks venomous, but its colors are a trick and it is actually nonpoisonous. Other snakes use different kinds of self-defense. The **pine snake** ⑯ from North America squirts out horrible-smelling fluid when threatened, while the European **grass snake** ⑰ turns upside down with its tongue hanging out and pretends to be dead. The South American **false water cobra** ⑱ has a dangerous

bite, and it warns away enemies in the same way as a true cobra by widening its neck. In places with cold winters, snakes hide away and hibernate. Most hide on their own, but North American **garter snakes** ⑲ gather together in hundreds in underground dens. They come to the surface in the spring and squirm in tangled masses as they fight for the chance to mate.

153

AFRICAN BUSH VIPER
This small but deadly snake hunts mostly at night. Although it eats small animals, its venom can cause serious illness or even death in humans. However, this hasn't stopped people from keeping it as a pet. This snake is sometimes called the variable viper because it exists in a variety of colors, including green, yellow, red, and orange, and because it may change color as it matures.

Size ❯ Males average 26 in (65 cm) in length; females average 28 in (71 cm) **Habitat ❯** Bushes and shrubs in tropical forests and other densely vegetated areas. **Distribution ❯** West and Central Africa **Diet ❯** Small nocturnal mammals such as rodents and shrews, small birds, frogs, and reptiles. **Breeding ❯** Mating occurs in the rainy season. Females give birth to up to nine live young, abandoning them immediately afterward. The young are venomous and able to hunt for themselves from birth. **Life span ❯** 10–20 years in the wild. Captive vipers may live longer. **Predators ❯** Adult African bush vipers have few, if any, predators. They may eat the young of their own species.

Crocodiles and alligators

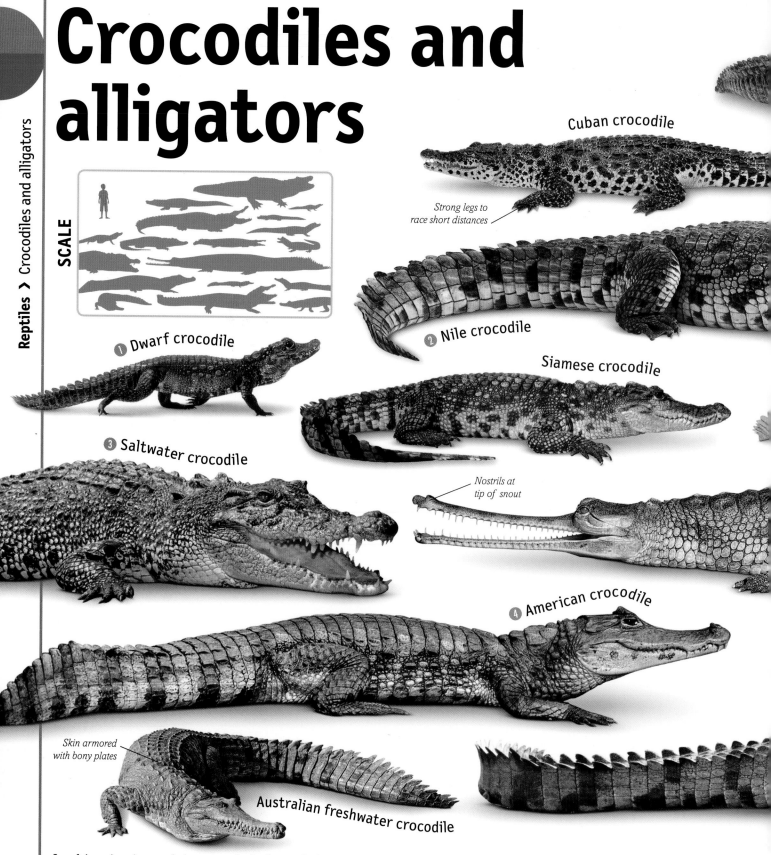

SCALE

Cuban crocodile

Strong legs to race short distances

❶ Dwarf crocodile

❷ Nile crocodile

Siamese crocodile

❸ Saltwater crocodile

Nostrils at tip of snout

❹ American crocodile

Skin armored with bony plates

Australian freshwater crocodile

Lurking in rivers, lakes, and sheltered shores, crocodiles and alligators use stealth and muscle power to ambush and kill their prey. Even the smallest kinds, such as the African **dwarf crocodile** ❶, have scales like armor plating, while the largest can smash open boats with their giant jaws. Crocodiles swallow small animals whole. They tear bigger ones apart, after pulling them underwater so they drown. The African **Nile crocodile** ❷ often lies in wait near the banks of rivers and water holes, where it attacks animals coming to drink. Females are devoted parents, guarding their eggs and carrying their young to water once they have hatched. Found in Australia and Southeast Asia, the **saltwater crocodile** ❸ is the biggest reptile in the world. Measuring up to 23 ft (7 m) long, it is

American alligator ❺

Chinese alligator ❻

Cuvier's dwarf caiman

Broad-snouted caiman ❼

Sharp teeth to tear prey apart

Orinoco crocodile

Spectacled caiman ❽

Gharial ❾

Schneider's dwarf caiman

Eyes high on head to spot prey from underwater

Yacare caiman

Marsh crocodile

Black caiman

a notorious man-eater, often attacking after dark. The **American crocodile** ❹ feeds mainly on fish, while the **American alligator** ❺ eats all kinds of animals, from frogs to deer. Like the rare **Chinese alligator** ❻, it can be told from true crocodiles by the shape of its head, and by the way its teeth fit together when its mouth is closed. Caimans are relatives of alligators from Central and South America. The **broad-snouted caiman** ❼ lives in marshes and swamps, while the **spectacled caiman** ❽ lives on coasts, as well as in inland lakes and rivers. The critically endangered **gharial** ❾ is a unique fish-eating species from India, with extremely narrow jaws and dozens of sharply pointed teeth. It lives in deep rivers and finds its prey mainly by touch.

Beak ❯ Birds use their beaks as their main tool. This parrot's beak is adapted for cracking open seeds, but other birds use theirs as drills, saws, or even strainers.

Blue-and-yellow macaw

Birds

The masters of the air, birds can fly higher, farther, and faster than any other creature. Their front limbs are adapted into wings, and their bodies are covered in feathers for warmth and for a streamlined shape. Their bones are partly hollow, making them light but strong and ideally suited for flying through the air.

Feathers > Different types of feather have different uses. Warm, fluffy down feathers keep the bird warm. Long, stiff feathers grow on the wings to direct the air in flight. Many species grow brightly colored feathers to attract a mate.

Features

Wings > All birds have wings, although not all of them can fly. The wings flap with great force to lift the bird off the ground. Once in the air, some birds simply hold their wings out to soar like a glider, while others can perform amazing aerobatics.

- Lay eggs to reproduce

- Have beaks instead of teeth

- Are covered in feathers

- Have wings and most can fly

- Are warm-blooded

Ostriches and relatives

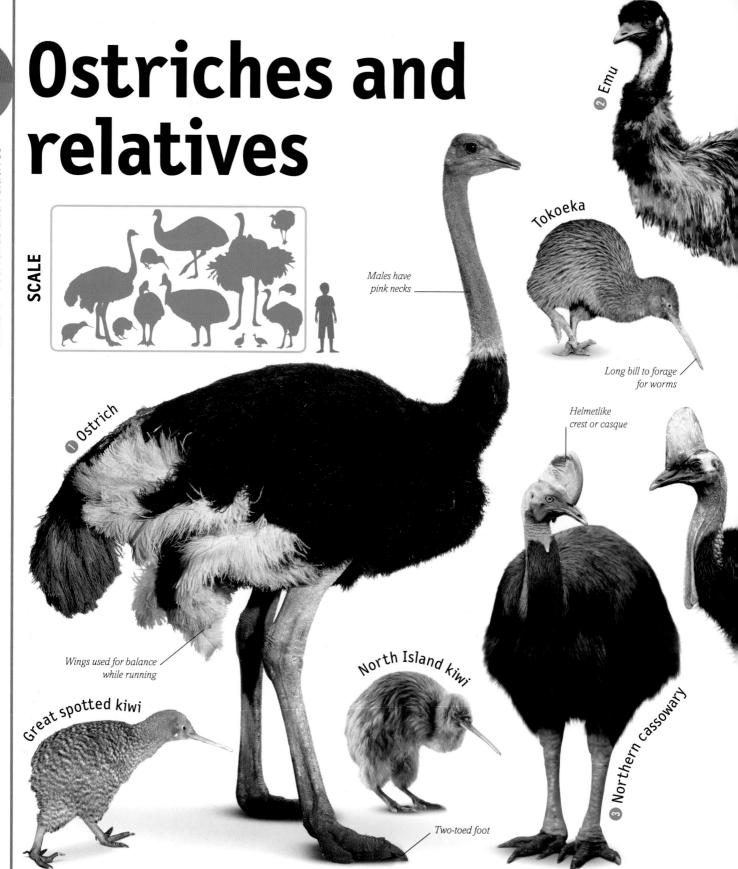

SCALE

② Emu

Tokoeka

Males have
pink necks

Long bill to forage
for worms

① Ostrich

Helmetlike
crest or casque

Wings used for balance
while running

Great spotted kiwi

North Island kiwi

③ Northern cassowary

Two-toed foot

Standing more than 8 ft (2.5 m) tall and weighing up to 350 lb (160 kg), twice as much as a man, **ostriches** ① are the world's biggest birds. Ostriches cannot fly but they are the fastest animals on two legs, with a cruising speed of 45 mph (70 kph). They live in Africa and feed on seeds and fruit, swallowing stones as big as golf balls to help them grind up their food. **Emus** ②, from Australia, are almost as big, with feathers that look like shaggy fur. They have tiny wings and three toes on each foot, whereas ostriches have two. Thousands of emus sometimes gather together in flocks, crossing deserts and raiding farmland in search of food. The **northern cassowary** ③ and **southern cassowary** ④ are rain-forest birds from Australia and New Guinea, with a helmetlike crest on their heads. They live

Gray neck

5 Lesser rhea

Somali ostrich

4 Southern cassowary

6 Little spotted kiwi

7 Greater rhea

Powerful legs for running and swimming

Gray-brown plumage for camouflage

8 Ornate tinamou

9 Elegant crested tinamou

on their own and can be dangerous if cornered, kicking out with their claws. Rheas come from South America. Males are hard-working parents, sitting on the eggs and taking care of the striped chicks. **Lesser rheas 5** live in flocks of up to 30 birds. During the breeding season, males fight for the attention of female partners. Kiwis come from New Zealand and are chicken-sized, flightless birds with long beaks. They live in forests and feed at night, sniffing out insects and worms. Some are very rare. The **little spotted kiwi 6** lives on offshore islands, safe from predators. **Greater rheas 7** live in flocks of up to 100. Males use impressive wing displays to attract potential mates. The **ornate tinamou 8** and **elegant crested tinamou 9** also come from South America. They can fly, but prefer to run away from danger instead.

161

Game birds

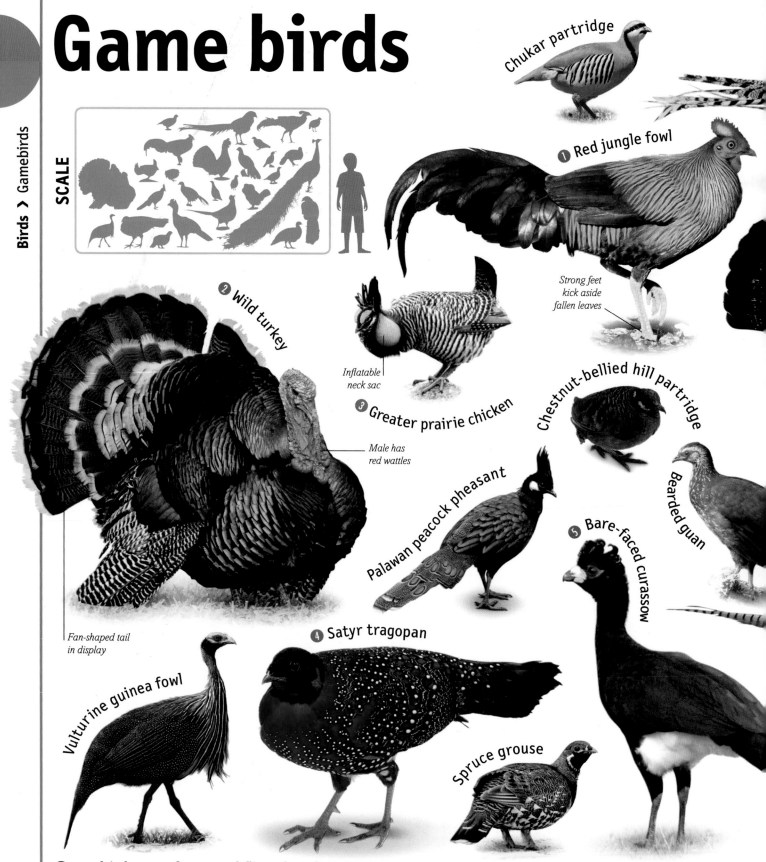

Chukar partridge

SCALE

❶ Red jungle fowl

Strong feet
kick aside
fallen leaves

❷ Wild turkey

Inflatable
neck sac

❸ Greater prairie chicken

Chestnut-bellied hill partridge

Male has
red wattles

Palawan peacock pheasant

❺ Bare-faced curassow

Bearded guan

Fan-shaped tail
in display

❹ Satyr tragopan

Vulturine guinea fowl

Spruce grouse

Game birds are often good fliers, but the majority of them spend most of their lives on the ground. They peck at seeds and small animals, and scratch up food with their feet. Unlike most other birds, they don't like washing in water, but they love taking a dust bath to keep their feathers clean. The **red jungle fowl** ❶ from southern Asia looks and sounds just like a barnyard rooster, with its

"cock-a-doodle-do" call. It is the distant grandparent of chickens, which are the most common birds on Earth. Found in North America, the **wild turkey** ❷ is another large game bird that has been tamed. Game birds live in a variety of habitats. Some, such as the **greater prairie chicken** ❸, live in open grassland, but others are found in forests, mountains, or wind-swept Arctic tundra. The **satyr**

162

6 Lady Amherst's pheasant

7 Siamese fireback

Roulroul

Gray francolin

Western capercaillie

Plain chachalaca

California quail

Gray-headed chachalaca

8 Indian peacock

9 Gray partridge

Common quail

Sooty grouse

Rock ptarmigan

Red patches around eyes

Common pheasant

10 Malleefowl

Male's extravagant tail used to attract females

Cauca guan

tragopan 4 lives in cool forests high in the Himalayan mountains. Most game birds roost, or sleep, in trees, but the **bare-faced curassow 5** feeds above ground, too. Male game birds are often much more eye-catching than females. Male **Lady Amherst's pheasants 6** are stunningly colored, and **Siamese firebacks 7** have red faces and a feathery crest. **Indian peacocks 8** have extraordinary plumes that open like fans, attracting peahens. Most game birds nest on the ground, and some produce incredible numbers of eggs. One **gray partridge 9** laid 25 eggs at one time, which is a world record for any bird. Females usually sit on the eggs to incubate them, but Australian **malleefowl 10** bury their eggs inside a nest that looks like a huge compost heap. The heap warms the eggs until they hatch.

Pigeons and doves

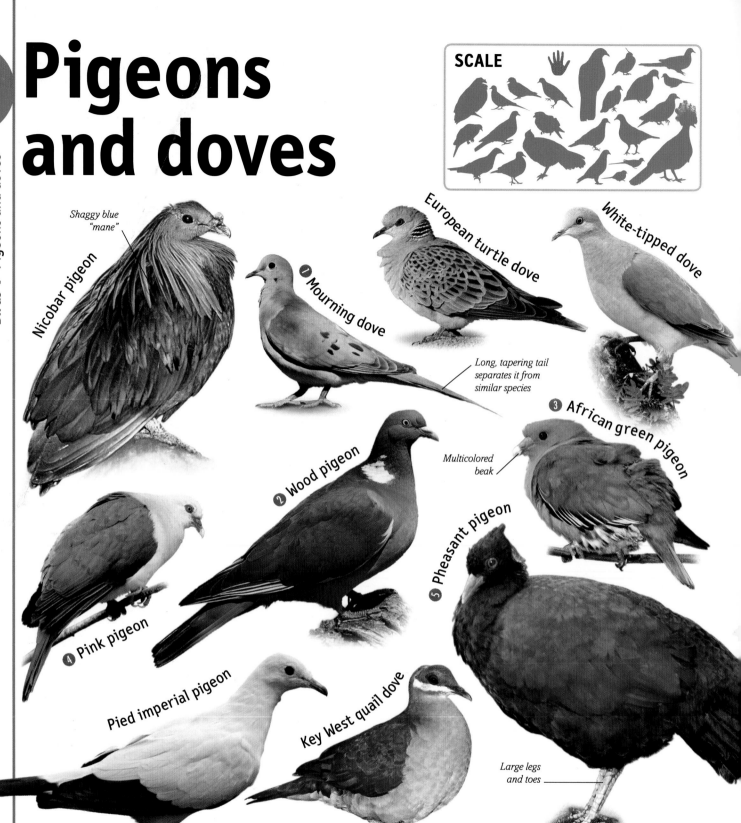

SCALE

Nicobar pigeon

Shaggy blue "mane"

European turtle dove

White-tipped dove

1 Mourning dove

Long, tapering tail separates it from similar species

3 African green pigeon

Multicolored beak

2 Wood pigeon

5 Pheasant pigeon

Pink pigeon **4**

Pied imperial pigeon

Key West quail dove

Large legs and toes

Pigeons and doves include many common birds, as well as others that are very rare. They have rounded bodies and short legs, and their heads often bob backward and forward when they walk. All of them are vegetarians, and many, including the **mourning dove** **1** and **wood pigeon** **2**, live near fields and farms, which provide a steady supply of food. Pigeons and doves are mostly brown or gray, but some tropical kinds are much more colorful. They include the **African green pigeon** **3**, which clambers around in trees like a parrot, and the very rare **pink pigeon** **4** from the island of Mauritius in the Indian Ocean. The pink pigeon almost became extinct in the 1990s, but was rescued by conservationists when just 10 birds were left in the wild. The **pheasant pigeon** **5** from New Guinea has strong legs and

Wompoo fruit dove

Permanently raised spiked crest

⑦ Spinifex pigeon

Brown cuckoo dove

Emerald dove

Sulawesi ground dove

Inca dove

Lacy crest bobs backward and forward as the bird walks

Speckled pigeon

White-speckled wings

Common bronzewing

Wonga pigeon

Spotted underparts

⑩ Southern crowned pigeon

⑧ Domestic pigeon

Namaqua dove

⑨ Diamond dove

feeds on the ground, while the **wompoo fruit dove** ⑥ lives high up in rain-forest trees. It swallows fruit whole and scatters the seeds in its droppings, helping trees to spread. Pigeons and doves are found in dry places, too. The crested **spinifex pigeon** ⑦ lives in the rocky hills of central Australia and feeds on the seeds of desert grasses. The most common of all, the **domestic pigeon** ⑧ thrives in

urban areas, where it dodges traffic, nests on buildings and eats scraps of leftover food. The tiny **diamond dove** ⑨ from Australia is often seen in pairs or small groups, feeding on the ground. It is only 8 in (20 cm) long. At the other extreme, the **southern crowned pigeon** ⑩ from New Guinea weighs as much as a chicken. It is one of the biggest pigeons in the world, measuring up to 30 in (75 cm) long.

Parrots and cockatoos

Red-fronted macaws

Australian king parrot

Olive-headed lorikeet

Pacific parrotlet ❶

Princess parrots

❷ Blue-and-yellow macaw

Chattering lory

Gray parrot ❸

Powerful beak to crack nuts

❹ Budgerigar

❺ Kakapo

Crest can be raised or lowered

Sharp beak shreds bark and leaves

Eastern rosella

❻ Sulfur-crested cockatoo

Parrots are some of the world's brainiest, noisiest, and most colorful birds. Most of them live in tropical forests, although a few favor open habitats. They use their curved beaks to crack open nuts and seeds and they vary greatly in size. The tiny **Pacific parrotlet** ❶ is smaller than a sparrow, but the bigger ones, such as the **blue-and-yellow macaw** ❷, can be nearly 3 ft (1 m) from head to tail. Big or small, all parrots have strong feet with fleshy toes. They use them for climbing around and for holding their food. The African **gray parrot** ❸ and the **budgerigar** ❹, from Australian grasslands, are amazingly good at mimicking human speech. One record-breaking budgerigar learned more than 1,700 words, while trained gray parrots can answer questions and even count. Found in New Zealand,

SCALE

Red-fronted parakeet

⑩ Kea

Yellow-collared lovebird

Blue-headed parrot

Female is red, with blue neck band

Male is mainly green

Red-fan parrot

⑨ Eclectus parrots

Scarlet macaw

⑧ Galah

Blue-crowned hanging parrots

Long, sharply pointed crest

Tail as long as body

⑦ Cockatiels

St. Vincent parrot

Red-tailed black cockatoo

Distinctive red patch on tail

kakapos ⑤ are the world's rarest and heaviest parrots. They cannot fly and come out only at night. These slow-moving birds are easily caught by predators, and only about 125 kakapos are left in the wild. Cockatoos are parrots with feathery crests. Found in Australia and New Guinea, the **sulfur-crested cockatoo** ⑥ sometimes flies into city gardens and parks, while the **cockatiel** ⑦, like the budgerigar, lives in dry scrub and grassland. Most parrots nest in tree holes, and many, including the **galah** ⑧, pair up for life. Male and female parrots often look the same, but **eclectus parrots** ⑨ are so dissimilar that they were once thought to be different kinds of bird. The **kea** ⑩ lives in the mountains of New Zealand. Unusually for a parrot, it eats almost anything, including live animals and carrion.

MILITARY MACAW
One of the largest and most dazzling members of the parrot family, the military macaw has spectacular plumage, with a bright green body, shimmering sky-blue wingtips, and scarlet patches on its head and tail. Its large beak is adapted for picking fruit and cracking open nuts. Highly intelligent and sociable, it is popular in zoos and is sometimes kept as a pet, although it can be noisy!

Size ❯ Body length up to 30 in (75 cm) **Wingspan ❯** Up to 3½ ft (1.1 m) **Weight ❯** Around 2 lb (900 g) **Habitat ❯** Lowland tropical forests and semiarid woodland. Lives in large flocks, nesting in treetops or on cliff faces. **Distribution ❯** Central America and northern South America. **Diet ❯** Fruit, vegetables, berries, nuts, and seeds. In the Amazon rain forest, they sometimes eat clay from riverbanks, possibly to remove toxins they have swallowed in their food. **Breeding ❯** They perform complex courtship flights and mate for life. **Life span ❯** Up to 60 years in the wild. **Predators ❯** Large mammals, some reptiles, primates, and birds of prey. **Conservation status ❯** Threatened by habitat loss and illegal trade in cage birds.

Cuckoos and turacos

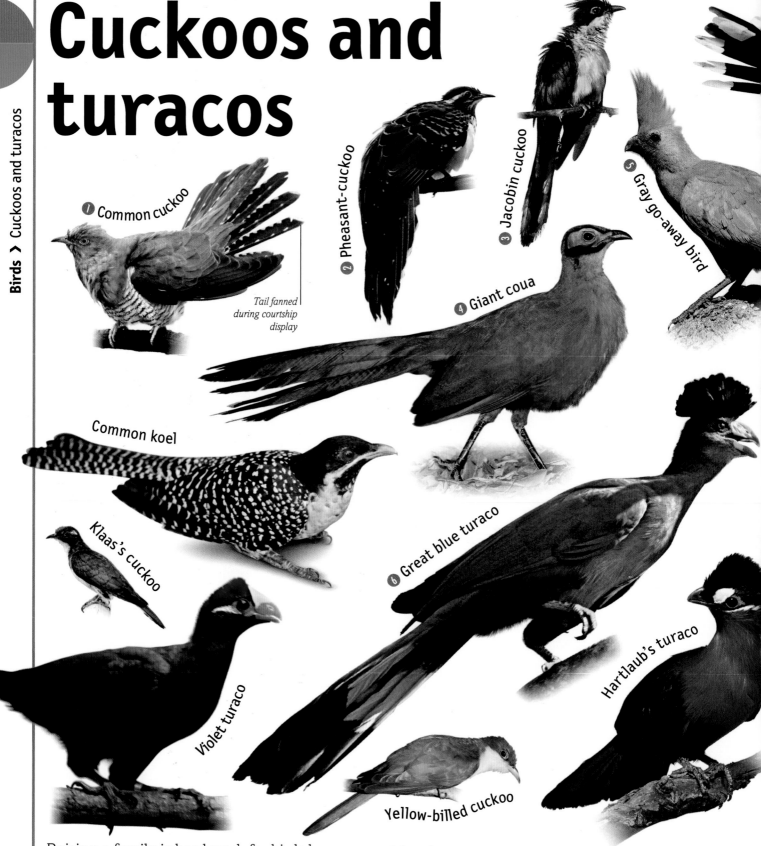

❶ Common cuckoo

Tail fanned during courtship display

❷ Pheasant-cuckoo

❸ Jacobin cuckoo

❺ Gray go-away bird

❹ Giant coua

Common koel

Klaas's cuckoo

❻ Great blue turaco

Violet turaco

Hartlaub's turaco

Yellow-billed cuckoo

Raising a family is hard work for birds because they have to build a nest and look after their young. Many cuckoos skip these tasks by laying their eggs in other birds' nests. The nests' owners do not realize that they have been tricked and raise the young cuckoos themselves. The **common cuckoo** ❶ is one of the best-known of these birds, with a loud "cuc-oo" call that gives it its name.

It breeds in Europe and Asia and spends the winter in Africa, undertaking a yearly journey of up to 9,300 miles (15,000 km). The **pheasant-cuckoo** ❷ from Central and South America and the **jacobin cuckoo** ❸ from Africa and Asia also cheat when they breed, but the **giant coua** ❹ from Madagascar makes its own nest in trees. Cuckoos feed mainly on small animals such as insects, spiders, and worms,

Guira cuckoo

SCALE

❼ Greater roadrunner

Greater coucal

Great spotted cuckoo

Wings used for balance when running

Fan-tailed cuckoo

Permanently raised spiked crest

❾ Hoatzin

Dideric cuckoo

❽ Green turaco

Strong toes grip branches tightly

Red-crested turaco

Short, stubby beak

but turacos live mostly on fruit. Found only in Africa, they include the noisy **gray go-away bird** ❺ and the **great blue turaco** ❻, which feeds high up in trees. Turacos have strong feet, and they run along branches like squirrels as they look for food. The **greater roadrunner** ❼, from the US and Mexico, spends much of its life on the ground. It is a great runner, as its name suggests, with a top speed of about 18 mph (30 kph). It sprints after lizards and snakes, battering them against rocks before swallowing them whole. The **green turaco** ❽ lays two eggs in a flimsy nest, and its young clamber out among branches before they learn to fly. The **hoatzin** ❾ from South America is a strange bird that feeds only on leaves. Its chicks are good climbers thanks to small claws on their wings.

Owls

SCALE

① Ural owl

③ Black-and-white owl

Cuban pygmy owl

② Northern hawk-owl

Long tail, like that of a hawk

④ Elf owl

Wing feathers muffle the sound of flight

Tawny owl

⑤ Great gray owl

Black-capped screech owl

Tropical screech owl

When the Sun sets, most birds settle down to sleep. Owls do the opposite, because this is when most of them start to hunt. Guided by their large eyes and supersensitive ears, they noiselessly swoop on their prey. Owls come in many different sizes, and they live all over the world. The **Ural owl ①** and the **northern hawk-owl ②** are from northern Eurasian forests, while the **black-and-white owl ③** lives in the jungles of Central and South America. The tiny **elf owl ④** is a desert-dweller from the southern US and Mexico. It weighs only 1½ oz (40 g), which is much lighter than a cell phone. The **great gray owl ⑤** is nearly 50 times heavier. It has a flat, rounded face and staring yellow eyes. Its face channels sound toward its ears, letting it pinpoint small mammals on the ground, or even under snow.

Eurasian scops owl

6 Snowy owl

Large ear tufts extend sideways

Buffy fish owl

White plumage flecked with black

Short-eared owl

Spectacled owl

7 Barn owl

8 Northern saw-whet owl

Southern white-faced owl

9 Great horned owl

Ferruginous pygmy owl

Long-eared owl

Desert eagle-owl

10 Eastern screech owl

Razor-sharp talons can tackle large prey

The **snowy owl** 6 lives in the high Arctic region, where its white plumage makes good winter camouflage. The Sun never sets during the Arctic summer, so the owl has to hunt by day. The ghostly **barn owl** 7 is one of the world's most widespread birds; it lives on every continent except Antarctica. It can hunt in total darkness, flying with slow wingbeats just a few yards above ground. Owls are silent

when they hunt, but many have strange or spooky calls. When it is alarmed, the **northern saw-whet owl** 8 makes a sound like a saw being sharpened, while the **great horned owl** 9 has a deep and echoing hoot. The **eastern screech owl** 10 is a short, stocky bird, with a large head and almost no neck. Despite its name, this owl doesn't screech; instead, it whistles and trills.

BARRED OWL
Named for its brown-and-white striped plumage, the barred owl is also known as the hoot owl for its distinctive, repeated call. Barred owls roost in trees during the day and hunt by night, seeking out animals such as rodents and rabbits. The feathers on their wings are specially shaped to allow them to fly almost silently so they can take their prey by surprise, swooping down to grab their victims with razor-sharp talons.

Size ❯ Up to 20 in (51 cm) long **Wingspan ❯** Up to 43 in (1.1 m) **Weight ❯** Males about 22 oz (630 g); females about 28 oz (800 g) **Habitat ❯** Forests, wooded swamps, and suburbs. **Distribution ❯** Originally found in the eastern US, down to Texas in the South. Now also found in California, Oregon, southwestern Canada, and Mexico. **Diet ❯** Rodents, rabbits, birds, frogs, reptiles, and fishes. **Breeding ❯** Females lay a clutch of one to five eggs. The chicks can fly at six weeks and mature at around two years. **Life span ❯** Up to 18 years in the wild. **Predators ❯** Great horned owls may occasionally take adult barred owls. Raccoons and weasels may eat eggs and young. **Conservation status ❯** Not threatened.

Hummingbirds and swifts

SCALE

① Racket-tailed puffleg

Brazilian ruby

② Andean hillstar

Broad-billed hummingbird

Hooded visorbearer

③ Calliope hummingbird

Buff-bellied hummingbird

④ Sword-billed hummingbird

Tongue protrudes from beak when feeding

Rufous hummingbird

Collared inca

Blue-throated hummingbird

Ruby-throated hummingbird

Allen's hummingbird

⑤ Stripe-breasted starthroat

Lucifer hummingbird

Scale-throated hermit

In different ways hummingbirds and swifts break all kinds of records as they speed through the air. Beating their wings up to 70 times a second, hummingbirds zip forward, backward, or hover on the spot like tiny helicopters. They include species such as the **racket-tailed puffleg** ①, with its eye-catching tail plumes, and the **Andean hillstar** ②, which lives high in the Andes at up to 16,500 ft

(5,000 m). The **calliope hummingbird** ③ spends the winter in Central America but migrates northward as far north as Canada every spring, an amazing feat for such a little bird. Most hummingbirds have long beaks that work like drinking straws to suck sugary nectar from flowers. The **sword-billed hummingbird** ④ is the only bird with a beak longer than its body. It feeds on large trumpet-shaped flowers, hovering

Violet saberwing

6 Bee hummingbird

1 Alpine swift

Anna's hummingbird

White-vented violet-ear

8 White-throated swift

Long-tailed sylph

9 Common swift

White-necked jacobin

Scythe-shaped wings for high-speed flight

Ruby topaz

Curved beak to drink nectar from flowers

White-tipped sicklebill

Orange-red tail fanned to attract females

underneath them to get at its food. The **stripe-breasted starthroat's** 5 folded wings are much longer than its tail. The tiny **bee hummingbird** 6 from Cuba is the smallest bird in the world. Males are 2 in (5 cm) long and weigh less than a sugar cube. Hummingbirds are found only in the Americas, but swifts live all around the world. They feed on insects that they catch on the wing. The **alpine swift** 7 and

white-throated swift 8 nest in rocky crevices. Like all swifts, they have tiny feet that cling but cannot perch. The **common swift** 9 from Europe, Africa, and Asia is one of the world's fastest birds. It spends most of its time on the wing, and even eats, drinks, and sleeps in flight. After leaving the nest, a young swift does not land until its second or third birthday, when it starts to breed.

Kingfishers and relatives

Racket-tipped tail can swing like a pendulum

1 Blue-crowned motmot

2 Red-billed hornbill

Large eyes with feathery eyelashes

Turquoise-browed motmot

Hollow chamber amplifies hornbill's call

3 Northern ground hornbill

4 Malabar pied hornbill

5 European bee-eater

6 White-throated bee-eater

Short claws on strong feet

Tail with central spike seen in adults

Kingfishers often live near water, but most of their relatives are land-based. Many of them hunt small animals, and nearly all dig nest holes in riverbanks or in trees. The biggest of these birds are ground hornbills, which can weigh twice as much as a farmyard hen. At the other extreme, some kingfishers weigh just ⅓ oz (10 g), which is less than a CD. The **blue-crowned motmot** **1** from Central and South America swoops on insects and other animals from a favorite perch. The African **red-billed hornbill** **2** lives on the ground and in trees, while the **northern ground hornbill** **3** patrols Africa's grasslands on its large scaly feet. Hornbills get their name from the helmet, or casque, that many have on top of their beaks. The **Malabar pied hornbill** **4** from South Asia has an extra-large casque,

Crest raised on takeoff and landing

Hoopoe ⑦

Racket-tailed roller

Buff-breasted paradise kingfisher

⑧ **Common kingfisher**

Blue-bellied roller

Trumpeter hornbill

Slender beak to probe for insects in trees

Flattened bill for catching insects in flight

Jamaican tody

Green wood hoopoe

African pygmy kingfisher

Brown plumage camouflages the bird in trees

Laughing kookaburra ⑩

⑨ **Belted kingfisher**

Little kingfisher

Pied kingfisher

Yellow-billed kingfisher

SCALE

and its wings make a distinct whooshing sound as it flies. **European bee-eaters** ⑤ and **white-throated bee-eaters** ⑥ are experts at catching bees while flying. After they have caught one, they wipe it against a perch to remove its sting. The **hoopoe** ⑦ is a migratory bird that breeds in Europe and Asia. It uses its slender beak to probe in the ground for grubs and worms. **Common kingfishers** ⑧ live along rivers and streams, where they dive for fish. The North American **belted kingfisher** ⑨ is another waterside hunter. Like its relatives, it hits its catch against a perch before swallowing it headfirst. The Australian **laughing kookaburra** ⑩ is the world's biggest kingfisher, with a noisy laughing call. It lives in woodland and swoops on anything that it can swallow, including insects, lizards, and snakes.

Toucans and woodpeckers

SCALE

Great barbet

Saffron toucanet

Beak with serrated edges

Red-breasted toucan ❶

Green-backed honeybird

❺ Collared aracari

❸ White-whiskered puffbird

Rusty-breasted nunlet

Spot-billed toucanet ❷

Beak has honeycomb-like air spaces

❹ White-eared puffbird

❻ Chestnut-eared aracari

Black-fronted nunbird

Long, slender tongue

Toucans and woodpeckers look very different, but they belong to the same group of birds. They live mainly in woods and forests, and usually nest in holes. All of them have specially shaped feet for clinging to tree trunks, but the most attention-grabbing feature of toucans is a giant multicolored beak. The **red-breasted toucan** ❶ feeds mainly on fruit. Like many toucans, its beak is filled with air spaces, saving a lot of weight. The **spot-billed toucanet** ❷ has a smaller beak, but it feeds in typical toucan style. After picking a piece of fruit, it tosses it in the air and then swallows it whole. The **white-whiskered puffbird** ❸ and **white-eared puffbird** ❹ feed mainly on insects, and they often nest in old termite mounds or in holes in the ground. Like toucans, **collared aracaris** ❺ and **chestnut-eared**

Toucan-barbet

Yellow-fronted tinkerbird

⑦ Toco toucan

⑧ Northern flicker

⑨ Great spotted woodpecker

Spotted piculet

Red-headed barbet

Beak more than half the bird's body length

D'Arnaud's barbet

Prominent red crest is always raised

Two toes face forward and two backward

Northern wryneck

Rufous-tailed jacamar

Long, thin, daggerlike beak

⑪ Pileated woodpecker

Red-and-yellow barbet

Yellow-fronted woodpecker

⑩ Heart-spotted woodpecker

Ochraceous piculet

Yellow-bellied sapsucker

Tail braces body against tree trunk

aracaris ⑥ live in the forests in Central and South America. They roam the treetops in small flocks and roost together in hollow trees. The **toco toucan** ⑦ is one of the largest birds in the toucan family. Its colossal beak allows it to reach fruit growing on the tips of branches. It also eats small animals such as insects and frogs. Some woodpeckers, including the **northern flicker** ⑧, feed on the ground, but most cling to tree

trunks and hammer into them with their beaks in search of insects to eat. The **great spotted woodpecker** ⑨ from Europe and Asia eats wood-boring grubs, while the **heart-spotted woodpecker** ⑩ from Southeast Asia probes for insects under bark. The North American **pileated woodpecker** ⑪ is one of the largest of these wood-busting birds. Despite its impressive size, it feeds mainly on ants.

Birds of prey

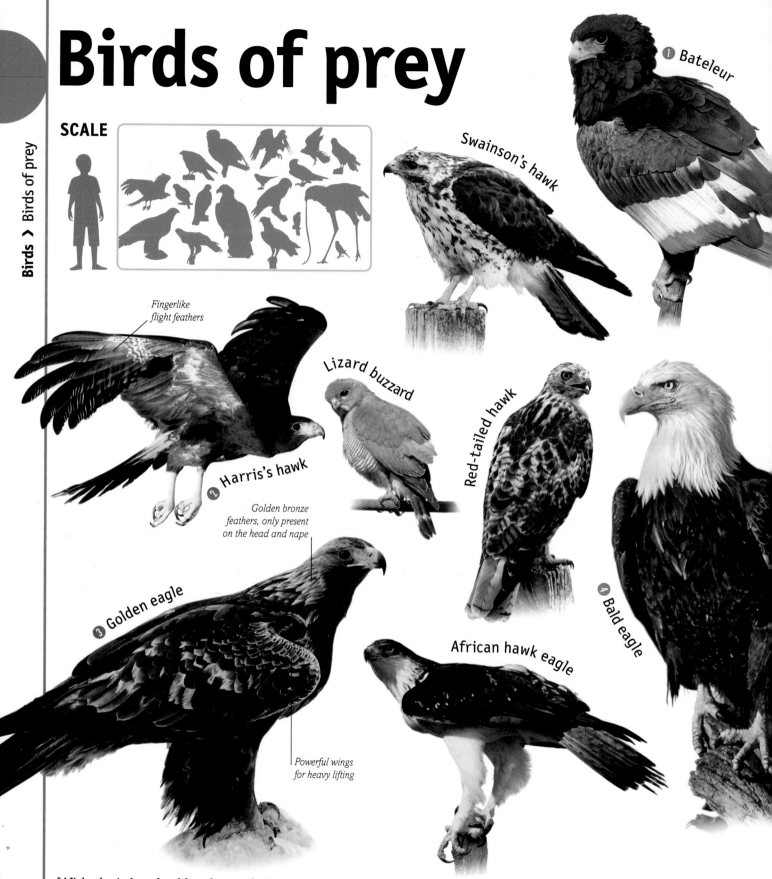

SCALE

① Bateleur

Swainson's hawk

Fingerlike flight feathers

Lizard buzzard

Red-tailed hawk

② Harris's hawk

Golden bronze feathers, only present on the head and nape

③ Golden eagle

④ Bald eagle

African hawk eagle

Powerful wings for heavy lifting

With their hooked beaks and piercing claws, birds of prey are natural killers. Most of them use their feet to grab food, and their hooked beaks to tear it apart. Some, such as the African **bateleur** ①, eat carrion as well as live prey. Vultures, on the other hand, are full-time scavengers, gulping down rotting remains. Birds of prey usually hunt alone, but the **Harris's hawk** ② from

North America is one of the few that works in teams. The **golden eagle** ③ hunts over mountains and the Arctic tundra. With its huge wings and powerful legs, it can lift prey as heavy as itself. North American **bald eagles** ④ often gather near water, where they catch live fish or eat dead ones that wash up on the shore. They build massive nests from sticks, and the biggest one on record weighed

⑤ Lanner falcon

Forward-facing eyes for judging distances

⑥ Common kestrel

Eurasian buzzard

Large, broad wings and a short tail

American kestrel

⑦ Peregrine falcon

Long-legged buzzard

Eaglelike head, with a hooked beak

Merlin

⑨ Secretary bird

Snake about to be swallowed whole

⑧ Osprey

Long, partly feathered legs

African pygmy falcon

Reversible outer toe for a better grip of prey

nearly 3 tons. Falcons and kestrels are much smaller birds, with slim bodies and slender wings. The **Lanner falcon ⑤** dives down on other birds, while the **common kestrel ⑥** hovers in midair before dropping on voles, insects, and even worms. The **peregrine falcon ⑦** is the fastest animal on Earth. Hurtling toward the ground with its wings partly folded, it can hit speeds of more than 185 mph (300 kph), which is almost as fast as a Formula 1 race car. Found all over the world, the **osprey ⑧** hunts fish, snatching them from the water's surface and then carrying them back to its perch. The African **secretary bird ⑨** has extra-long legs and hunts on the ground. An expert snake-eater, it uses its wings as shields and often stamps on its prey before swallowing it whole.

183

Yellow-headed caracara

Adult has black streak behind the eye

⑪ Turkey vulture

Striated caracara

⑩ Crested caracara

White collar in adults

⑬ Andean condor

⑫ Black vulture

Hooked beak for tearing food apart

⑭ Red kite

White-tailed kite

⑮ Snail kite

Mississippi kite

SCALE

Many birds of prey won't touch food unless it is alive. Caracaras are less picky; they don't mind if their food is living or dead. The **crested caracara** ⑩ feeds mainly on the ground, but it also behaves like an airborne raider, chasing other birds to make them drop their prey. Most vultures have weak claws and rarely hunt for themselves. Instead, they work like a clean-up crew, tracking down and feeding on dead

remains. American **turkey vultures** ⑪ often feed on animals killed on roads, although **black vultures** ⑫ sometimes push them aside so they can get all the food for themselves. The **Andean condor** ⑬ from South America is the largest vulture, and one of the world's biggest flying birds. With its huge 10½ ft (3.2 m) wingspan, it soars over remote mountains and rocky shores, feeding on all kinds of animal casualties, including

Head and neck almost bald

16 Rüppell's vulture

17 Egyptian vulture

Bare skin around eyes

18 Palm-nut vulture

Northern goshawk

Streaked chest

Northern harrier

19 African white-backed vulture

stranded whales. Kites are hunters and scavengers that patrol near the ground. The **red kite** 14 often feeds on dead rabbits and birds, but the **snail kite** 15 eats freshwater apple snails. Holding them down with one foot, it uses its slender beak to pull the snails out of their shells. Africa and Asia have many vultures of their own. The **Rüppell's vulture** 16 is almost bald on its head and neck, since feathers in this area would get clogged with blood when the bird feeds on animal carcasses. The **Egyptian vulture** 17 uses stones to crack open ostrich eggs. The **palm-nut vulture** 18 is partly vegetarian. It swallows oil-palm fruit, as well as insects, scorpions, and crabs. The **African white-backed vulture** 19 uses its large wings to soar and circle in the air, looking for carrion. Like the Rüppell's vulture, it jostles for food at big carcasses.

KING VULTURE
Found in Central and South America, the king vulture may have gotten its name from its habit of driving smaller birds away from its food. Like all vultures, this odd-looking, colorful scavenger feeds on carrion. It is one of the largest and most powerful scavenging birds, and its sharp beak and strong muscles can rip open the carcasses of dead animals that other, smaller birds cannot get into.

Size ❯ Body up to 32 in (80 cm) long. **Wingspan ❯** Up to 6½ ft (2 m) **Weight ❯** Up to 10 lb (4.5 kg) **Habitat ❯** Lowland tropical forests and nearby grasslands. **Distribution ❯** Tropical areas of Central and South America, from Mexico to Argentina. **Diet ❯** Dead animals **Breeding ❯** Females lay one creamy white egg, which takes up to 58 days to hatch. Both parents care for the young, feeding it with carrion that they store in a throat pouch called a crop. **Life span ❯** Unknown in the wild. More than 30 years in captivity. **Predators ❯** Snakes may take the eggs. Jaguars may eat sick or injured adults. **Conservation status ❯** Not currently in danger, but numbers are declining possibly due to habitat loss.

Ducks, geese, and swans

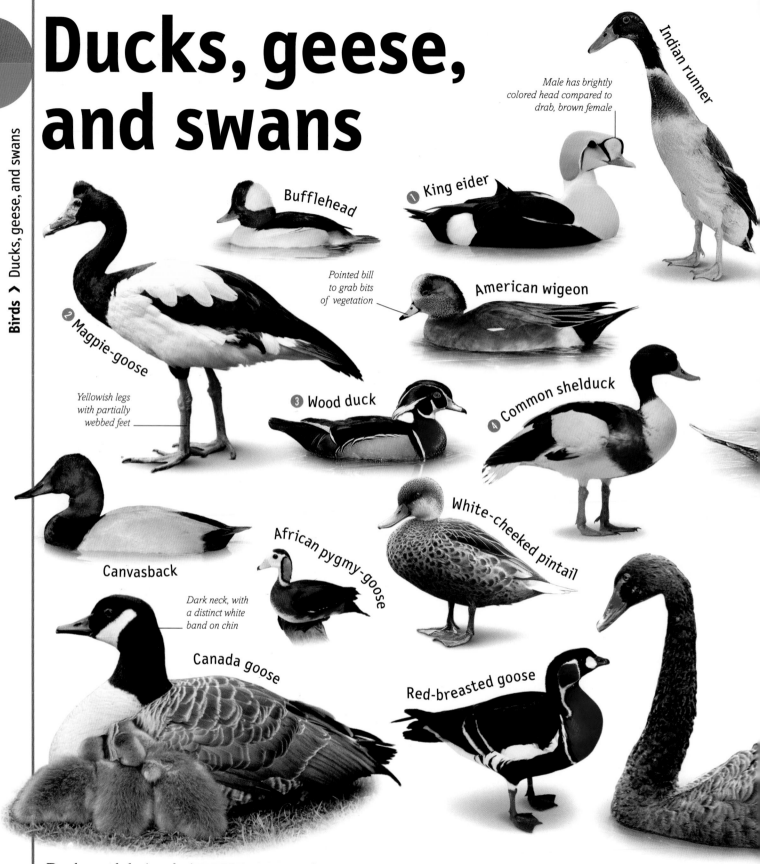

Indian runner

Male has brightly colored head compared to drab, brown female

1 King eider

Bufflehead

Pointed bill to grab bits of vegetation

American wigeon

2 Magpie-goose

3 Wood duck

4 Common shelduck

Yellowish legs with partially webbed feet

Canvasback

African pygmy-goose

White-cheeked pintail

Dark neck, with a distinct white band on chin

Canada goose

Red-breasted goose

Ducks and their relatives are expert swimmers, which is why they are also known as waterfowl. Nearly all of them have webbed feet and waterproof feathers. Most live on lakes and rivers, but some ducks, including the **king eider** **1**, breed on coasts and spend the winter at sea. **Magpie-geese** **2** lay up to 12 eggs a year. Despite having large families, they face lots of predators and only a few of

the young survive. The North American **wood duck** **3** nests high up in tree holes. Soon after the ducklings hatch, their mother leads them to water, and they have to jump all the way to the ground. The **common shelduck** **4** often breeds in rabbit burrows, but most other waterfowl nest in the open, near the water's edge. Geese feed mainly on grass, but ducks and swans usually eat while afloat. **Northern**

⑤ Northern shoveler

Large crest can be expanded

Hooded merganser

SCALE

⑥ Red-breasted merganser

Long-tailed duck

Sawlike red beak for gripping fish

① Mute swan

Male is black, with white patch on forehead

Surf scoter

⑧ Bar-headed goose

Plumed whistling duck

Gray head with a feathery crest

⑨ Mallard

Southern screamer

⑩ Domestic duck

⑪ Black swan

Baikal teal

Smew

shovelers ⑤ use their flat beaks to filter small animals from water, while **red-breasted mergansers** ⑥ have saw-edged beaks for catching slippery fish. **Mute swans** ⑦ tip up on end as they swim, using their long necks to reach for food buried in mud. When threatened, these swans curve their necks and half-raise their wings to scare off attackers. The **bar-headed goose** ⑧ is a long-distance migrant, climbing to over 20,000 ft (6,000 m) as it crosses the Himalayas. Waterfowl include some well-known farmyard birds. The **mallard** ⑨ is the most widespread duck in the world. The **domestic duck** ⑩, a descendant of the mallard, has been farmed for thousands of years. Found only around wet habitats, the Australian **black swan** ⑪ is a large, nomadic bird that flies to lakes that fill up after rain.

Penguins

SCALE

① Galápagos penguin

② Adélie penguin

Small, stiff wings act like flippers

③ Emperor penguin

Snares penguin

Long, yellow feathery crest

Rockhopper penguin

④ Little penguin

⑤ Jackass penguin

Yellow-eyed penguin

On television, in movies, and in real life, penguins have true star appeal, with their upright bodies and black-and-white plumage. Penguins cannot fly but they are superb swimmers. They use their wings like flippers to speed after fishes and other prey in some of the world's coldest and stormiest seas. **Galápagos penguins** ① live in the Galápagos Islands north of the equator. They are the only penguins to breed in tropical waters. All other penguins live in much colder waters in the Southern Hemisphere. **Adélie penguins** ② are among the few that breed in Antarctica, building nests out of stones among the rocks in spring. Another Antarctic species, the **Emperor penguin** ③ is the biggest penguin, growing up to 4 ft (1.2 m) in height. It breeds on the ice, and males keep the eggs warm during the long polar winter by balancing

Humboldt penguin ❻

Chinstrap penguin

Gentoo penguin

Fiordland penguin

Long beak for catching fishes and squid

Magellanic penguin ❼

❽ King penguin

❾ Macaroni penguin

Erect-crested penguin

Short legs and strong feet for swimming

them on their feet. The females, meanwhile, stay out at sea to feed, returning to land when the chicks hatch. The **little penguin** ❹, at 16 in (40 cm), is the smallest of all penguins. It nests in burrows on the shores of New Zealand and Australia, coming ashore after dark. The **African** or **jackass penguin** ❺ gets its name from its donkeylike call. It is a close relative of the **Humboldt penguin** ❻ and **Magellanic**

penguin ❼, both of which nest in the far south of South America. The **king penguin** ❽ looks like a smaller version of the emperor penguin. It nests on remote rocky islands in Antarctica and incubates its eggs in the same way as the emperor penguin. The **macaroni penguin** ❾ is one of several kinds of penguin with feathery crests. It comes to land to breed, but spends the rest of the year far out at sea.

EMPEROR PENGUINS
These tall, stately birds are the largest of all penguin species. Emperor penguins live on pack ice and hunt in the freezing waters of the Antarctic Ocean, darting after fish with incredible agility. Their dense feathers and thick layer of fat protect them from the intense cold. On land, adults and chicks huddle together in large colonies, taking turns enjoying the warmth at the center of the group.

Size > About 3¾ ft (1.15 m) tall **Weight >** Up to 82 lb (37 kg)
Habitat > Coastal areas, islands, and pack ice. **Distribution >**
Antarctica **Diet >** Fishes, squid, crustaceans, and krill.
Breeding > Emperor penguins breed once a year. Females lay a
single egg, then leave to find food. Males rest the eggs on their
feet, covering them with a warm layer of skin called a brood
pouch. The females return once the eggs have hatched. Both
parents then care for the chick. **Predators >** Adults may be
eaten by killer whales, sharks, or leopard seals. The chicks may
be taken by birds such as Antarctic skuas and giant petrels.
Conservation status > Scientists suspect this species will
become threatened as sea ice melts due to climate change.

Storks, ibises, and herons

SCALE

① Great egret

Yellow "saddle" on top of beak

⑥ Saddle-billed stork

Beak turns deep orange during mating season

S-shaped neck straightens to stab prey

Reddish egret

② Cattle egret

④ Eurasian spoonbill

Indian pond heron

Beak with sensitive spoon-shaped tip

⑤ Roseate spoonbill

Little bittern

③ Eurasian bittern

Little egret

With their long beaks and even longer legs, storks and their relatives are built for hunting by stealth. Many of them stride through shallow water in search of food, but some species feed on land. The **great egret** ① waits patiently for fish and frogs and then spears them with a sudden jab of its beak. The **cattle egret** ② hunts in rough grassland, snapping up grasshoppers and other insects stirred up by animal hooves. Bitterns hunt by the water's edge, with their necks hunched and ready to strike. The **Eurasian bittern** ③ is perfectly camouflaged to match dead reeds. If anyone comes nearby, it stands up straight and sways slowly from side to side, just like reeds blowing in the wind. **Eurasian spoonbills** ④ and American **roseate spoonbills** ⑤ catch their prey by wading through water and

Tricolored heron

Wood stork

❼ Black-crowned night heron

Short, thick beak

Boat-billed heron

❽ Gray heron

Partially webbed toes

❿ Scarlet ibis

Black wingtips

❾ European white stork

Large eyes for hunting in dim light

Yellow-crowned night heron

Green heron

Glossy ibis

Long, sturdy legs

Black-faced ibis

sweeping their flattened beaks from side to side. If they feel food with the tips of their beaks, the "spoon" instantly snaps shut. African **saddle-billed storks** ❻ have a wingspan of up to 9 ft (2.75 m). Like other storks, they fly with their necks stretched out and their legs trailing behind. While storks and ibises usually hunt by day, night herons are active after dark. The **black-crowned night heron** ❼ lives in wetlands all over the world, creeping along the water's edge and ambushing its prey. **Gray herons** ❽ live year-round in western Europe, but **European white storks** ❾ migrate northward every year from Africa and South Asia, soaring high on outstretched wings. The beautiful **scarlet ibis** ❿ lives in South America and the Caribbean. It gets its amazing scarlet color from its diet of small crustaceans.

Pelicans and relatives

Sharp eyes can spot prey beneath the water

1 Shoebill

2 White-tailed tropicbird

3 Red-billed tropicbird

Little pied cormorant

5 Flightless cormorant

Flexible neck helps with grabbing fish

4 Great cormorant

6 Anhinga

Red-legged cormorant

Double-crested cormorant

Pygmy cormorant

Pelicans and their relatives nearly all have webbed feet, and most swim or dive to catch their food. The **shoebill** **1** is the odd-one-out. It lives in African swamps, where it scoops up frogs and fish in its enormous beak. The **white-tailed tropicbird** **2** and **red-billed tropicbird** **3** are always on the move. They flutter above tropical oceans, splashing down with their wings partly

folded and quickly taking off with their catch. The **great cormorant** **4** chases fish in rivers, lakes, and on coasts. It dives down beneath the surface, using its feet as propellers and steering with its wings. Like other cormorants, its feathers are not waterproof and when it has finished fishing it holds its wings out to dry. The **flightless cormorant** **5**, from the Galápagos Islands, has stumpy wings and is the

SCALE

Hammerkop

Red-faced shag

Masked booby

American white pelican ⑦

Black-and-white coloring develops in adulthood

Brown booby

Beak has pouch for catching fish

Brown pelican ⑧

Densely streaked head

Magnificent frigatebird ⑨

Blue-footed booby

European shag

Northern gannet ⑩

Blue feet impress potential mates

Spot-billed pelican

only cormorant that cannot fly. The **anhinga** ⑥, or snakebird, swims with its body below the waterline, so that only its head and neck can be seen. Pelicans are famous for the huge pouches hanging below their beaks, which they use for catching fish. The **American white pelican** ⑦ fishes from the surface, but the **brown pelican** ⑧ cruises just above the waves and dive-bombs its prey. The **magnificent**

frigatebird ⑨ soars over the ocean on amazingly long and slender wings. It feeds by snatching fish from the surface, or by chasing other birds so that they drop their catch. Boobies and gannets feed by diving into the sea at high speed to grab passing fish. The **northern gannet** ⑩ plummets from 100 ft (30 m) up. It folds back its wings as it slams through the water, disappearing with an impressive splash.

FLAMINGOS
With their amazingly long necks and legs, and their brilliant pink coloring, flamingos are easy to recognize. These greater flamingos, one of six species in the family, live in huge flocks of up to 250,000 birds, which feed, nest, and breed together. They feed by wading through the shallows with their heads partly underwater. Their specially adapted beaks have a built-in strainer to filter out tiny pieces of food.

Size ❯ Up to 5 ft (1.5 m) tall **Wingspan** ❯ 5½ ft (1.7 m)
Weight ❯ Up to 9 lb (4 kg) **Habitat** ❯ Lagoons, salt lakes, and
shallow, muddy coasts. **Distribution** ❯ Central and South
America, Caribbean, Africa, southwest Europe, and Asia.
Diet ❯ Shrimp, worms, microscopic algae, and small pieces
of water plants. Their pink color is a by-product of the
flamingos' diet. **Breeding** ❯ Females lay a single egg in
a nest that looks like a miniature volcano made out of
mud. **Life span** ❯ 30 years in the wild, longer in captivity.
Predators ❯ Adults have few natural enemies, but chicks
may be eaten by hyenas, birds of prey, and marabou storks.
Conservation status ❯ Not threatened.

Cranes and relatives

Clapper rail ➊

❷ King rail

❸ Common moorhen

Red band develops in adulthood

❺ Brolga

Black rail

❹ Water rail

Ruffled wings can scare off rivals

❻ Common crane

Buff-banded rail

Sunbittern

Virginia rail

African finfoot

Cranes and rails look very different, but they belong to the same, very varied group of birds. All of them have long legs, and many of them have long, pointed beaks. Cranes live in the open, but rails have slender bodies so they can hide away among waterside plants. The **clapper rail** ➊ likes mangrove swamps, while the **king rail** ❷ from North and Central America lives in marshes. Although these birds are timid, many of them have noisy calls. The **common moorhen** ❸ makes a loud "kurruk," while the **water rail** ❹ grunts and squeals. The **brolga** ❺ is an Australian crane with a red band on its head. It spends its life on the move, traveling to places where it has recently rained. The **common crane** ❻, from Europe, Asia, and Africa, is a long-distance migrant, traveling thousands of miles each

SCALE

Red-knobbed coot

Long beak picks food out of mud

❾ Red-crowned crane

❿ American coot

Sungrebe

Black crake

Distinctive feather crown

Red-legged seriema

Corncrake

❼ Great bustard

❽ Gray crowned crane

Only breeding males have patterned necks

Purple gallinule

Little bustard

Long toes to walk on floating plants

Black "tail" is actually wing feathers

year. Like other cranes, it is legendary for its courtship dances and its amazingly loud trumpeting call. The **great bustard** ❼ is a massive grassland bird from Europe and Asia. Males can weigh up to 46 lb (21 kg), making them some of the heaviest flying birds. **Gray crowned cranes** ❽ live in Africa. Unlike most cranes, they can perch, and they spend the night roosting in trees. The beautiful **red-crowned crane** ❾ lives in Russia,

China, and Japan. Standing up to 6 ft (1.8 m) tall, it is one of the largest cranes, and one of the rarest, with fewer than 3,000 left in the wild. The **American coot** ❿ is much more common, and it can easily be seen in wetlands across North America. Coots are good swimmers, with paddle-shaped flaps on their toes. They can also be quarrelsome, often kicking and splashing when they fight.

201

Waders, gulls, and auks

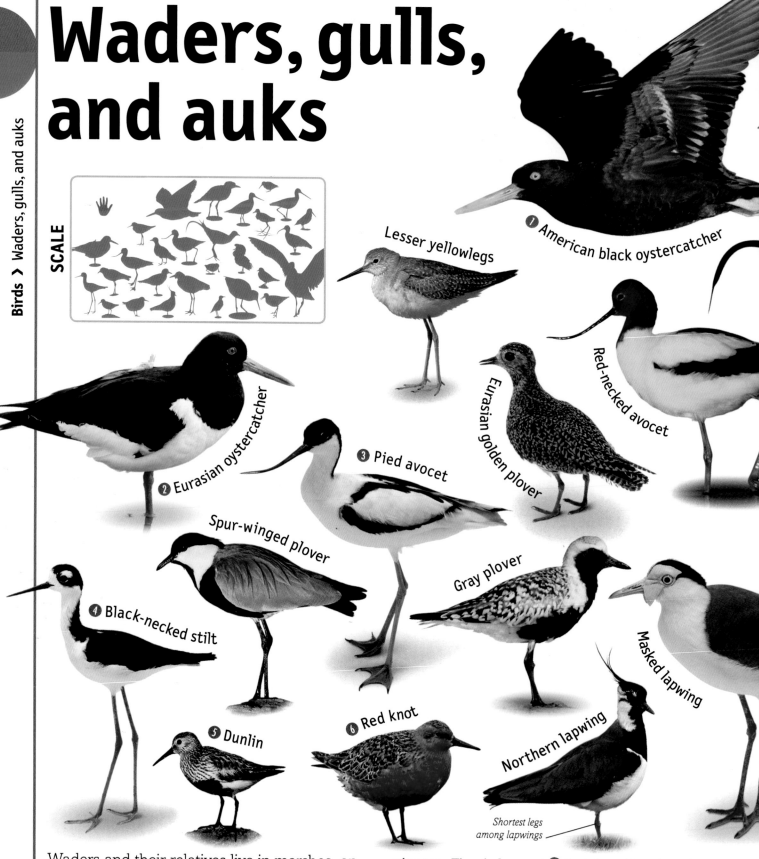

SCALE

Lesser yellowlegs

① American black oystercatcher

② Eurasian oystercatcher

Red-necked avocet

Eurasian golden plover

③ Pied avocet

Spur-winged plover

Gray plover

④ Black-necked stilt

Masked lapwing

Northern lapwing

⑤ Dunlin

⑥ Red knot

Shortest legs among lapwings

Waders and their relatives live in marshes, on coasts, and in the open sea. Most of them lay their eggs on the ground, and some travel record distances to breed. The **American black oystercatcher** ① feeds on shrimp and worms, but is also an expert at smashing open shells of oysters and crabs. The **Eurasian oystercatcher** ② uses the same hunting technique to get at mussels and other prey. The **pied avocet** ③ feeds by striding through shallow water and sweeping its upturned beak from side to side. The tip of its beak is amazingly sensitive, helping it catch insects, shrimps, and other small animals entirely by touch. **Black-necked stilts** ④ wade through water on pencil-thin, bright-red legs. Relative to their bodies, their legs are gigantic, and they stick out behind when

Eurasian stone curlew

Hudsonian godwit

Jack snipe

Black-tailed godwit

Long, narrow beak digs into mud for food

❼ Wattled jacana

❽ American woodcock

Pheasant-tailed jacana

Long toes to spread weight

Curved beak can probe under rocks

Ibisbill

❾ Ruff

Breeding males sport brown, black, or white neck ruffs

❿ Long-billed curlew

Spoon-billed sandpiper

Ruddy turnstone

Banded stilt

Common redshank

Cream-colored courser

these birds sit on their eggs. The **dunlin** ❺ and the **red knot** ❻ breed in the Arctic tundra and then migrate south in enormous flocks. The red knot travels as far as the tip of South America and New Zealand, an epic round trip of 18,500 miles (30,000 km). The **wattled jacana** ❼ from South America has giant toes for walking over lily pads in shallow lakes. The **American woodcock** ❽ has 360-degree vision, thanks to eyes near the top of its head. During their courtship displays, male woodcocks fly at just 5 mph (8 kph), a slow-flying record for a bird, equivalent to a gentle jog. The male **ruff** ❾ has bright courtship plumage, with a feathery collar around its neck. The **long-billed curlew** ❿ is specially equipped to pull up worms, with a curved beak more than half its body length.

⑪ Little auk

⑫ Razorbill

Beak flattened from side to side

Black skimmer

South polar skua

Marbled murrelet

Great black-headed gull

⑬ Tufted puffin

Black guillemot

⑭ Atlantic puffin

Crested auklet

⑮ Brown noddy

⑯ Arctic tern

Swallow-tailed gull

⑰ Caspian tern

Greater crested tern

Short, sturdy legs

Webbed feet for paddling in water

Gulls and auks are good swimmers, with waterproof feathers and webbed feet. Gulls often wander inland, but auks are true seabirds, using their wings to fly and to swim. The **little auk** ⑪ is the smallest auk, growing up to 7 in (19 cm) long. It has a black-and-white body and a short, stubby beak. It nests among boulders in the high Arctic and feeds in huge flocks that look like swarms of bees.

The **razorbill** ⑫ breeds on rocky ledges, but the **tufted puffin** ⑬ and **Atlantic puffin** ⑭ nest in clifftop burrows. Puffins use their multicolored beaks to catch sand eels and other fish. Holding them crosswise, they can carry up to a dozen at a time. Terns and noddies are relatives of gulls, with long tails and pointed wings. The **brown noddy** ⑮ breeds on tropical islands, while the **Arctic tern** ⑯

Sooty gull

⓲ Ross's gull

Dolphin gull

Gray gull

Powerful beak to stab at prey

⓳ Great black-backed gull

⓴ Common gull

Breeding adults have white heads

Laughing gull

Heermann's gull

Inca tern

SCALE

Black-legged kittiwake

migrates between the Arctic and the Southern oceans. In its 30-year life span, it can travel up to 1.5 million miles (2.4 million km), six times the distance from Earth to the Moon. The **Caspian tern ⓱** stays close to coasts, and often breeds near lakes. Like most terns, it is a fiercely protective parent, dive-bombing anyone who comes close to its nest. Auks catch all their food at sea, but gulls often scavenge

along the shore and inland. **Ross's gull ⓲** lives near the edge of the Arctic pack-ice and rarely strays further south. The **great black-backed gull ⓳** is the biggest gull, at 31 in (78 cm) long, and it has a fearsome appetite. It often preys on other seabirds, and it can swallow young rabbits in a single gulp. The **common gull ⓴** often follows tractors plowing fields, swooping down to snap up worms.

ALBATROSSES
Perhaps the ultimate seabirds, albatrosses spend most of their lives gliding over the oceans. They may fly hundreds of miles in a single day, and they are able to lock their enormous wings open so they can glide with little or no effort. Black-browed albatrosses, like the ones above, are the most common and widespread species, but even they are endangered by human activity.

Size ❯ 33–37 in (83–95 cm) tall **Wingspan ❯** Up to 8 ft (2.4 m) **Weight ❯** Up to 11 lb (5 kg) **Habitat ❯** They spend most of the year at sea but return to land to breed. **Distribution ❯** South Atlantic Ocean **Diet ❯** Crustaceans, fishes, squid, and also dead penguins. They pick food from the ocean surface or dive for it, and sometimes follow trawlers for discarded fishes. **Breeding ❯** Albatrosses mate for life. The female lays one egg, which both parents care for. **Life span ❯** Usually about 30 years, but may live as long as 70 years. **Predators ❯** Tiger sharks may take adults. Rats or skuas may take the eggs. **Conservation status ❯** Endangered; they often die after becoming tangled in fishing lines.

Perching birds

SCALE

Scarlet-chested sunbird ❶

Great kiskadee

Northern cardinal ❷

Conical beak for cracking open seeds

Orange-bellied leafbird

Eastern wood-pewee

Pin-tailed manakin

Blue manakin ❸

Vermilion flycatcher

White-bearded antshrike

White-throated dipper ❹

Common tody-flycatcher

Blue-winged pitta ❺

Black-capped vireo

Dunnock

There are thousands of kinds of perching birds, outnumbering all other birds put together. Most are small, with special feet that lock tightly when they perch, keeping them in place. During the daytime most perching birds are constantly busy as they search for food, build their nests, and look after their young. The **scarlet-chested sunbird** ❶ from Africa feeds on sugary nectar from flowers using a curved beak. The **northern cardinal** ❷ lives in Canada, the US, and Mexico. In the winter the male's brilliant red plumage stands out against the snow. **Blue manakins** ❸ come from the rain forests of Brazil. Males attract females with elaborate dances but play no part in raising a family. The **white-throated dipper** ❹ from Europe and Asia is one of the few perching birds that can dive and swim. It

Variegated fairy-wren

Rufous hornero **6**

7 Andean cock-of-the-rock

Males have blue skin around eyes, throat, and neck

8 Bare-throated bellbird

Scarlet tanager

Males turn bright red in breeding season

Rufous gnateater

9 Golden bowerbird

Green catbird

Green broadbill

Wide beak almost covered by feathers

10 Red crossbill

Mustached antpitta

Penduline tit

Chaffinch

Yellow warbler

American redstart

feeds underwater, collecting small animals in rivers and streams. The **blue-winged pitta 5** lives in Southeast Asia, where it eats insects on the forest floor. **Rufous horneros 6** from South America make soccer-ball-shaped nests out of mud. Both parents help in the construction, which includes a slit-shaped entrance and a curved inner corridor. Male **Andean cock-of-the-rocks 7** put all their energy into

courtship, but the females raise the young. **Bare-throated bellbirds 8** from South America are some of the world's loudest birds, with piercing metallic calls. Male **golden bowerbirds 9** attract partners by piling sticks around small trees. These bowers are up to 6½ ft (2 m) high, decorated with fruit and flowers. The **red crossbill 10** has a cross-tipped beak for extracting seeds from pine cones.

Spotted pardalote

Lapland longspur

⑪ African paradise flycatcher

Spotted towhee

⑫ Eastern paradise whydah

Scarlet honeyeater

Long beak for feeding at flowers

⑬ Black-capped chickadee

Crested drongo

Varied tit

Common waxbill

⑭ Gouldian finch

Chipping sparrow

⑯ Lesser bird-of-paradise

⑮ Eurasian golden oriole

Red-backed shrike

Lark bunting

Yellow plumes along sides

SCALE

Perching birds need lots of high-energy food because they are very active. **African paradise flycatchers** ⑪ catch insects on the wing, while **eastern paradise whydahs** ⑫ collect seeds and insects on the ground. During the breeding season male whydahs grow spectacular tail feathers that can be three times their body length. The **black-capped chickadee** ⑬ from North America often visits bird feeders in the winter months. Like other chickadees, it is a natural acrobat, hanging upside down from twigs as it searches for insects and spiders. The multicolored **Gouldian finch** ⑭ is a seed-eater from northern Australia. It is rare in the wild but is sometimes kept as a cage bird. The **Eurasian golden oriole** ⑮ feeds mainly on fruit. Males have striking plumage but they are

Yellow-headed blackbird

⑰ Yellow-headed blackbird

Crimson-breasted gonolek

Brown-throated wattle-eye

Baltimore oriole

⑱ Eastern meadowlark

Common iora

⑲ Brown-headed cowbird

Masked woodswallow

Green jay

Buff-rumped thornbill

⑳ Red-billed blue magpie

Eastern yellow robin

Strong perching feet

hard to see because they feed in treetops. The **lesser bird-of-paradise** ⑯ lives in the forests of New Guinea. Males are much more colorful than females, and they show off their finery in remarkable courtship displays. The **yellow-headed blackbird** ⑰ has a call that sounds like a creaky, rusty gate. It breeds in North America and forms enormous flocks in winter that often feed in fields. The **eastern meadowlark** ⑱ is another North American bird, with a loud whistling call. It feeds on the ground, probing for insects with its sharply pointed beak. **Brown-headed cowbirds** ⑲ lay their eggs in the nests of other birds. Asian **red-billed blue magpies** ⑳ are nest raiders, stealing and eating other birds' eggs and chicks. They belong to the crow family, which contains the world's biggest perching birds.

Apostle bird

㉒ Barn swallow

㉑ European robin

Adults have orange-red breasts

Yellow wagtail

Subalpine warbler

Eurasian nuthatch

㉓ Winter wren

Splendid glossy starling

㉔ Bohemian waxwing

Collared sand martin

Common stonechat

Silver-eared mesia

Mistletoebird

Blue-and-white flycatcher

㉕ Long-tailed tit

Perching birds include some long-distance travelers as well as some that stay put throughout the year. The **European robin** ㉑ is one of the stay-at-homes. It often lives in backyards, where it feeds on insects and worms. The **barn swallow** ㉒ catches insects in midair. It breeds in North America, Europe, and Asia but flies south when fall arrives, a round trip of up to 12,500 miles (20,000 km).

Winter wrens ㉓ live across the Northern Hemisphere. In cold weather they often roost together, and more than 60 winter wrens have been found in a single nest box. The **Bohemian waxwing** ㉔ comes from the forests of North America, Europe, and northern Asia but sometimes migrates southward in winter if insects and berries get hard to find. The **long-tailed tit** ㉕ forms busy winter flocks that flutter

SCALE

26 Eurasian blackbird

27 Song thrush

Broad-ringed white eye

28 Western bluebird

Eurasian treecreeper

Asian fairy-bluebird

Vinous-throated parrotbill

Red-whiskered bulbul

Wren-tit

Northern mockingbird

30 House sparrow

Chestnut weaver

Short, broad wings

31 Eurasian skylark

Blue-gray gnatcatcher

White outer tail feathers

through European woodlands in a single file. The thrush family is famous for its tuneful singers. They include the **Eurasian blackbird** 26, **song thrush** 27, and the North American **western bluebird** 28. Like most perching birds, the male western bluebird sings to attract females and also to warn other males to keep away. The **northern mockingbird** 29 sings for hours at a time. It copies the songs of other birds, and even the ringtones of cell phones. The **house sparrow** 30 has followed humans all over the Earth and is now the world's most widespread bird. It often nests under roofs and in holes in walls. House sparrows are a common sight inside supermarkets and warehouses, eating spilled food. The **Eurasian skylark** 31 feeds on the ground but sings high up in the air.

213

RED-BACKED SHRIKE
This gruesome display is the pantry of the red-backed shrike. A small but efficient hunter, this shrike is sometimes called the butcher bird because of its habit of sticking its prey on thorns. This dries out the bodies, so that they decay slowly and the bird can save them to eat later. The shrike eats larger animals such as lizards by pulling them off the thorns piece by piece.

Size ❯ Up to 7 in (18 cm) long **Wingspan ❯** 10 in (25 cm)
Weight ❯ 1 oz (30 g) **Habitat ❯** Heathlands and commons
with thorny bushes in Europe, and dry scrublands in Africa.
Distribution ❯ Continental Europe, western and central Asia.
Winters in central-southern Africa. **Diet ❯** Bees, beetles, and
other large insects. Also small mammals, birds, and reptiles.

It may chase and catch insects in flight or swoop at prey on
the ground. **Breeding ❯** From late May to early July. Females
lay up to six eggs. **Life span ❯** Up to eight years. **Predators ❯**
None known. **Conservation status ❯** Not threatened.
However, the bird has almost disappeared from the UK
due to habitat loss and possibly pesticide use.

Mammals

All mammals feed their young with milk produced in special glands in the mother's skin. They are warm-blooded, generating heat inside their bodies, and often have fur to protect them from the cold. Most mammals have large brains relative to their body size and are capable of learning, remembering, and forming social relationships.

Ears > Mammals have tiny bones inside their ear canals. Sound waves make these bones vibrate, passing signals to the brain. This system gives mammals exceptionally good hearing.

Fur > Warm-blooded creatures such as mammals need to insulate themselves from outside temperatures. Fur traps air next to their skin, helping them to stay warm.

Tiger

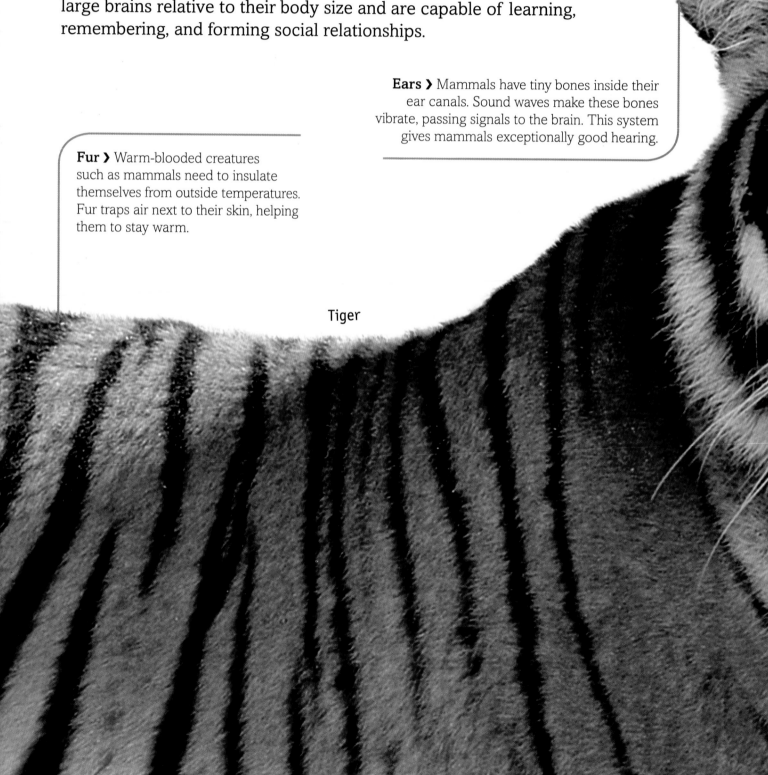

Head ❯ Mammals generally have larger heads and brains compared to their body size than other animals. They include the most intelligent creatures on the planet.

Features

- Almost all give birth to live young

- Feed their young on milk

- Most have hair or fur

- Are warm-blooded

- Include human beings

Teeth ❯ Mammals have a very varied diet. Some eat only plants, others eat meat, and many eat both. This tiger's long, sharp fangs are perfect for killing and eating other animals.

Mammals with pouches

Long, stiff whiskers are touch-sensitive

1 Virginia opossum

2 Parma wallaby

Ears swivel to pinpoint sounds

3 Red-necked wallaby

Brush-tailed bettong

Tail used to carry nesting material

Striped possom

4 Honey possum

Long-nosed potoroo

Bushy, white-tipped tail

5 Sugar glider

Tail acts as a prop

Instead of growing inside their mothers, these animals, known as marsupials, develop inside a pouch. They are born very early and find the pouch by crawling through their mother's fur. Some baby marsupials have their mother's pouch to themselves, but young **Virginia opossums** *1* share it with up to 12 siblings, and have to hang on tight to survive. They live in the US, Mexico, and Central America, often straying into urban areas. Virginia opossums are good climbers and feed at night, sometimes raiding trash cans for leftover food. Marsupials also live in South America, but most of them come from Australia. The **parma wallaby** *2* and **red-necked wallaby** *3* have powerful back legs for jumping, but the **honey possum** *4* has tiny paws and a slender wrap-around tail. Weighing just ½ oz (14 g), it is one of the

Eyes placed on sides of head for wider view

Bearlike body with short legs

⑦ Doria's tree kangaroo

⑧ Common ringtail

⑥ Red kangaroo

⑨ Gray four-eyed opossum

Tail used for balance when climbing

Musky rat-kangaroo

⑩ Bare-tailed woolly opossum

Pouch tightens while hopping

SCALE

world's smallest marsupials, and it feeds on sugary nectar from flowers. The **sugar glider** ⑤ eats insects, fruit, and sap. It can glide up to 165 ft (50 m) between trees, using the stretchy skin between its legs as a parachute. The **red kangaroo** ⑥ is the largest and fastest marsupial, with a top speed of 30 mph (50 kph). Young kangaroos, or joeys, stay in their pouch for up to six months before exploring the world outside.

Doria's tree kangaroos ⑦ from New Guinea spend their lives off the ground. The heaviest tree-climbing marsupials, they feed on leaves, flowers, and fruit. **Common ringtails** ⑧ also eat leaves, but the **gray four-eyed opossum** ⑨ and **bare-tailed woolly opossum** ⑩ have a more varied diet, including earthworms, insects, and birds' eggs. Both live in the Americas and feed mainly at night.

219

⑪ Southern hairy-nosed wombat

SCALE

Single young carried in pouch

⑭ Greater bilby

Distinctive large ears

⑬ Numbat

Powerful forefeet rip open termite nests

⑫ Common wombat

Australia's marsupials come in many different shapes and sizes. Some live in trees, but they also include burrowers that live and feed on the ground. The **southern hairy-nosed wombat** ⑪ digs a network of tunnels, coming out after dark to feed on grass. The burrows are handed on from one generation to the next and can be more than 50 years old. **Common wombats** ⑫ are bigger and more powerful.

Like other wombats, they have a backward-opening pouch. This stops soil from getting in when they are digging and protects their young from roots and twigs. The **numbat** ⑬ lives in forests and feeds on termites. It can eat 20,000 of these insects a day, lapping them up with its long, sticky tongue. The **greater bilby** ⑭ is one of Australia's strangest-looking marsupials, with rabbitlike ears, a pointed snout, and long, silky

⑮ Tasmanian devil

⑯ Koala

Fingers and toes clamp around branches

⑰ Western quoll

Prominent eyes for nighttime hunting

⑱ Mountain brushtail possum

Southern brown bandicoot

⑲ Common spotted cuscus

Male's coat is spotted

Strong, curved claws

Eastern barred bandicoot

fur. It lives in dry places and digs burrows that spiral downward like a corkscrew, making it harder for predators to get inside. The **Tasmanian devil** ⑮ is the world's biggest meat-eating marsupial, with a thick-set body, powerful jaws, and sharp teeth. It is mainly a scavenger, swallowing the skin and even bones of dead animals. Far more appealing and much better known, the **koala** ⑯ lives in gum trees and feeds on their leaves. It eats for about six hours a day and spends the rest of its time asleep. The **western quoll** ⑰ is active at night and hunts like a cat, while the **mountain brushtail possum** ⑱ lives in thick forests and sleeps in hollow trees. The **common spotted cuscus** ⑲ is another tree-dweller, with a tail adapted for grasping branches. The female carries her young on her back after they have left her pouch.

Armadillos, sloths, and anteaters

SCALE

Northern naked-tailed armadillo

Protective plates do not cover the tail

Larger hairy armadillo

Underside covered in dense hairs

Giant armadillo

❶ Three-banded armadillo

❷ Pichi

❸ Nine-banded armadillo

❹ Giant anteater

Long, toothless snout

Six-banded armadillo

Armadillos are the only mammals to have a hard, protective shell. They have flexible bands to let their bodies bend and some kinds, including the **three-banded armadillo** ❶, can roll themselves up into a ball. The **pichi** ❷ has another way of keeping out of trouble. It wedges itself in its burrow, making it hard for predators to drag it out. Most armadillos live in Central and South America, but the **nine-banded armadillo** ❸ lives as far north as the United States. Its family life is very unusual because it always has identical quadruplets each time it breeds. Armadillos feed mainly on ants and termites, although they do eat other animals such as grubs and worms. The **giant anteater** ❹ is one of the biggest insect-eating mammals, swallowing up to 30,000 ants a day. It rips open

Maned sloth

Southern two-toed sloth **5**

Tough armor of overlapping scales

Brown-throated sloth **6**

Ground pangolin **8**

Northern tamandua

Silky anteater **1**

Long-tailed pangolin

Prehensile tail used to grip branches

Collared anteater

Indian pangolin **9**

anthills or termite mounds with its claws and licks up its food with its sticky 2 ft (60 cm) long tongue. Sloths are distant relatives of anteaters, but they hang from branches and feed on leaves. The **southern two-toed sloth 5** never moves in a hurry, and the **brown-throated sloth 6** is one of the slowest mammals in the world. Its top speed in trees is about ¼ mph (0.3 kph), and it eats, sleeps, and even gives

birth upside down. The **silky anteater 7** from Central and tropical South America can climb just as well as a sloth. Large, curved front claws and a prehensile tail help it to live in trees, where it nests in holes. Pangolins are unmistakable animals with their covering of overlapping scales. The African **ground pangolin 8** and **Indian pangolin 9** are so well protected that they can even keep lions and tigers at bay.

Hedgehogs and moles

SCALE

Desert hedgehog ❶

Long ears help in keeping cool

Long-eared hedgehog

North African hedgehog ❷

European hedgehog ❸

Long, furry tail

Pygmy shrew ❹

Southern African hedgehog

Eurasian water shrew

North American least shrew ❺

When the Sun sets, hedgehogs set off to find food. Armed with up to 5,000 sharp spines, they rummage through the undergrowth, rolling up into a spiked ball if they are threatened with attack. They eat invertebrates, fruit, and carrion. The **desert hedgehog** ❶ from Africa and the Middle East usually prefers insects and their larvae but can also tackle scorpions and venomous snakes. The **North**

African hedgehog ❷ gives birth to about six babies, or "hoglets," each time it breeds. At first their spines are soft, but they harden within a day. The **European hedgehog** ❸ lives in lots of different habitats, including farms and yards. Despite its dumpy shape, it is a great climber, scrambling up fences and walls and dropping unharmed onto the other side. The **pygmy shrew** ❹ has a vicious bite. This tiny mammal

Pyrenean desman

⑥ Hispaniolan solenodon

Front legs have powerful claws for burrowing

⑦ Moonrat

Small Japanese mole

Alpine shrew

⑧ European mole

Sensitive tentacles to find food

Common shrew

Bicolored white-toothed shrew

Reddish-gray musk shrew

Tiny eyes

⑨ Star-nosed mole

Northern short-tailed shrew

Greater white-toothed shrew

is just 2 in (5 cm) long but can attack earthworms many times its size. The **North American least shrew** ⑤ is almost as small and has venomous saliva that helps it to overpower its prey. The **Hispaniolan solenodon** ⑥ looks like a giant shrew. It is only found on Hispaniola, an island in the Caribbean. The **moonrat** ⑦ from Southeast Asia is related to hedgehogs and eats fruit as well as animal prey. The **European mole** ⑧

lives underground and digs tunnels with its spadelike front paws. It feeds on earthworms, storing them in special "pantries" and biting off their heads to stop them from getting away. The **star-nosed mole** ⑨ from North America looks for food with 22 pink tentacles on its nose. A good swimmer, it is amazingly quick on the draw, taking just a quarter of a second to sense and grab its food.

AFRICAN ELEPHANTS
The largest land animals, African elephants are equipped with a long trunk, which they use not only for breathing, smelling, and trumpeting, but also to grip and move objects and to suck up water. Their huge ears allow heat to escape, keeping them cool. Elephants are known for their intelligence, and they form strong family relationships.

Size ❯ Males up to 13 ft (4 m) tall; females up to 8½ ft (2.6 m) tall **Weight ❯** Males up to 6 tons and females up to 3½ tons **Habitat ❯** Savanna **Distribution ❯** Sub-Saharan Africa **Diet ❯** Leaves and bark from trees, and grass. They can eat up to 350 lb (160 kg) of food a day. **Breeding ❯** Females (cows) give birth to one baby every two to four years.

Elephant herds consist mainly of females, and other members may help the mother to care for the baby. **Life span ❯** Around 60 years in the wild. **Predators ❯** Adults have no predators. Calves may be killed by lions, leopards, hyenas, or crocodiles. **Conservation status ❯** Vulnerable because they are hunted for their ivory tusks.

Rabbits, hares, and pikas

1 Lop-eared rabbit

2 Angora rabbit

Soft fur can be used to make wool

Dwarf rabbit

3 European rabbit

4 Eastern cottontail

Swamp rabbit

5 European hare

6 Arctic hare

SCALE

Rabbits and hares have many predators but their keen senses and long legs give them a head start in the race for safety. At the first sign of danger, most rabbits sprint into their burrows. Hares stay above ground, bounding away at up to 50 mph (80 kph). Rabbits and hares have big ears and large front teeth, and they feed entirely on plants. There are more than 50 breeds of rabbit, including the **lop-eared rabbit** 1, whose dangly ears can measure 27 in (70 cm) long. The **Angora rabbit** 2 is valued for its long, soft hair, which is spun into yarn. These two breeds, and many others, are descendants of the **European rabbit** 3, which has been kept in captivity for hundreds of years. In the wild, European rabbits live in big burrow systems called warrens. They breed amazingly quickly, raising up to 40 babies, or "kits," each year.

Marsh rabbit

8 American pika

Short legs and no tail

White-tailed jackrabbit

Large eyes for feeding at night

7 Mountain hare

9 Antelope jackrabbit

Large ears used for hearing and keeping cool

Cape hare

Wide-set eyes provide all-around vision

10 Snowshoe hare

Black-tailed jackrabbit

Coat turns white in winter

The American **eastern cottontail** 4 looks very similar to the European rabbit but breeds above ground. Hares are usually bigger than rabbits and live on their own. The **European hare** 5 stays brown all year round, but many other kinds, including the **Arctic hare** 6 and **mountain hare** 7, turn white in winter for camouflage against the snow. Pikas are relatives of rabbits and hares, but they are much smaller and have shorter ears. The **American pika** 8 lives in rocky burrows high up in mountains. To survive the winter, it collects plants and dries them like tiny piles of hay, to eat when other food is scarce. The **antelope jackrabbit** 9 has the biggest ears of all wild hares. The **snowshoe hare's** 10 ears and paws are thickly furred, keeping it warm in the bitterly cold winters of Canada and Alaska.

Rodents

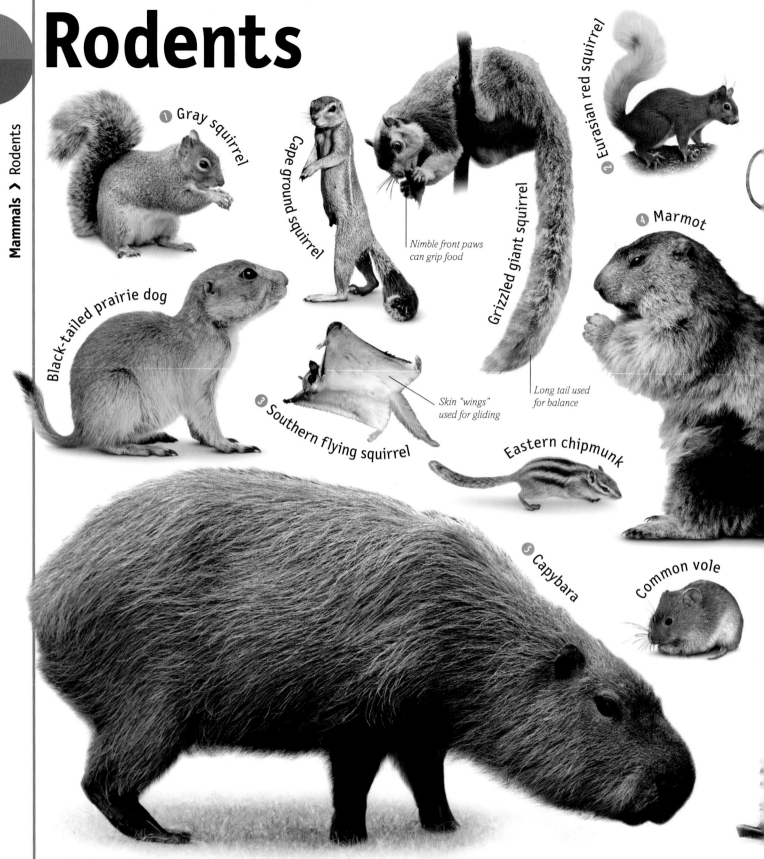

① Gray squirrel

Cape ground squirrel

Black-tailed prairie dog

Nimble front paws can grip food

③ Southern flying squirrel

Skin "wings" used for gliding

Grizzled giant squirrel

Long tail used for balance

② Eurasian red squirrel

④ Marmot

Eastern chipmunk

⑤ Capybara

Common vole

Added together, rodents easily outnumber all other mammals on Earth. They live almost everywhere on dry land and in freshwater too. Most rodents feed on plants. Their front teeth grow nonstop, enabling them to gnaw through their food and anything in their way. The **gray squirrel ①** is an expert climber with nimble front paws. Originally from North America, it has pushed out the **Eurasian red squirrel ②** in many parts of the British Isles. The red squirrel uses its long tail to balance itself while jumping from one tree to another. The North American **southern flying squirrel ③** glides between trees on folds of stretchy skin. It can travel almost 100 ft (30 m) in a single flight, landing right on target even in the dark. The **marmot ④** lives in mountain burrows and hibernates for up to nine months every year. The world's

Lesser Egyptian jerboa

⑥ Beaver

Meadow jumping mouse

⑦ Desert pocket mouse

Merriam's kangaroo rat

Paddle-shaped tail for swimming and signaling to other beavers

African dormouse

South African springhare

⑧ Azara's agouti

Long legs for high-speed running

Kangaroo-like hind legs

⑨ Norway lemming

Muskrat

Roborovski's desert hamster

⑩ Golden hamster

SCALE

largest rodent is the **capybara** ⑤ from the swamps of South America. It grows to the size of a small pig. To escape its enemies, it dives into water and can hold its breath for up to five minutes. The **beaver** ⑥ is a good swimmer and is renowned for building dams. The biggest beaver dam on record, in Canada, is ½ mile (850 m) long and was first spotted by satellite. Many other rodents, such as the **desert**

pocket mouse ⑦, get all their water from their food. **Azara's agouti** ⑧ from South America has small families with just two young, but **Norway lemmings** ⑨ sometimes produce more than 50 babies a year. When their burrows get overcrowded, young lemmings pour across the Arctic tundra in search of food. The **golden hamster** ⑩ from the Middle East is very rare in the wild, but millions are kept as pets.

⑪ Domestic guinea pig

Long teeth used for digging tunnels

⑫ Naked mole rat

⑬ Chinchilla

Thick-set body without tail

⑭ Mara

Short, thick spines

Harvest mouse

Pallid gerbil

⑮ Brown rat

Brazilian porcupine

Botta's pocket gopher

Wood mouse

⑯ Albino house mouse

Rodents include some rare animals as well as common ones found all over the world. The **domestic guinea pig** ⑪ from South America was once raised for food but is now a popular pet, with many different breeds. The **naked mole rat** ⑫ from east Africa lives in big families and spends its whole life tunneling underground. It is one of the world's weirdest-looking mammals, with big front teeth, bare wrinkly skin, and tiny eyes. **Chinchillas** ⑬ have luxurious fur coats that protect them from the cold. Found in the South American Andes, these rodents are hunted for their fur and are now endangered in the wild. The **mara** ⑭ looks a lot like a hare. It lives in South America's grasslands and is one of the fastest rodents, bounding along at 28 mph (45 kph). The **brown rat** ⑮ is a worldwide pest. Adaptable and intelligent,

Dense fur for protection against cold

⑰ Mountain viscacha

⑱ Coypu

Quills detach and stick in attacker's skin

⑲ Dassie rat

Bare feet give good grip

Degu

⑳ Crested porcupine

it survives in all kinds of habitats, from remote islands to urban drains. An expert climber and a good swimmer, it eats almost anything, including seeds, eggs, leather, and even soap. The **house mouse** ⑯ is another rodent that lives alongside people, although it keeps out of sight. It is found on every continent except Antarctica and has even been discovered aboard planes and deep down in mines. The **mountain** **viscacha** ⑰ is a close relative of the chinchilla and lives high up in mountains. The South American **coypu** ⑱ feeds in lakes and swamps. African **dassie rats** ⑲ live in rocky hillsides. They have flat skulls and flexible ribs for squeezing into cracks. The African **crested porcupine** ⑳ is the world's best-armed rodent. When threatened, it charges backward into its enemy, stabbing it with its sharp, hollow quills.

Bushbabies, lemurs, and tarsiers

White-footed sportive lemur ①

Young rides on its mother's back

Coquerel's sifaka ③

Verreaux's sifaka ②

Senegal bushbaby ④

Moholi bushbaby ⑤

Strong back legs good for jumping

Ring-tailed lemur ⑥

Brown greater galago

Mongoose lemur

Long tail used for balancing

Bushbabies and their relatives belong to a group of mammals called primates, which includes monkeys, apes, and also humans. Most of these animals live in trees and all of them have forward-facing eyes, allowing them to judge distances in three dimensions. Bushbabies come from Africa, but lemurs are found in Madagascar and nowhere else in the world. There are many different kinds of lemur and each has its own way of living. The **white-footed sportive lemur** ① feeds mainly on leaves, but **Verreaux's sifaka** ② also eats fruit, flowers, and bark. **Coquerel's sifaka** ③ is an amazingly acrobatic climber, even with a baby on board. The **Senegal bushbaby** ④ and **moholi bushbaby** ⑤ come out after dark. They can leap 25 times their own body length as they spring from branch to branch. The

234

7 Black-and-white ruffed lemur

Red-bellied lemur

8 Slow loris

Forward-facing eyes give good 3D vision

Pygmy slow loris

Spectral tarsier

Red slender loris

Horsfield's tarsier

Head can turn through 180 degrees to keep watch behind

Potto

Gray mouse lemur

Greater dwarf lemur

10 Aye-aye

9 Philippine tarsier

Tail used to store fat in wet season

SCALE

Slender middle finger for picking grubs out of wood

ring-tailed lemur 6 climbs well, but spends much of its time on the ground. It is very sociable and always keeps together in groups. The **black-and-white ruffed lemur** 7 is the largest lemur at 24 in (60 cm) long, but only weighs about 9 lb (4 kg), about the same as a pet cat. Lorises are plant- and insect-eaters from tropical forests in Asia. The **slow loris** 8 creeps along branches once the sun has gone

down. The **Philippine tarsier** 9 is a pocket-sized primate with enormous staring eyes. Like other tarsiers, it leaps on to insects in the dark and crunches them up with its sharp teeth. The nocturnal **aye-aye** 10 from Madagascar is the world's strangest primate, with skinny hands and scraggly fur. It feeds on fruit, eggs, and insects, and uses its extra-long middle finger to tweak out insect larvae from wood.

Gibbons, apes, and humans

Müller's Bornean gibbon

SCALE

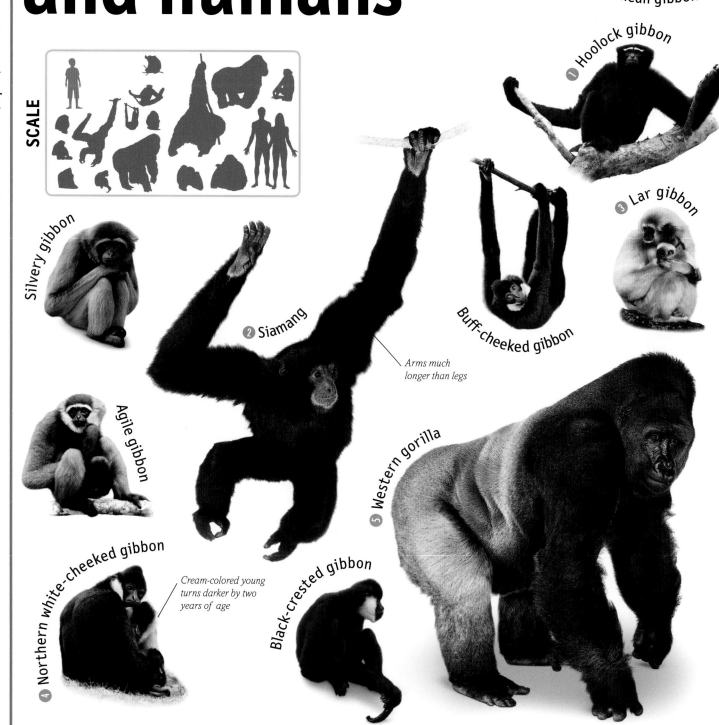

❶ Hoolock gibbon

❸ Lar gibbon

Silvery gibbon

❷ Siamang

Arms much longer than legs

Buff-cheeked gibbon

Agile gibbon

❺ Western gorilla

❹ Northern white-cheeked gibbon

Cream-colored young turns darker by two years of age

Black-crested gibbon

236

Gibbons and apes include our closest relatives in the living world. Not only are they similar to people in appearance, but they are also highly intelligent animals. The **hoolock gibbon** ❶ lives in South and Southeast Asia, which is where all wild gibbons are found. Like other gibbons, it uses its hands like hooks to swing from branch to branch, speeding through the forest almost as fast as a man can run. The

siamang ❷ is the biggest gibbon. It eats leaves and fruit, and starts the day with a loud dawn chorus that can be heard from far away. The skin on its throat is elastic and inflates to the size of a grapefruit, amplifying its amazingly loud calls. The **lar gibbon** ❸ is black or brown, but **northern white-cheeked gibbons** ❹ start life with creamy fur and turn darker as they grow up. Gorillas come from Africa and spend most

Mature males have "saddle" of silvery fur

⑥ Eastern gorilla

⑦ Chimpanzee

⑧ Sumatran orang-utan

Can grip with hands and feet

⑩ Human male

Human female

⑨ Bornean orangutan

Bonobo

of their lives on the ground. The **western gorilla** ⑤ can weigh three times as much as an adult man, but the **eastern gorilla** ⑥ is even bigger, weighing a massive 485 lb (220 kg). Despite their size, gorillas are peaceful plant-eaters and rarely attack people unless their young are threatened. Also from Africa, the **chimpanzee** ⑦ is the primate most similar to us. It lives in large groups and eats all kinds of food, from termites to monkeys, which it ambushes in trees. The **Sumatran orangutan** ⑧ and **Bornean orangutan** ⑨ are two fruit-eaters from Southeast Asia. Like chimps, they are highly intelligent and are good at problem-solving and making simple tools. **Humans** ⑩ are the only living primates that walk upright on two legs. Today there are more than 7 billion of us, spread over every land habitat on Earth.

237

ORANGUTANS
These apes are some of humans' closest relatives. In fact, their name means "person of the forest" in Malay. These shy treetop-dwellers are very intelligent animals. Long arms and flexible hands and feet help them to move around in trees, looking for fruit and other food. Young orangutans stay with their mothers for up to seven years, learning the skills they need to survive as adults.

Size ❯ Males up to 5 ft (1.5 m); females up to 4¼ ft (1.3 m) tall **Weight ❯** Males 110–175 lb (50–80 kg); females 65–100 lb (30–45 kg) **Habitat ❯** Rain forest. Orangutans are solitary animals, but females and their offspring may be seen together. **Distribution ❯** Tropical forest in Borneo and in northern Sumatra, Indonesia. **Diet ❯** Mainly figs and other fruit, leaves, occasionally insects, honey, and birds' eggs. **Breeding ❯** Orangutans start breeding in their teens. Females give birth once every eight years and infants stay with them for six to seven years. **Life span ❯** Up to 50 years in the wild and 60 years in captivity. **Predators ❯** Tigers **Conservation status ❯** Critically endangered due to habitat loss.

New World monkeys

Long tail used for balance

① Black-capped squirrel monkey

Common squirrel monkey

Goeldi's monkey

② White-faced saki

Colombian spider monkey

⑤ Pygmy marmoset

Long, white crest

③ Red bald-headed uakari

Long waterproof fur

④ Northen night monkey

Collared titi monkey

Common marmoset

Cotton-top marmoset

Black-bearded saki

New World monkeys come from Central and South America. Many of them have flat noses and tails that wrap around branches like an extra hand. **Black-capped squirrel monkeys** ① live in large groups in the treetops, feeding on fruit and insects. They have more than two dozen separate calls, including special alarm sounds if they spot a predator such as an eagle or a snake. The **white-faced**

saki ② has shaggy fur and feeds closer to the ground. The **red bald-headed uakari** ③ looks as if its head has been shaved. Its red face is thought to attract potential mates. Most New World monkeys feed during the day, but the **northern night monkey** ④ wakes up after dark and is most active on moonlit nights. The tiny **pygmy marmoset** ⑤ is the world's smallest monkey, weighing just five times as much

6 Southern muriqui

7 Venezuelan red howler

Throat works like an amplifier

Emperor tamarin

Weeper capuchin

Thick, prehensile tail can grip tree branches

8 Golden lion tamarin

Long, silky mane

9 Gray woolly monkey

10 White-headed capuchin

Golden-headed lion tamarin

SCALE

as a mouse. Like other marmosets it scampers along branches, and has hands with sharp claws. It gnaws holes in the bark of trees and licks up the sap that oozes out. The **southern muriqui** **6**, also known as the woolly spider monkey, is the largest New World monkey. The **Venezuelan red howler** **7** is the noisiest land animal with a roar that can be heard up to 3 miles (5 km) away. Howlers live in trees and eat leaves.

They call at dawn to claim their feeding territory high above the ground. The beautiful **golden lion tamarin** **8** is one of the most endangered monkeys in the world. It was rescued from extinction in the 1980s when fewer than 200 were left. The **gray woolly monkey** **9** stays high up in trees, but the **white-headed capuchin** **10** sometimes feeds on the ground and is good at walking on all fours.

Old World monkeys

SCALE

① L'Hoest's monkey

② Rhesus macaque

③ De Brazza's monkey

④ Proboscis monkey

Nose is largest in males

Blue monkey

⑤ Patas monkey

Old World monkeys live in Africa and Asia, as far north as Japan. Most of them are tree-dwellers, although baboons spend much of their time on the ground. Unlike New World monkeys, they cannot grip with their tails, but they include some amazingly good climbers as well as the fastest monkey on all fours. **L'Hoest's monkey** ① from Central Africa lives in mountain forests. It mainly eats fruit and leaves and has cheek pouches for storing food. The **rhesus macaque** ② is found in South Asia, Thailand, and China. It lives in all kinds of habitats, from forests to the outskirts of towns. **De Brazza's monkey** ③ from Africa has a long, white beard, while the **proboscis monkey** ④ from Borneo has a huge, fleshy nose. Proboscis monkeys live in mangrove swamps and are great swimmers and divers.

Toque macaque

Southern pig-tailed macaque

7 Hamadryas baboon

6 Olive baboon

8 Grivet

Tufted gray langur

*Muscular limbs
for fast movement*

*Long tail
for balance*

9 Yellow baboon

10 Mandrill

*Females
are smaller
than males*

They leap from a height of 50 ft (15 m), hitting the water in a noisy belly flop. The African **patas monkey 5** is a ground-dweller and a great runner, with a record-breaking top speed of 34 mph (55 kph). Baboons also come from Africa, but they have big teeth and a much heavier build. The **olive baboon 6** forages in open grassland, while the **hamadryas baboon 7** lives in rocky places. If baboons are threatened, the biggest males face up to the enemy, giving the rest of the troop time to escape. The **grivet 8** eats insects and plant food. Its predators include the **yellow baboon 9**, which hunts smaller monkeys for food. The multicolored **mandrill 10** from West Africa has a vivid blue-and-red face. It lives in giant troops called hordes, which can contain 800 animals, a record for any primate.

Bats

1 Lyle's flying fox

Wing membrane attached to hind legs

Long, clawed thumbs

2 Geoffroy's tailless bat

Franquet's epauletted bat

3 Kitti's hog-nosed bat

Mouse-tailed bat

Tail almost as long as body

4 Egyptian rousette

5 Vampire bat

Razor-sharp teeth to pierce skin of victims

Wings used like legs on ground

Lots of small mammals can glide, but bats are the only ones that can really fly, using muscle power to flap their wings. These wings are made of skin stretched between amazingly slender finger bones, which can be as thin as a human hair. Small bats usually feed on flying insects, but most big ones eat fruit, which they find using keen eyesight and a superb sense of smell. **Lyle's flying fox 1** is a fruit-eater from the forests of Southeast Asia. Named for its foxlike face, it spends the daytime roosting upside down in trees, using its large clawed thumbs to move along branches. **Geoffroy's tailless bat 2** comes from Central and South America and feeds on sugary nectar with its brush-tipped tongue, but **Kitti's hog-nosed bat 3** from Thailand and Myanmar hunts insects, snatching them out of the air or

Proboscis bat

6 Large flying fox

Large eyes for seeing after dark

7 Spectacled flying fox

Body wrapped in wings when roosting

8 Wahlberg's epauletted fruit bat

9 Lesser horseshoe bat

Seba's short-tailed bat

Nose leaf helps in echolocation

picking them off plants. It is the world's tiniest mammal with large ears but a body as small as a bumblebee's. The **Egyptian rousette** ❹ eats fruit, but the legendary **vampire bat** ❺ from Central and South America drinks blood from mammals and birds. Silent and stealthy, it scuttles up to its victims on all fours, slicing through their skin with its sharp teeth and lapping up a meal of blood. The **large flying fox** ❻ is one of the world's biggest bats, with a wingspan of 5 ft (1.5 m). Like the **spectacled flying fox** ❼ from Australia and New Guinea, it sets off to feed at sunset, flying up to 30 miles (50 km) in search of food. **Wahlberg's epauletted fruit bat** ❽ is a fruit-eater from Africa, but the **lesser horseshoe bat** ❾ is an insect-eater, with a small body and surprisingly big wings.

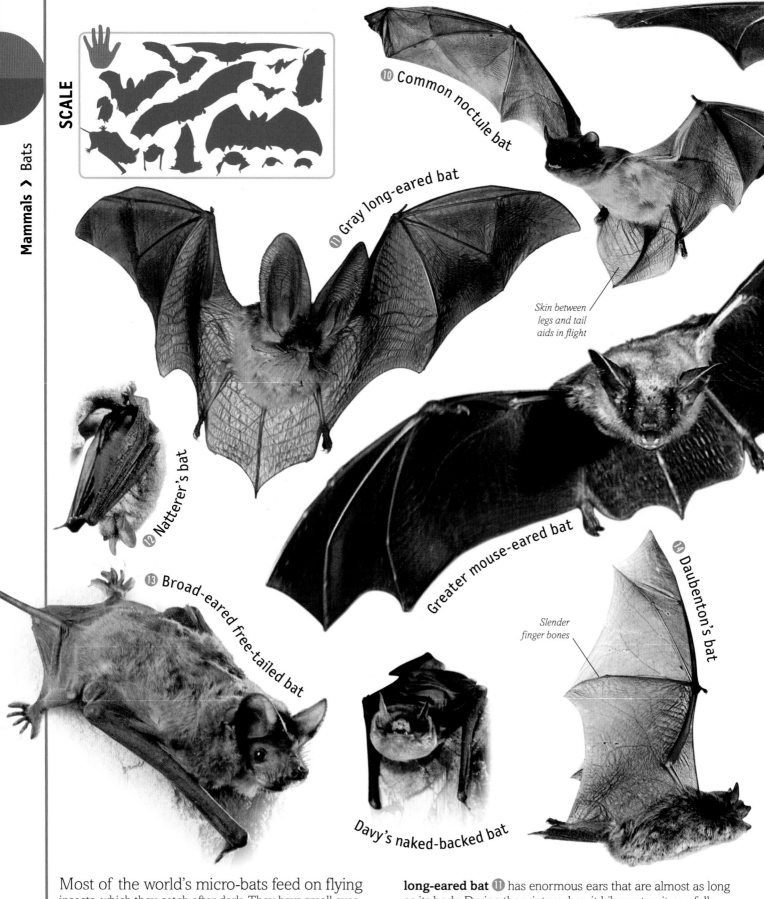

SCALE

⑩ Common noctule bat

⑪ Gray long-eared bat

Skin between legs and tail aids in flight

⑫ Natterer's bat

⑬ Broad-eared free-tailed bat

Greater mouse-eared bat

Slender finger bones

⑭ Daubenton's bat

Davy's naked-backed bat

Most of the world's micro-bats feed on flying insects, which they catch after dark. They have small eyes and find their prey by echolocation, using bursts of high-frequency sound to form an "image" of their surroundings. The **common noctule** ⑩ from Europe and Asia catches most of its food in the air. It also snatches insects off leaves and swoops on them on the ground. The European **gray**

long-eared bat ⑪ has enormous ears that are almost as long as its body. During the winter when it hibernates, it carefully tucks them away under its wings. **Natterer's bat** ⑫ from Europe hibernates in caves and mines. During its long winter sleep, its body temperature can drop to just 35°F (2°C), and it may breathe just once an hour. The **broad-eared free-tailed bat** ⑬ lives in Central and South America, where it is warm all

⑮ European free-tailed bat

⑯ Common pipistrelle

Kuhl's pipistrelle

Big brown bat

⑰ Ghost bat

Long-fingered bat

⑱ Spix's disk-winged bat

Nathusius' pipistrelle

Suction disk for gripping leaves

year round. It roosts in small groups, but some of its relatives sleep and breed in huge colonies, numbering a million bats or more. **Daubenton's bat** ⑭ scoops up insects from the surface of lakes and ponds, hunting mainly at dawn and dusk. The **European free-tailed bat** ⑮ spends the whole night on the wing. Like other free-tailed bats, it has a distinctive mouselike tail. The **common pipistrelle** ⑯ is the smallest bat in Europe. It often roosts in old buildings and hunts around streetlights, catching insects that are attracted by the light. The **ghost bat** ⑰ is the biggest predatory species in Australia. In addition to catching insects, it eats frogs, lizards, birds, and even other bats. **Spix's disk-winged bat** ⑱ lives in Central and South American forests. It has suction cups on its wrists and ankles for roosting underneath leaves.

HONDURAN WHITE BATS
These tiny Central American bats have fluffy white fur, making them look like little cotton balls. They also have eye-catching, golden-yellow ears, black wings, and a snout with a pointed top. They are often found huddled in a colony of four to eight bats roosting under a *Heliconia* leaf, which they adapt to make a tent for themselves.

Size ❯ 1½–1¾ in (3.5–4.5 cm) **Weight ❯** About ¼ oz (6 g)
Habitat ❯ Tropical rain forest. The bats chew through the veins of *Heliconia* leaves, so that the two sides of the leaf hang down to form a tent. They roost inside this tent, which protects them from sun, rain, and predators. **Distribution ❯** Lowlands of Central America. **Diet ❯** Fruit **Breeding ❯**

Females produce one baby in the rainy season. Males and females roost together until the young are born, then the males leave. The young suckle for 20–21 days. **Predators ❯** Snakes and small mammals such as opossums.
Conservation status ❯ Numbers have declined sharply in recent years due to destruction of their habitat.

Dogs, foxes, and relatives

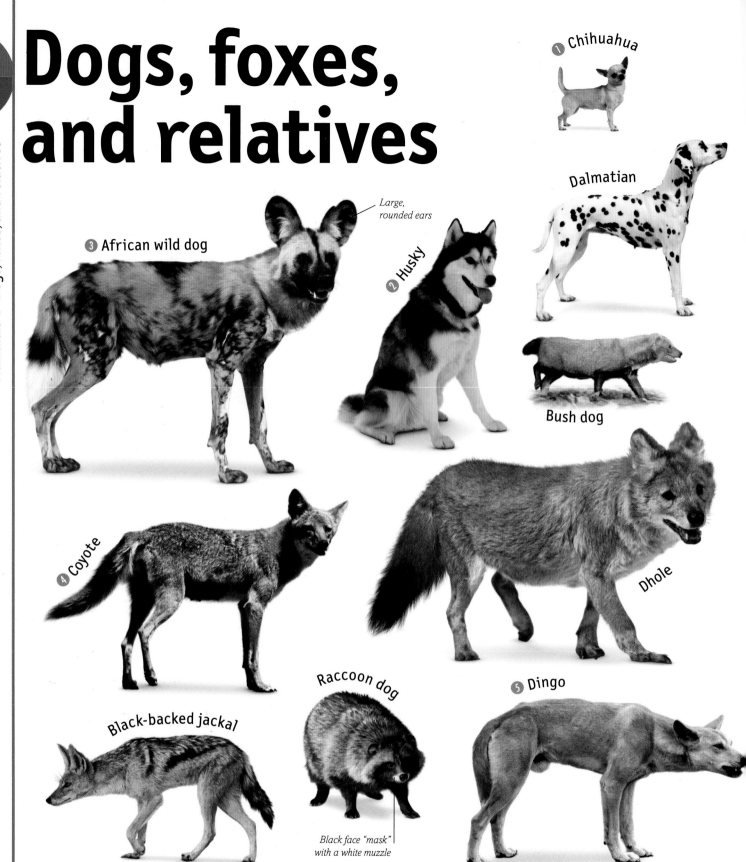

① Chihuahua

Dalmatian

③ African wild dog

Large, rounded ears

② Husky

Bush dog

④ Coyote

Dhole

Black-backed jackal

Raccoon dog

Black face "mask" with a white muzzle

⑤ Dingo

Dogs and foxes are expert hunters, although most of them also eat plants and carrion. Dogs originally developed from wolves, which people gradually learned to tame. There are now hundreds of different breeds of dog, from the tiny **chihuahua** ①, the smallest of domestic dog breeds, to the hardy **husky** ②, which is used for pulling sleds. Huskies can work in temperatures as low as -58°F (-50°C). They are

the only mammals, aside from humans, that have walked to both the North and South Pole. **African wild dogs** ③ live in highly organized packs, rearing young cooperatively and hunting together to kill animals much bigger than themselves. Each wild dog has its own coat pattern, which is as unique as a fingerprint. **Coyotes** ④ come from North and Central America. They hunt alone, in pairs, or in packs, and they can

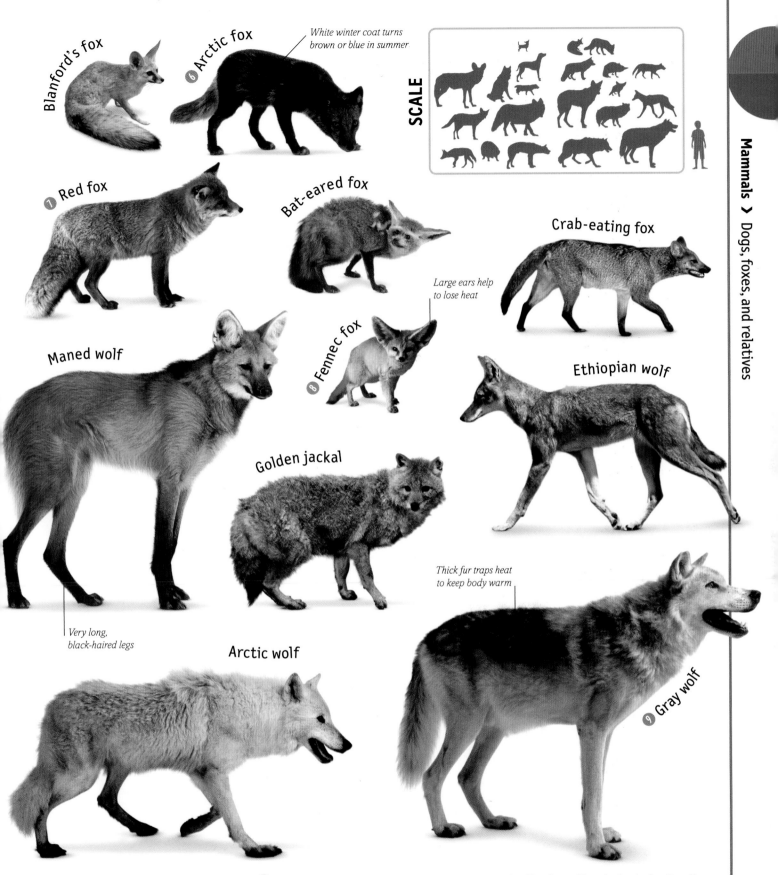

Blanford's fox

Arctic fox 6

White winter coat turns brown or blue in summer

Red fox 7

Bat-eared fox

Crab-eating fox

Maned wolf

Fennec fox 8

Large ears help to lose heat

Ethiopian wolf

Golden jackal

Thick fur traps heat to keep body warm

Very long, black-haired legs

Arctic wolf

Gray wolf 9

SCALE

run at up to 40 mph (65 kph). **Dingoes** 5 were introduced into Australia from Asia by humans about 4,000 years ago. They hunt small animals on their own but band together to attack kangaroos. **Arctic foxes** 6 are specially suited to life in the far north. In winter their coats turn pure white, and they can hunt on drifting ice hundreds of miles out at sea. The **red fox** 7 is one of the world's most widespread predators, occuring throughout the Northern Hemisphere. It often lives in cities, where it scavenges leftover food from garbage cans and dumps. The North African **fennec fox** 8 is smaller than a cat. It pounces on rodents and insects, pinpointing them with its giant ears. The **gray wolf** 9 is the biggest member of the dog family. It lives in packs and communicates with an eerie howl that can be heard from far away.

Bears

SCALE

① Asiatic black bear

Pale patch gives this species alternate name "moon bear"

② American black bear

Strong legs allow bear to walk upright

③ Brown bear

④ Grizzly bear

"Grizzled" hairs lighter at tip than at base

Legendary for their size and strength, bears are some of the world's biggest land mammals, with stocky bodies and flat paws. Most of them stay well away from people but some can be highly dangerous, particularly when they are hungry or protecting their cubs. The **Asiatic black bear** ① lives in forests from India to Japan. It spends more than half its life in trees and feeds on fruit, nuts, and small animals. The **American black bear** ② is slightly bigger but also good at climbing. Like all bears, it has a superb sense of smell, and sometimes breaks into cars or campsites to get at stored food. The **brown bear** ③ is the most widespread, with several forms found in different parts of the world. Most famous is the **grizzly bear** ④, which lives in western North America. Standing up to 10 ft (3 m) tall on

6 Polar bear

White fur provides camouflage in snow and ice

5 Kodiak brown bear

Large front paws used as paddles while swimming

7 Sun bear

Furry soles provide good grip on ice

10 Giant panda

8 Sloth bear

9 Spectacled bear

Long claws for breaking open termite mounds

its back legs, it is strong enough to drag away a moose or a horse. It eats almost anything that it can catch or collect, including deer, fish, berries, and even moths. The **Kodiak brown bear** 5 from Alaska is even bigger, but the **polar bear** 6 is the largest of all. It is the only bear that actively hunts people, although seals are its usual prey. The **sun bear** 7 and **sloth bear** 8 live in southern Asia. The sun

bear's tongue can protrude up to 10 in (25 cm) to extract food such as honey and grubs from holes and crevices. The **spectacled bear** 9 comes from forests high up in the South American Andes. It feeds on fruit, plant shoots, and meat. The **giant panda** 10 lives in central China, where it feeds entirely on bamboo. Like all bears, it has tiny cubs. They weigh only about 4 oz (120 g) when they are newly born.

253

POLAR BEAR
This powerful Arctic predator is the largest land-based meat-eater. Instantly recognizable by its thick white fur, the polar bear is a strong swimmer and a lethally effective hunter. Its usual prey is seals, which it ambushes as they surface through holes in the ice to breathe. The polar bear is often curious about people and can be dangerous if it comes too close to human settlements.

Size › Males up to 10 ft (3 m); females up to 7 ft (2.2 m) tall, standing on their hind legs **Weight** › Males weigh 660–1,760 lb (300–800 kg); females about 330–660 lb (150–300 kg) **Habitat** › Arctic tundra and sea ice. Spends a lot of its time hunting on sea ice. **Distribution** › Arctic Circle; Canada and northern Alaska; Greenland; northern Scandinavia, Russia, and Siberia. **Diet** › Seals, narwhals, walruses, and seabirds. They may go without food for months, living off their body fat. **Breeding** › They mate from March to May. Cubs are born from November to January. **Life span** › Up to 30 years. **Predators** › None. **Conservation status** › Vulnerable. Melting of ice due to climate change is reducing their habitat.

Seals and walrus

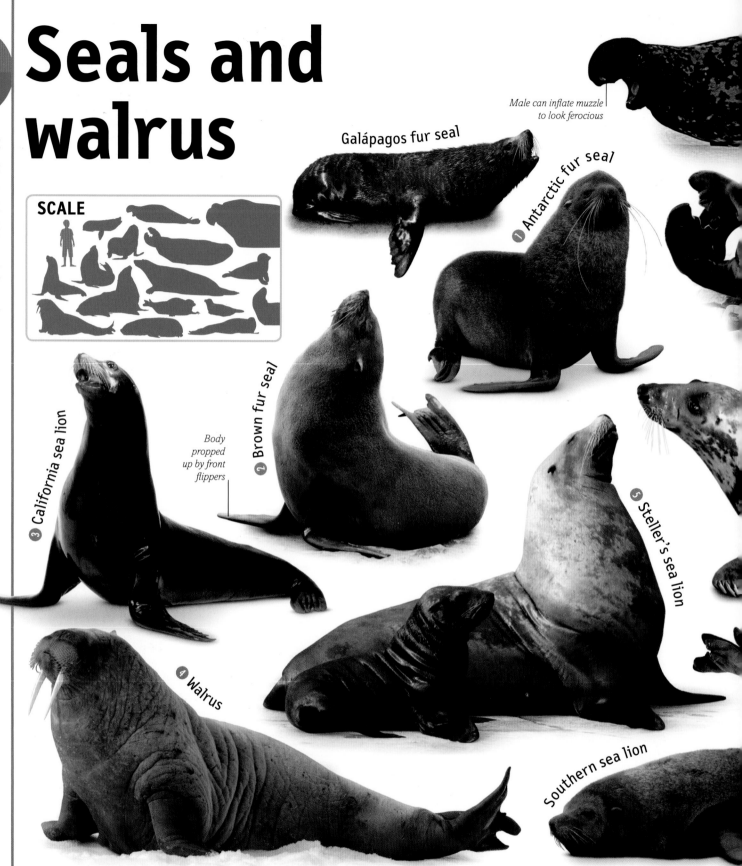

SCALE

Male can inflate muzzle to look ferocious

Galápagos fur seal

① Antarctic fur seal

③ California sea lion

Body propped up by front flippers

② Brown fur seal

⑤ Steller's sea lion

④ Walrus

Southern sea lion

Seals are awkward on land but fast and graceful in the water. All of them have streamlined bodies and flippers instead of legs. The smallest seals are just over 3 ft (1 m) long, but the biggest measure more than 13 ft (4 m) around their blubbery waists and weigh more than 3 tons. The **Antarctic fur seal ①** breeds on islands in the Southern Ocean, while the **brown fur seal ②** lives along the coasts of Australia and South Africa. The **California sea lion ③** is an expert at catching fish, and is a star performer at wildlife parks and zoos. At full speed it can swim at 25 mph (40 kph). **Walruses ④** have huge wrinkly bodies, bristly mustaches, and white tusks up to 3 ft (1 m) long. They live in the Arctic and feed on clams and other seabed animals, sucking them out of their shells. **Steller's sea lion ⑤** from the North

Hooded seal

Trunklike nose in males

6 Southern elephant seal

Thick layer of blubber keeps body warm

7 Weddell seal

Front flippers used for steering

Common seal

8 Gray seal

Streamlined body for speedy swimming

9 Leopard seal

Harp seal

Large eyes for good vision in deep water

Baikal seal

Flippers have short claws

Bearded seal

Pacific is the biggest of its kind. Like all sea lions and fur seals it can walk on its flippers, while other seals crawl on their stomachs when they come ashore. The **southern elephant seal 6** is the largest seal and a record-breaking diver. It can plunge more than 1¼ miles (2 km) deep to catch fish and squid, holding its breath for an hour and a half. **Weddell seals 7** live around Antarctica. These expert divers specialize in long, deep dives under Antarctic ice shelves. In the winter season, they gnaw holes in the sea ice so that they can come to the surface to breathe. **Gray seals 8** are fish-eaters from the North Atlantic, but the Antarctic **leopard seal 9** is a ferocious killer of warm-blooded animals, including penguins and other seals. Unusually for a true seal, it uses its front flippers to swim and steer.

257

Cats

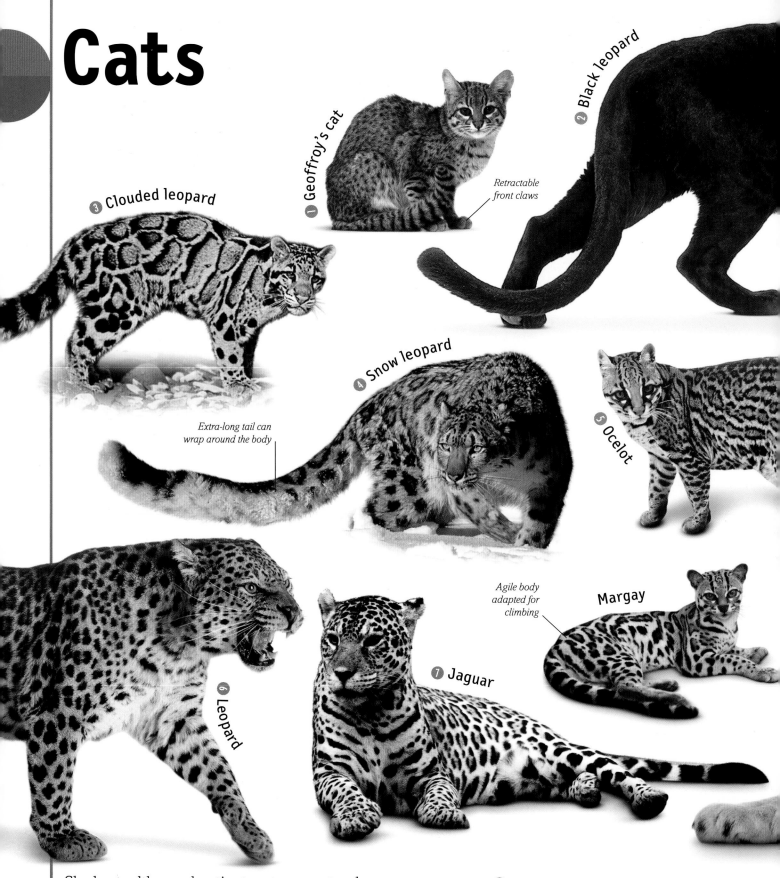

③ Clouded leopard

① Geoffroy's cat

② Black leopard

Retractable front claws

④ Snow leopard

Extra-long tail can wrap around the body

⑤ Ocelot

Agile body adapted for climbing

Margay

⑦ Jaguar

⑥ Leopard

Sleek, stealthy, and patient, cats are natural killers. Except for lions, most of them hunt on their own, using their claws and teeth to catch their prey. They include the fastest animals on four legs as well as some of the world's laziest predators, which snooze up to 20 hours each day. **Geoffroy's cat ①** from South America is a typical small cat. It hunts at night, catching mammals, birds, and fishes. The

black leopard ② is a variety of the regular leopard, with unusually dark fur. The **clouded leopard ③** gets its name from its cloud-shaped markings. It comes from the forests of South and Southeast Asia, and often hunts in treetops. The **snow leopard ④** lives in the mountains of Central Asia, where its thick coat and wrap-around tail protect it from the cold. **Ocelots ⑤** are forest cats from Central and

Dark fur with black spots

Fishing cat

⑩ Tiger

⑧ Lion

⑨ Rusty-spotted cat

Vertical stripes for camouflage

Males have thick mane

Long legs and large feet to knock down big prey

South America. Night hunters, they prey on rodents but can climb trees to stalk monkeys and birds. **Leopards ⑥** live in Africa and Asia. To safeguard their food from scavengers, they sometimes haul prey high into trees. The **jaguar ⑦** is the biggest cat in the Americas. It is a good swimmer and often feeds on turtles, crushing their shells with its powerful bite. The **lion ⑧** is the only wild cat that lives in groups, known as prides. Although males are bigger than females, or lionesses, the females do most of the hunting and take sole charge of raising the young. The **rusty-spotted cat ⑨** from India and Sri Lanka is the smallest wild cat, while **tigers ⑩** are the biggest and the most dangerous. Tigers range from Asia's tropical rain forests to eastern Siberia, but fewer than 5,000 are left in the wild.

Sphynx cat

Thin, very short fur

11 Cheetah

12 Persian cat

13 Siamese cat

Sand cat

Jungle cat

Tail balances legs when sprinting

Tabby cat

Long ear tufts

14 Cornish Rex

15 Manx cat

Pallas's cat

16 Caracal

SCALE

Most cats hunt after dark, creeping up on their prey and pouncing. The **cheetah** **11** is different because it hunts by day, relying on speed to make a kill. This lean African cat is the world's fastest sprinter. It speeds after antelope at up to 60 mph (100 kph), tripping up its victims with a swipe of its front paws. Domestic or pet cats are found all over the world, and have lived alongside people for about 10,000 years. There are many different breeds, including the fluffy **Persian cat** **12**, with its long hair and short muzzle, and the elegant **Siamese** **13**. The **Cornish Rex** **14** has ultrasoft fur, while the **Manx cat** **15** does not have a tail. Most pet cats are good hunters and they sometimes go back to living in the wild. Both domestic and wild cats are renowned for their agility. The **caracal** **16** is a long-legged

17 European wild cat

Black-footed cat

Eurasian lynx

Short, bobbed tail

Iberian lynx

18 Canadian lynx

Large paws for running over snow

Asian golden cat

Indian desert cat

19 Bobcat

Marbled cat

20 Puma

Powerful jaw for attacking large prey

Serval

Tail used for balance while climbing

wild cat from Africa and western Asia. A stunning acrobat, it leaps up to 10 ft (3.1 m) off the ground to knock birds out of the air. The **European wild cat** **17** feeds mainly on rodents, but it also attacks ground-nesting birds, swallowing everything including their feathers and bones. Lynxes and bobcats have stubby tails and tufted ears. The **Canadian lynx** **18** is found mostly across Alaska, Canada, and in a few areas of the

northern US. Its main prey is the snowshoe hare, while the North American **bobcat** **19** stalks and pounces on all kinds of animals, from insects to young deer. The **puma** **20**, also known as the cougar or mountain lion, is one of the most widespread cats in the world, found all the way from western Canada to the tip of South America. It is normally shy but it sometimes attacks humans and can kill.

LIONS
Perhaps the most famous of all wild animals, lions are instantly recognizable by their size, brownish-orange coat, and the male's bushy mane. They are renowned for their strength and ferocity. These African lion cubs are practicing hunting skills, play-fighting with each other and their mother. These games may look like fun, but they teach the cubs how to stalk, ambush, and kill prey. These will be essential skills when they reach adulthood.

Size ❯ Males up to 8 ft (2.5 m) long; females up to 5½ ft (1.7 m) long. **Weight ❯** Males weigh 420 lb (190 kg), females 280 lb (126 kg) **Habitat ❯** Hot, dry grassland, scrubland, and occasionally forests. Lions live in groups called prides. Males defend the pride's territory, which can be up to 100 sq miles (260 km²). **Distribution ❯** Asian lions live in the Gir Forest in western India. African lions are found in sub-Saharan Africa. **Diet ❯** Antelope, zebra, and wildebeest, hunted by the females. **Predators ❯** None, but may be killed by rival males, hyenas, and humans. **Breeding ❯** Lions breed all year round. Females give birth to up to six cubs per litter. **Conservation status ❯** Lions are in danger due to hunting and habitat loss.

Otters, raccoons, and weasels

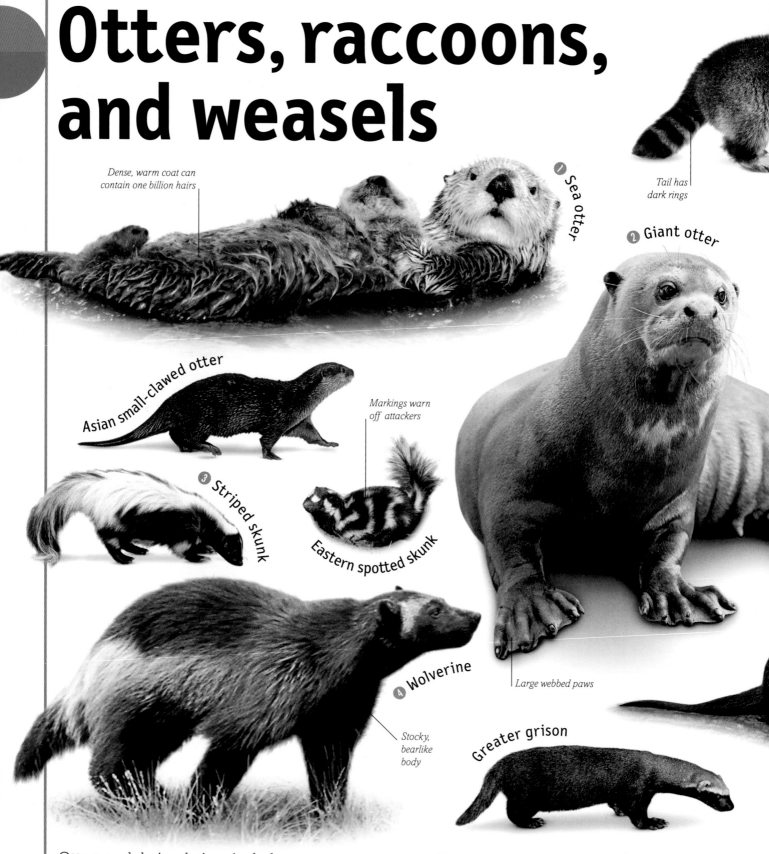

Dense, warm coat can contain one billion hairs

1 Sea otter

Tail has dark rings

2 Giant otter

Asian small-clawed otter

Markings warn off attackers

3 Striped skunk

Eastern spotted skunk

Large webbed paws

4 Wolverine

Stocky, bearlike body

Greater grison

Otters and their relatives include many expert hunters as well as the smelliest mammals on Earth. They have slender bodies and short legs, with small ears and thick fur. Most of these animals catch their food on land or in freshwater. The **sea otter** **1** is the only one that lives offshore. It feeds on shellfish, breaking them open with a stone using its stomach as a work surface. The rare **giant** otter **2** from South America's rivers is longer but lighter and has a paddle-shaped tail. North American **striped skunks** **3** have an overpowering method of self-defense. If anything or anyone comes too close, they squirt a foul-smelling liquid from glands beneath their tails. The liquid smells like a mixture of burning rubber and rotting eggs and takes days to fade away. **Wolverines** **4** live in northern parts of Canada, the

SCALE

⑤ Raccoon

⑥ Least weasel

Skunklike stripes extend from head to tail

African zorilla

South American coati

① Kinkajou

Large eyes for good night vision

European polecat

Black-footed ferret

⑧ Honey badger

Paddlelike tail for swimming

North American river otter

American mink

⑨ Eurasian badger

Beech marten

Stoat

US, Europe, and Asia. Up to 3½ ft (1.05 m) long, they are the world's strongest mammals for their size, capable of killing a caribou or a moose. In North America the **raccoon** ⑤ is a common nocturnal visitor to gardens and backyards. Intelligent and curious, it often raids trash cans for leftover food, and catches fish and frogs in ponds. The **least weasel** ⑥ is the smallest meat-eating mammal. As thin as a finger, it hunts mice in their burrows underground. **Kinkajous** ⑦ from South America feed mainly on fruit, while the **honey badger** ⑧ from Africa breaks into bees' nests. It has very thick fur, which protects it from angry bees' stings. The **Eurasian badger** ⑨ eats plants and animals, and lives in burrow systems called setts. Some setts contain more than 1,000 ft (300 m) of tunnels, and can be 100 years old.

Mongooses, civets, and genets

SCALE

Banded mongoose

Yellow mongoose

Bushy white-tipped tail

Meerkat

Tail with brushlike tip

❸ Egyptian mongoose

Ruddy mongoose

Cape genet

Common dwarf mongoose

White-tailed mongoose

❹ Indian gray mongoose

Mongooses are famous for fighting snakes, although they eat lots of other animals, including insects, lizards, birds, frogs, and even scorpions. Alert and watchful, their quick movements protect them from getting bitten or stung by their prey. They often live in groups and are generally active during the day. The African **banded mongoose** ❶ makes its home in old termite mounds, while **meerkats** ❷ use their long front claws to burrow underground. The **Egyptian mongoose** ❸ hunts in thick undergrowth and sometimes catches fishes and crabs at the edge of streams and ponds. The **Indian gray mongoose** ❹ often lives near towns and villages where it helps out by killing rats, snakes, and scorpions for food. Civets and genets are different from mongooses in that they usually feed at

⑤ Asian palm civet

⑥ Binturong

Sharp claws for climbing

Oriental civet

Small Indian civet

⑦ Masked palm civet

African palm civet

African civet

⑧ Small-spotted genet

Large eyes to see in the dark

⑨ Banded linsang

night and live on their own. The **Asian palm civet** ⑤ eats fruit and flowers as well as small animals, and stays mainly in trees. The **binturong** ⑥ from Southeast Asia has shaggy black fur, tufted ears, and a prehensile tail. **Masked palm civets** ⑦ live in forests in Southeast Asia and China. Like other civets, they can squirt attackers with a powerful-smelling fluid, produced by glands at the base of their tails.

The **small-spotted genet** ⑧ looks like an extra-long cat with a slender tail. Found in southern Europe and Africa, it is an expert climber and often catches birds roosting in trees. In some areas it raids farms and is considered a pest. The **banded linsang** ⑨ from Southeast Asia has a beautifully striped and spotted coat. It nests in trees and spends most of its life off the ground.

MEERKATS
These mischeivous, sociable animals are related to mongooses. Meerkats live in groups called mobs. They dig burrows to protect them from the hot African sun and from predators. Mobs feed and hunt together, with some meerkats acting as lookouts, standing on their hind legs to watch for danger. If a predator approaches, the lookout gives a warning cry and the whole mob dives for cover.

Size › Up to 24 in (60 cm) long. Males are slightly larger than females. **Weight ›** Up to 2 lb (1 kg) **Habitat ›** Open plains, dry, hot grasslands, and savanna. **Distribution ›** Southern and southwestern Africa **Diet ›** Insects, birds and birds' eggs, lizards, rodents, and fruit. **Life span ›** 5–15 years in the wild. **Breeding ›** Meerkats breed all year round, but more so in the warmer months between August and March. Usually only the dominant female breeds. She may have up to four litters a year, with two to four young per litter. Males and siblings help raise the young, teaching them hunting and survival skills. **Predators ›** Hawks, eagles, and jackals. **Conservation status ›** Not currently in danger.

Rhinos and tapirs

African black rhinoceros ❶

② Javan rhinoceros

Long front horn

❸ Sumatran rhinoceros

❹ Indian rhinoceros

❺ Mountain tapir

Three-toed feet

After elephants, rhinos are the world's largest land animals, with barrel-shaped bodies and thick, folded skin. They have few natural enemies, but most rhinos are threatened by illegal hunting for their horns. **African black rhinos** ❶ weigh up to 1½ tons. They have a reputation for grumpiness, but, in fact, they just startle easily because they have poor eyesight. They eat twigs and leaves, which they grasp with their flexible upper lips. The **Javan rhino** ② and **Sumatran rhino** ❸ are found in the forests of Indonesia. Javan rhinos have a single horn and are some of the rarest mammals in the world, with fewer than 50 left in the wild. Sumatran rhinos are also critically endangered. They have two horns and are born with a wiry coat of brown fur. Smallest of all rhinos, they can still grow to a height of 5 ft (1.5 m).

Baird's tapir 6

SCALE

Malayan tapir 8

South American tapir 7

Long, flexible snout to grasp leaves overhead

Thick, gray protective skin

White rhinoceros 9

Square mouth for grazing

The **Indian rhino** 4 is the biggest Asian species, with a single horn and armor-plated skin. It lives in tall grasslands and almost became extinct in the early 1900s, when fewer than 200 were left. About 3,000 live in India today, protected by armed guards. Tapirs are distant relatives of rhinos, with long noses like miniature trunks. They eat fruit and leaves and find their food mainly by smell. The **mountain tapir** 5,

Baird's tapir 6, and **South American tapir** 7 come from Central and South America. The largest of all, the **Malayan tapir** 8 is the only Asian species, and the only one that is black and white when fully grown. The African **white rhino** 9 is the giant of its family. It has two horns and can weigh around 3 tons. Despite its colossal size, it is astonishingly quick and agile, galloping at nearly 30 mph (50 kph).

Horses and relatives

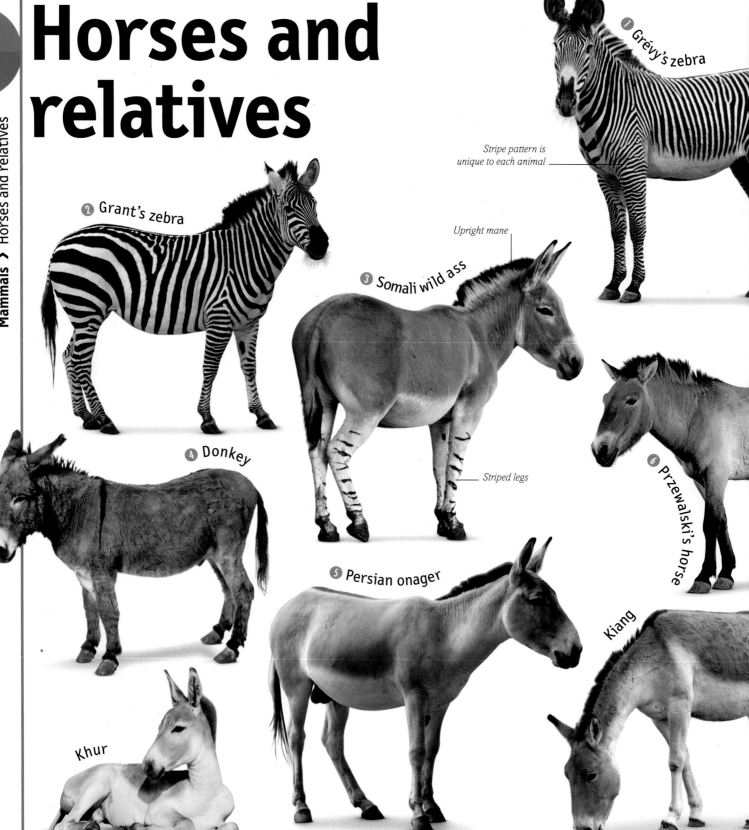

Grévy's zebra ❶

Stripe pattern is unique to each animal

❷ **Grant's zebra**

❸ **Somali wild ass**

Upright mane

❹ **Donkey**

Striped legs

❻ **Przewalski's horse**

❺ **Persian onager**

Kiang

Khur

The horse family contains some of the fastest and best-known mammals in the world. They live in herds and have very good eyesight and hearing. At the first sign of danger they quickly gallop away. Zebras are wild animals and so are most asses, but donkeys and horses were tamed thousands of years ago. **Grévy's zebra** ❶ is the biggest wild member of the horse family, with narrow stripes and a white underside. It lives in East Africa and is in danger of dying out, with fewer than 5,000 alive in the wild. **Grant's zebra** ❷ also comes from East Africa. It is the smallest zebra, growing up to 4½ ft (1.4 m), and it has thick stripes and a black upright mane. The **Somali wild ass** ❸ lives in the rocky deserts of northeast Africa. It is the ancestor of the **donkey** ❹, a sure-footed animal used by humans to carry

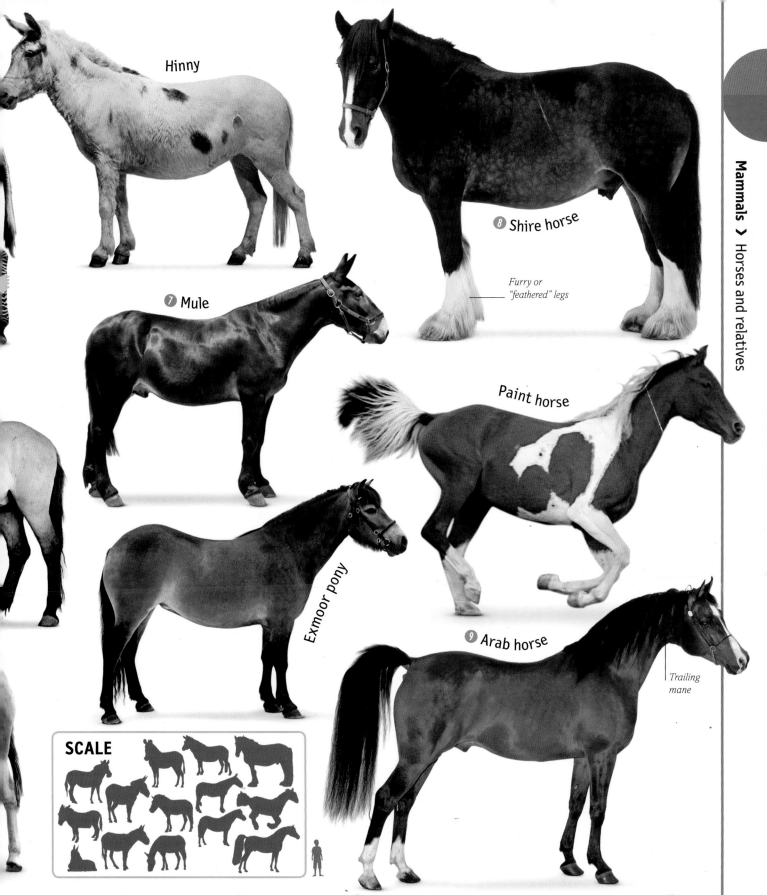

Hinny

8 Shire horse

Furry or "feathered" legs

7 Mule

Paint horse

Exmoor pony

9 Arab horse

Trailing mane

SCALE

burdens in many parts of the world. The **Persian onager** **5** is a wild ass from Asia and is now found only in Iran. **Przewalski's horse** **6** from Mongolia is the last true wild horse in the world. It almost died out in the 20th century, but is slowly recovering thanks to the work of conservationists. The **mule** **7** is a hybrid, or mixture, between a male donkey and a female horse. However, there are also more than 1,000 pure horse and pony breeds. The **Shire horse** **8**, bred in Britain, is one of the biggest and the best at pulling loads. The heaviest Shire horse on record, born in 1848, weighed more than 1½ tons. Today, Shire horses are quite rare, but some are still used in forestry. **Arab horses** **9** are the fastest breed and are used in horse racing. The most valuable can command a price of more than $10 million.

PLAINS ZEBRAS
They may look like peaceful creatures, but zebras can be vicious when it comes to defending themselves or their territory. Males sometimes fight for a chance to breed with females, kicking and biting at each other. Even predators such as lions and cheetahs have to be careful around zebra herds, since they can be injured or even killed in battles with large males.

Size ❯ Up to 4½ ft (1.4 m) tall **Weight ❯** Males weigh around 800 lb (360 kg); females around 700 lb (320 kg) **Habitat ❯** Grasslands and open savannas. They usually keep close to water holes. In the dry season, they move in huge herds to find food and water. **Distribution ❯** Southern Africa **Diet ❯** Grass, occasionally shrubs. **Breeding ❯** Plains zebras breed all year round. Foals are often born in the rainy season and can walk within an hour of being born. **Life span ❯** 15–20 years in the wild. **Predators ❯** Lions, cheetahs, leopards, and hyenas. Zebras may team up with each other or even with other species such as wildebeest for protection against predators.

Cows, antelope, and sheep

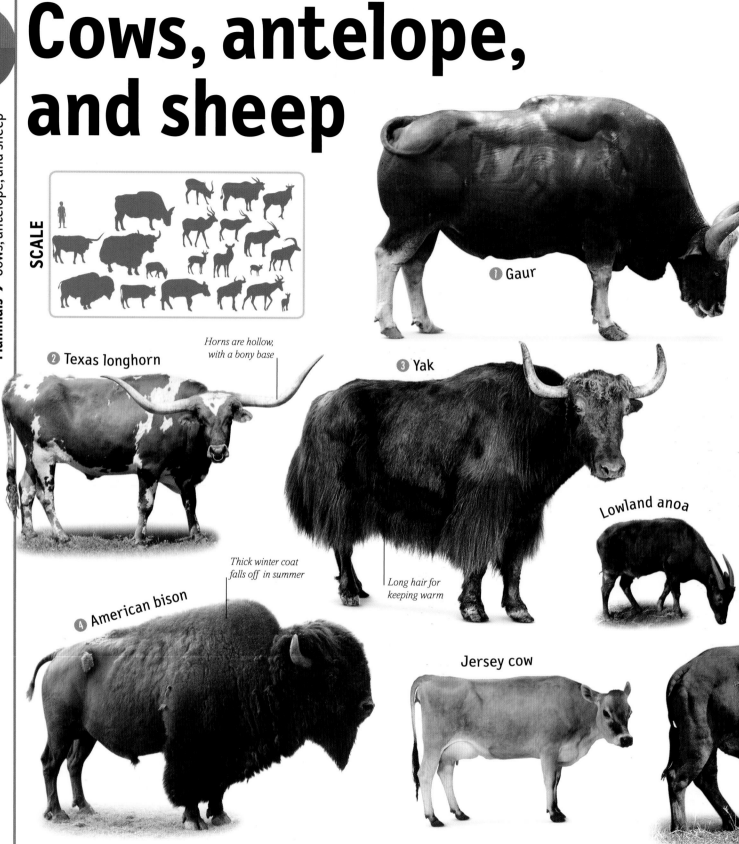

SCALE

❶ Gaur

❷ Texas longhorn

Horns are hollow, with a bony base

❸ Yak

Lowland anoa

Long hair for keeping warm

Thick winter coat falls off in summer

❹ American bison

Jersey cow

Cattle and their relatives all have hooves and special stomachs for digesting leaves and grass. Some of them live on their own, but most keep together in herds. The **gaur** ❶ is the largest kind of wild cattle, weighing up to 20 times as much as an adult man. It comes from the forests of tropical Asia and has few natural enemies, aside from tigers and crocodiles. Domesticated cattle such as the **Texas**

longhorn ❷ can be almost as big. This breed has some of the world's biggest horns, measuring an incredible 10 ft (3 m) from tip to tip. The **yak** ❸ comes from the mountain pastures of Central Asia, while the **American bison** ❹, or buffalo, is a grassland animal from the Great Plains in Canada and the US. At one time there were more than 50 million of these massive grazers, but after years of hunting only about 500,000

Sitatunga

Feet have two main hooves

⑤ Common eland

Nilgai

Greater kudu

Addax

⑥ Gemsbok

Horns have knobby rings

Sable antelope

Bohor reedbuck

⑦ Common waterbuck

Stripes provide camouflage

Zebra duiker

⑧ African buffalo

⑨ Wildebeest

Hartebeest

⑩ Klipspringer

are left. Antelope live in Africa and Asia. The African **common eland** ⑤ is one of the biggest kinds. It is a gentle animal and is sometimes farmed. **Gemsboks** ⑥ live in the deserts of southern Africa. Like most antelope, both males and females have horns. The **common waterbuck** ⑦ lives in grassland and woods but runs into lakes and swamps when threatened. The **African buffalo** ⑧ is one of the biggest and most

dangerous grassland animals. Adult males can even kill lions and demolish cars. **Wildebeest** ⑨ are some of the most common African antelope, migrating in huge herds that follow the yearly rains. Each migration involves up to 1.5 million wildebeest and thousands of other animals, including zebras. The **klipspringer** ⑩ lives on rocky outcrops in eastern and southern Africa. Its rubbery hooves give it a good grip.

277

SCALE

⑪ Thomson's gazelle

⑫ Springbok

Ridge of hair along back

Steenbok

Impala

Goitered gazelle

⑬ Günther's dik dik

Grant's gazelle

Extra-long neck

⑮ Blackbuck

Alpine chamois

⑭ Gerenuk

There are more antelope in Africa than anywhere else in the world. **Thomson's gazelle** ⑪ lives in East Africa's grasslands, where it often mixes with herds of zebras and wildebeest. It keeps a constant lookout for predators, sleeping in five-minute bursts for just an hour every day. The **springbok** ⑫ from southern Africa can leap more than six times its own length. Males lock horns during the breeding season, when they fight for the right to mate. **Günther's dik dik** ⑬ is a miniature antelope that lives in shrubby places, while the **gerenuk** ⑭ stands on its back legs to feed in shrubs and trees, helped by its long, slender neck. The **blackbuck** ⑮ lives in India and Nepal. Females are mainly brown, but males are black and white with spiraled, twisted horns. The **musk ox** ⑯ is named after the strong

⑰ Mountain goat

Markhor

⑯ Musk ox

Sharp hooves have soft inner pads for better grip

Thick, curved horns longer in males

Angora goat

Takin

Wool is used to make mohair, a costly fabric

⑱ Alpine ibex

Cotswold sheep

Curved horns

⑲ Mouflon

Barbary sheep

⑳ Bighorn sheep

smell emitted by males during the breeding season. It looks like a buffalo, but is actually a relative of wild goats and sheep. It lives in the high Arctic and has a thick, shaggy coat to protect it from the intense winter cold. The North American **mountain goat** ⑰ is a fearless and agile climber. It can leap along narrow ledges just a few hours after being born. The **Alpine ibex** ⑱ is just as sure-footed. It lives high

above the treeline in the European Alps and is famous for its horns, which can be up to 3 ft (1 m) long. The **mouflon** ⑲ from Europe and Asia is the wild ancestor of sheep that live on farms. Male **bighorn sheep** ⑳ from North America use their horns to fight with their rivals. They crash head-on with enormous force and their fights can last several hours, until one of the contestants walks away.

HIPPOPOTAMUSES
Hippopotamus means "river horse," and these animals love water. They spend the day submerged to stay cool and keep their skin moist, coming ashore to graze at night. Hippos can close their nostrils to hold their breath and sometimes even fall asleep underwater, coming up to breathe without waking up. With their long tusks, hippos can be dangerous, especially if their young are threatened.

Size ❯ Up to 5½ ft (1.7 m) tall **Weight ❯** Males up to 4½ tons; females up to 1½ tons **Habitat ❯** Shallow lakes, rivers, swamps, and grassland around these areas. **Distribution ❯** Sub-Saharan, Eastern, and Central Africa. **Diet ❯** Grass, reeds, and small shoots of plants. **Breeding ❯** Hippos breed about once every two years and have just one calf each time. The calves suckle for nearly a year and can do so even underwater. **Life span ❯** About 50 years. **Predators ❯** Adults have no predators except for humans. Young hippos may be eaten by crocodiles, lions, and hyenas. **Conservation status ❯** Numbers have fallen sharply in recent years due to habitat loss and because they are hunted for their teeth.

Pigs, peccaries, and deer

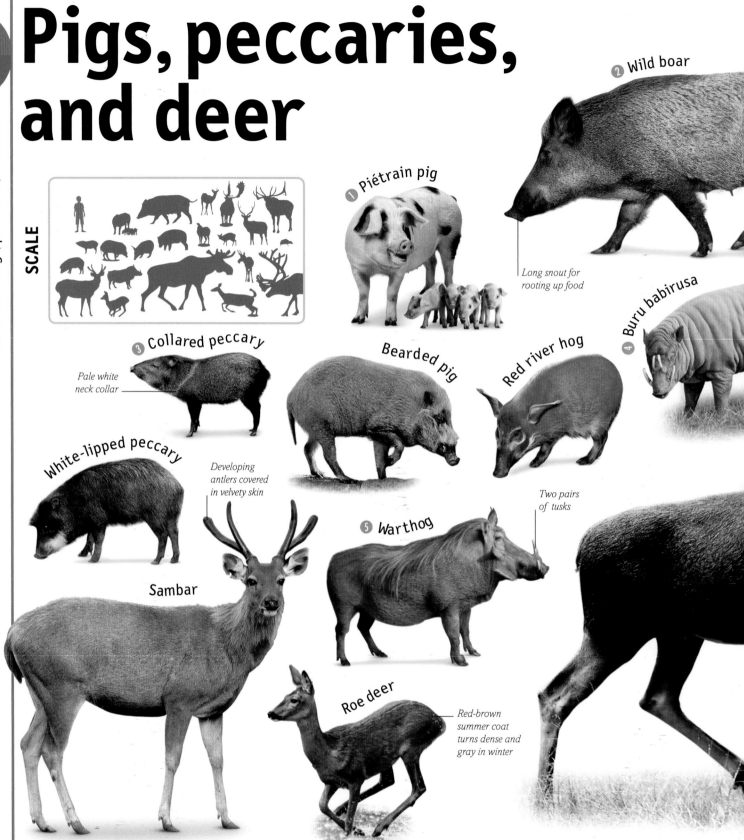

SCALE

① Piétrain pig

② Wild boar

Long snout for rooting up food

④ Buru babirusa

③ Collared peccary

Pale white neck collar

Bearded pig

Red river hog

White-lipped peccary

Developing antlers covered in velvety skin

Two pairs of tusks

⑤ Warthog

Sambar

Roe deer

Red-brown summer coat turns dense and gray in winter

Pigs come in many shapes and colors.
Domestic varieties are raised for their meat in farms across the world. The spotted **Piétrain** ① pig, originally from Belgium, is one popular variety. Domestic pigs have descended from the **wild boar** ②. With its bristly fur and bulldozerlike snout, this formidable creature digs up roots, burrowing animals, and also crops in fields. It originally comes from Europe,

North Africa, and Asia, but has been released in many other places, where it is sometimes a serious pest. The **collared peccary** ③ is found from Southern US to South America and is similar to a wild boar. The **Buru babirusa** ④ from Indonesia has some of the strangest tusks of any pig. It has two growing out of its mouth and two more growing upward through its snout. The **warthog** ⑤ lives in Africa's grasslands.

Pampas deer

Fallow deer ⑥

Antlers fall off when winter ends

⑦ Wapiti

Musk deer

Southern pudu

Axis deer

⑧ Java mouse deer

⑨ Moose

Sika deer

Both males and females grow antlers

White-tailed deer

⑩ Caribou

Like other wild pigs, it can be dangerous if cornered, particularly if it has piglets to protect. Pigs eat almost anything, but deer are vegetarians, feeding on leaves, lichens, and bark. Most male deer have antlers, which they shed and regrow each year. The **fallow deer's** ⑥ antlers are flat like the palm of a hand, but the **wapiti** ⑦ has branching antlers that end in sharp points. Every fall, male wapiti, or stags, clash head-on in a trial of strength that decides who gets a chance to breed. The tiny **Java mouse deer** ⑧ is the world's smallest hoofed mammal, no bigger than a rabbit, while the **moose** ⑨ is by far the largest deer, with a record weight of more than 1,750 lb (800 kg). Moose live on their own, but **caribou** ⑩ are much more sociable. In the Canadian Arctic, half a million of them can travel in a single herd.

Camels, llamas, and giraffes

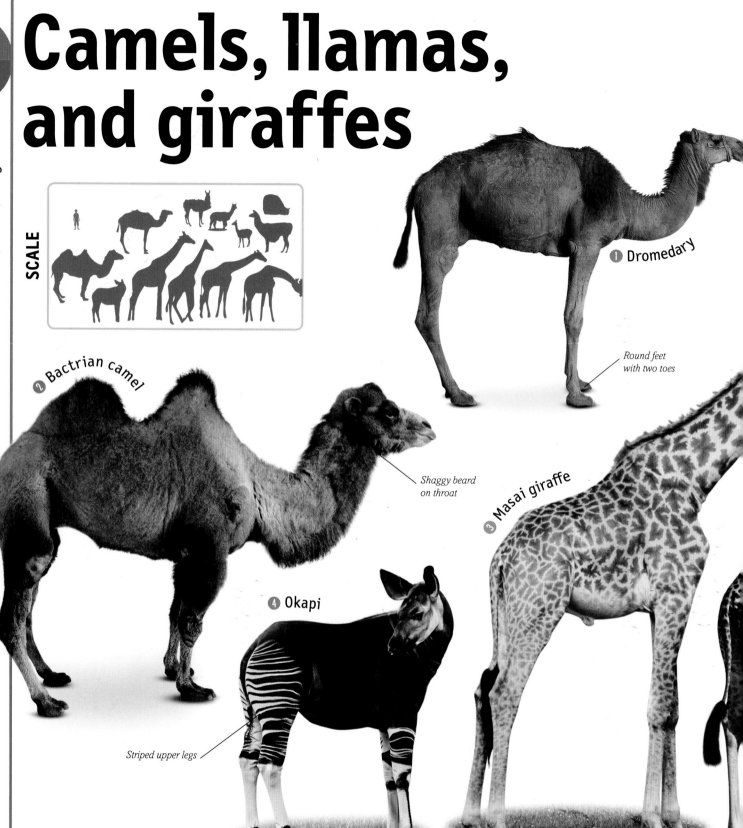

SCALE

① Dromedary

Round feet
with two toes

② Bactrian camel

Shaggy beard
on throat

③ Masai giraffe

④ Okapi

Striped upper legs

For thousands of years, the one-humped camel, or **dromedary** ①, has been used as a working animal in North Africa and the Middle East. Nicknamed the "ship of the desert," it can go for two weeks without drinking, and when it does find water it can swallow enough to fill four kitchen sinks. Its hump stores an emergency reserve of fat, and it has cushioned feet that stop it from sinking in the desert sand. The **Bactrian camel** ② from Central Asia is even tougher because it has to cope with extreme winter cold. It has two humps instead of one and a thick winter coat that falls off when spring arrives. Giraffes are the world's tallest animals. They live in Africa's tree-studded grasslands, feeding on leaves and twigs that other mammals cannot reach. The **Masai giraffe** ③ is the largest, with a record height of

⑤ Guanaco

⑥ Alpaca

⑦ Suri alpaca

Long, woolly coat

⑨ Llama

⑧ Vicuña

Bony horns covered in skin

Thornicroft's giraffe

Reticulated giraffe

Large ears for keeping cool

⑩ Rothschild's giraffe

20 ft (6 m). The **okapi** ④ from Central Africa is a forest-dwelling relative of giraffes, while the **guanaco** ⑤ belongs to the camel family. It lives high in the Andes like the South American **alpaca** ⑥. Alpacas are raised for their silky fleece. Some breeds have short coats but **suri alpacas** ⑦ can have a fleece so long that it trails along the ground. All alpacas are descendants of the **vicuña** ⑧. This wild grazer, also from

the Andes, can survive at 16,500 ft (5,000 m), a height that would leave many people gasping for breath. The **llama** ⑨, a tame relative of the guanaco, is used for carrying burdens on narrow mountain paths. Back in Africa, **Rothschild's giraffe** ⑩ is easily recognizable, with its big spots and long white "socks" on its lower legs. Loss of habitat has threatened its existence, and there are fewer than 670 left in the wild.

GIRAFFES

With their amazingly long necks reaching into the treetops, giraffes are the tallest living animals. They have only seven bones in their necks, the same number as humans. Their long, slender legs allow them to gallop as fast as a horse, but become a problem when they have to bend down to drink. Giraffes also have long, bluish-purple tongues and hornlike growths on their heads. Each giraffe can be recognized by its unique pattern of blotches.

Size › Males up to 20 ft (6 m); females up to 15½ ft (4.7 m) tall **Weight ›** Males weigh up to 1.6 tons; females up to 1.1 tons **Habitat ›** Grassland, savanna, and open woodland. **Distribution ›** Sub-Saharan Africa **Diet ›** Giraffes mainly feed on acacia trees. They have tough mouths and tongues to cope with the thorns. **Breeding ›** Giraffes breed in the rainy season, and calves are born in the dry season. Females give birth standing up, and a calf can walk within an hour of being born. **Life span ›** About 25 years in the wild. **Predators ›** Lions, but young giraffes may also be killed by leopards, hyenas, wild dogs, and crocodiles. **Conservation status ›** Numbers of some giraffe species are reducing due to habitat loss.

Dolphins and porpoises

① Striped dolphin

Pygmy killer whale

Atlantic white-sided dolphin

② Risso's dolphin

Distinctive blunt, rounded head

Mostly gray body becomes lighter with age

Southern right whale dolphin

Burmeister's porpoise

③ Vaquita

④ Dall's porpoise

Steeply sloping head

Franciscana

⑤ Amazon River dolphin

⑥ Indus River dolphin

Finless porpoise

Dolphins and porpoises are related to whales, but they are smaller and faster, with sharply pointed teeth. Some live alone, but most travel in groups called pods or schools. Intelligent and playful, they communicate with clicks and whistles. Like some whales, dolphins use sound waves to find their food. The **striped dolphin** ① lives worldwide, mainly where the sea is warm. It feeds on fishes and squid,

and often surfs the bow waves in front of fast-moving boats. **Risso's dolphin** ② has a flattened head instead of a beak. As it gets older, its body often becomes scarred from fighting with other dolphins and grappling with squid. Porpoises are usually shorter than dolphins, with barrel-shaped bodies and blunt jaws. The tiny **vaquita** ③ is one of the rarest and smallest species, measuring just 4 ft (1.2 m) long, while

⑦ Bottlenose dolphin

Peale's dolphin

Commerson's dolphin **⑧**

Hector's dolphin

⑨ Killer whale

Atlantic spotted dolphin

Powerful body suited for hunting

Hourglass dolphin

Short-beaked common dolphin

SCALE

Dall's porpoise ④ is the fastest, with a top speed of about 34 mph (55 kph). The **Amazon River dolphin** ⑤ has small eyes and the **Indus River dolphin** ⑥ is almost blind. Both of these dolphins live in freshwater and rely on sound waves to hunt. The **bottlenose dolphin** ⑦ is smart and agile, making it a popular performer at aquariums. It frequently interacts with humans in the wild, too. **Commerson's dolphin** ⑧, on the other hand, is a much rarer species from icy southern seas. The **killer whale** ⑨, or orca, is by far the biggest member of the dolphin family, weighing up to 7 tons. A cunning, quick-witted predator, it attacks other dolphins and whales, and sometimes tips over ice floes to make seals slide into the sea. It is even known to attack seals on beaches, using waves to wash itself back out to sea after grabbing its prey.

Whales

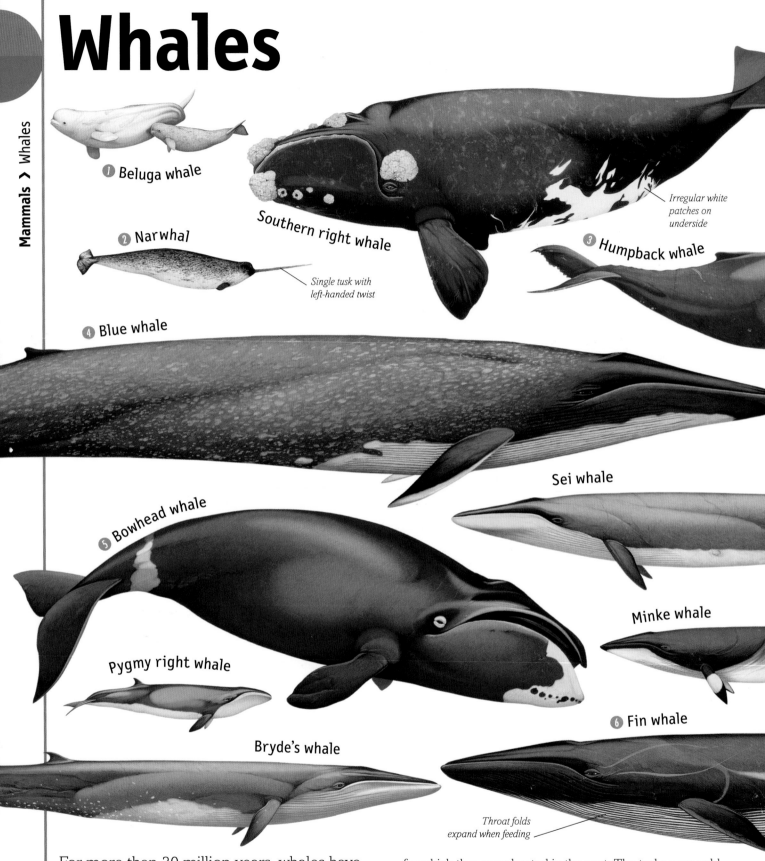

① Beluga whale

② Narwhal

Single tusk with left-handed twist

Southern right whale

Irregular white patches on underside

③ Humpback whale

④ Blue whale

Sei whale

⑤ Bowhead whale

Minke whale

Pygmy right whale

⑥ Fin whale

Bryde's whale

Throat folds expand when feeding

For more than 30 million years, whales have roamed the open seas. They include some of the biggest animals that have ever lived. They breathe air through blowholes on top of their heads and swim by beating their flukes, or horizontal tails. The **beluga ①** and **narwhal ②** are two small whales from the Arctic. Belugas have white skin that blends with Arctic ice floes. Narwhals have a long twisted tusk,

for which they were hunted in the past. The tusks were sold as "unicorn horns" and were thought to have magical powers. The **humpback whale ③** is a fish-eater and an incredible acrobat. It sometimes bursts completely out of the water, crashing back onto the surface with a massive splash. The humpback is much longer than a bus, but it is only half the size of the **blue whale ④**, the largest animal on Earth.

Wrinkled skin

⑦ Sperm whale

Scars from battling prey

Pygmy sperm whale

Strap-toothed whale

Blainville's beaked whale

⑧ Gray whale

Clumps of barnacles may grow on whale's skin

⑨ Baird's beaked whale

Gray's beaked whale

Teeth at tip of protruding lower jaw

Shepherd's beaked whale

Hubbs' beaked whale

Ginkgo-toothed whale

Northern bottlenose whale

⑩ Cuvier's beaked whale

Backward-sloping upper fin

SCALE

This mega-mammal weighs about 165 tons (150 metric tons), which is more than the heaviest dinosaur, and it grows up to 90 ft (27 m) long. It feeds on tiny animals called krill, filtering them out of the water, swallowing up to 8 billion every day. The **bowhead whale ⑤** and **fin whale ⑥** are also filter-feeders, but the **sperm whale ⑦** is the world's biggest hunter-killer, with a huge head and about 50 enormous teeth. It feeds on giant squid, diving up to 10,000 ft (3,000 m) beneath the waves to find prey. The **gray whale ⑧** makes the longest migrations of any mammal, a round trip of 12,500 miles (20,000 km) from Alaskan waters to warmer waters off Mexico. Beaked whales feed in seabed canyons, sucking up squid and fishes. **Baird's beaked whale ⑨** is the biggest of these mysterious animals, while **Cuvier's beaked whale ⑩** is the most widespread.

HUMPBACK WHALE

These whales are famous for the males' complex, haunting songs, which carry for thousands of miles through the ocean. Humpback whales are remarkably agile for their size. They can push themselves completely out of the water, twisting in the air to land on their backs with an enormous splash. This movement is known as breaching. Many whales do it, but scientists do not know why.

Size › Males up to 46 ft (14 m) long; females up to 52½ ft (16 m) long **Weight ›** Up to 44 tons (40 metric tons)
Habitat › Ocean; humpback whales breed in warm tropical and subtropical waters but migrate to cooler waters to feed.
Distribution › Oceans and coastal areas across the world.
Diet › Plankton, krill, and small fishes, which they filter out of the water. **Breeding ›** Females breed once every two to three years and nurse their calves for about 12 months. Humpback whales become adult at about five years. **Life span ›** Up to 95 years. **Predators ›** Killer whales may hunt young humpbacks. **Conservation status ›** No longer threatened since hunting by humans was banned in 1966.

INDEX

A

abdomens 81, 97

adders 150

African bush vipers 154–155

African savanna elephants 226–227

agoutis 231

albatrosses 206–207

algae 16–17, 20, 27, 61

alligators 139, 156, 157

alpacas 285

alpine swifts 177

anacondas 151

anemone cups 26

anemonefish 114

anemones 53, 114

angelfish 114

Angora rabbits 228

anhingas 196, 197

anteaters 222–223

Antelope jackrabbits 229

antelopes 277, 278

antennae 78, 79, 81, 121

antlers 283

ants 102–103, 222

antshrikes 208

apes 236–237

apollos 94

Arab horses 273

aracaris 180–181

armadillos 222

arthropods 48

ash trees 44

asses 272

atlas moths 97

auks 204

avocets 202

axolotls 137

aye-ayes 235

azure vase sponges 51

B

babies see young

babirusas 282

baboons 242–243

bacteria 14–15, 27

badgers 265

bald eagles 182–183

banana slugs 61

bandicoots 221

barbets 180, 181

barn owls 173

barnacles 78

barred owls 174–175

bateleurs 182

bats 244–247, 248–249

bat flies 100, 101

beaks 158

   birds 168, 176, 180, 181, 195, 198, 202

   whales 291

bears 252–253, 254–255

beavers 231

bedbugs 88, 89

bee-eaters 178, 179

bee flies 100, 101

bee hummingbirds 177

bees 102–103

beetles 92–93, 103

bellbirds 209

beluga whales 290

bettongs 218

big cats 258–261, 262–263

bilbies 220–221

binturongs 267

birch trees 46

birds-of-paradise (birds) 210, 211

birds-of-paradise (plants) 40

bird's nests (fungi) 24–25

birds of prey 182–185

birth 217

   mammals 222, 223, 224, 227, 228, 239, 255, 263, 269, 287

   reptiles 144, 152, 155

   sharks 108, 111

bitterns 194

black bears 252

black-browed albatrosses 206–207

black leopards 258

black rhinoceros 270

black-striped salemas 118–119

black swans 189

black widow spiders 71

black vultures 184

blackbirds 211, 213

blind animals see sight

blindsnakes 151

blood pythons 152

bloodsuckers 88, 89, 100, 245

blue whales 290–291

bluebirds 213

bluebottle flies 100

boa constrictors 150–151

boars 282

bobcats 261

bones 137, 158, 216, 244, 286

bonobos 237

boobies 197

boring sponges 50–51

Bornean orangutans 237

bottlenose dolphins 289

bowerbirds 209

bowhead whales 290, 291

box turtles 140

boxfish 112

brackens 35

brains 126

   intelligence 217, 226, 237, 288

bread crumb sponges 50

bream 114

breathing 104, 106, 115, 126

   lungs 139

   mammals 226, 231, 246, 257, 280, 290

breeding see birth, reproduction

brittle stars 64, 65
brolgas 200
brown bears 252, 253
brown noddies 204
brown rats 232–233
budgerigars 166
buffaloes 276, 277
bugs 88–89
bull sharks 109
bullfrogs 130, 131, 133
bumblebees 103
burbots 124
burrows
  badgers 265
  marsupials 220, 221
  moles 225
  rabbits 188, 228
  spiders 70
bushbabies 234–235
bustards 201
butterflies 94–97
buzzards 182–183

C

cacti 39
caimans 157
calls
  birds 173, 179, 200, 201, 209, 211, 213
  bugs 89
  frogs 130–131

primates 236, 240, 241
  whales 292
camels 284
camouflage 58, 94, 112,
  as eyes 88–89, 95, 97
  as plants 85, 88, 129, 134, 194
  against snow 173, 229, 253
  stripes 259, 277
cane toads 126–127
caps (fungi) 22
capsids 88
capuchins 241
capybaras 230–231
caracals 260–261
caracaras 184
carapaces 49
caribou 283
carnivores (meat-eaters) 43, 54, 139, 217
carpenter bees 102
carpenter moths 96
carps 122
cases 52, 80 see also shells
cassowaries 160–161
catbirds 209
caterpillars 95, 96, 98–99
catfish 113, 122
cats 258–261, 262–263
catsharks 107, 108
cedar trees 36
centipedes 68–69
chachalacas 163
chaffinches 209
chambered nautiluses 65
chameleons 138–139, 146–147
chanterelles 25
chars 124–125
cheetahs 260, 274
chestnut trees 46, 47
chickadees 210
chickens 162
chihuahuas 250
chimaeras 106
chimpanzees 237
chinchillas 232, 233
chipmunks 230

chlorophyll 31
cicadas 89
civets 266–267
clams 58, 61, 62–63
claws 77, 184, 223, 244, 253
  see also pincers, talons
click beetles 93
climbing animals 128, 152, 219, 224, 234, 259, 279
clostridia 14
clouded leopards 258
clover 38
coats 250, 264, 285
  fur 103, 216, 228, 229, 232, 253, 265
cobras 150, 151, 153
cockatiels 167
cockatoos 166, 167
cocks-of-the-rock 209
cocoa trees 44, 45
cod 116–117
cold-blooded animals 105, 127, 138
collective nouns see groups
colonies 192, 247, 248
colors 31, 154, 198
  to attract food 42, 120
  to attract mates 83, 159, 240
  as camouflage 64, 88, 107, 131, 147
  as mimicry 65
  as warnings 22, 56, 66, 86, 88, 113, 129, 130, 136
comet darners 83
communication see calls
conches 58–59
condors 184
conifers 36–37
constrictors 150–151
coots 201
coral spots (fungi) 26

coral weeds (seaweed) 21
corals (fungi) 24
corals (marine animals) 52–53
cormorants 196–197
Cornish Rexes 260
cottontails 228, 229
couas 170
coucals 171
cougars 261
courtship see mating
cowbirds 211
cows 276
coyotes 250–251
coypus 233
crab spiders 70
crabs 76–77
crakes 201
cramp balls 26–27
cranes 200–201
crickets 86–87
crocodile newts 136
crocodiles 156–157
crossbills 209
crows 211
crustaceans 18, 48, 76–79
ctenopomas 124
cuckoo doves 165
cuckoos 170–171
cup fungi 28–29
curassows 162, 163
cushion stars 64–65
cuttlefish 62, 63
cytoplasm 12

D

daddy longlegs spiders 71

daisies 41

damselflies 82–83

dandelions 41

darners 82, 83

dead man's fingers 26–27

death cap mushrooms 25

deep-sea fish 120–121

deer 282, 283

defenses 40, 49, 67, 85, 153, 264

armor 112, 140, 156, 223, 271

confusing predators 64, 88–89, 118, 134, 145

see also camouflage, poisonous animals, venomous animals

degus 233

desmans 225

diatoms 17

diet 195, 235, 257

feeding 43, 75, 96, 160, 264, 284, 286

carnivores 43, 54, 139, 217

herbivores 80, 217, 237

see also bloodsuckers, scavengers

dingoes 250, 251

dippers 208–209

disease carriers 14, 15, 56, 100–101

diving animals

birds 196, 208–209

mammals 231, 242–243, 257, 290

reptiles 145

DNA 12

dogfish 108

dogs 27, 250

dolphins 288–289

domesticated animals 146, 154, 168, 232, 250, 273, 282, 284, 285

donkeys 272–273

dormice 231

doves 164, 165

dragonflies 82–83

dromedaries 284

ducks 188–189

dunlins 203

E

E. coli 15

eagles 182–183

ears 216, 224, 226, 228, 229, 246, 251

hearing 172, 216, 229, 272

earthworms 57

echolocation (sound waves) 246, 288, 289

eels 112, 121, 123, 124

eggs 51, 105, 127, 159

amphibians 132, 135, 139

birds 163, 170, 187, 193, 211

fishes 108–109, 117, 119

insects 91, 92, 96, 100, 102, 103

invertebrates 79

plankton 19

reptiles 143, 152

egrets 194

elands 277

electric eels 124

electric shocks 124

elephants 226–227

elks (wapitis) 283

emperor penguins 190, 192–193

emus 160

endangered species see threatened species

energy from sunlight 15, 17, 30, 31, 43

ergots 26

evolution 104

exoskeleton 49

see also shells, skeletons

extinction 126, 164, 241, 271

see also threatened species

eyes 81, 101, 109, 116, 124, 147

as markings 88–89, 95, 97

see also sight

F

falcons 183

fallow deer 283

fangs 70, 72, 150, 217

see also teeth

feathers 159, 162, 174, 185, 196, 210

feeding 43, 75, 96, 160, 264, 284, 286

bloodsuckers 88, 89, 100, 245

see also scavengers

feet 133, 162, 193, 197, 208

hooves 276, 277, 279, 283

fennec foxes 251

ferns 34–35

ferrets 265

fighting 93, 114, 124, 153, 161, 201

mammals 226, 266, 274, 278, 279, 288

finches 209, 210

fin whales 291

fins 105, 107, 113, 121

fire ants 103

fire salamanders 136

fire worms 57

firs 36, 37

flagella 13

flamingos 198–199

flatworms 56

fleeces see coats

flickers 181

flies 100–101

flightless birds 160, 161, 167, 190, 196–197

flightless insects 80, 87, 89, 101

flippers 140, 257

flocks 161, 198, 211

flowering plants 31, 38–41

flowering trees 44–47

fly agarics 22–23, 25

fly catchers 208, 210

flying foxes 244, 245

flying squirrels 230

food storage 187, 197, 214, 242, 284

football fish 120

foxes 250, 251

foxgloves 41, 44

francolins 163

freshwater fish 122–125

frigatebirds 197

frogs 128–133, 134–135

fruit bats 245

fruit trees 44–45, 47

fruitbodies (fungi) 23

funnel-web spiders 72

fur 103, 216, 228, 229, 232, 253, 265

coats 250, 264, 285

fur seals 256

G

galahs 167

gallinules 201

gamebirds 162–163

gannets 197

gars 125

gazelles 278

geckos 144, 146, 147

geese 188

gender changes 115

genders, differences between

birds 163, 167, 169, 211

fishes 121

invertebrates 71

mammals 237, 243, 259, 278

genets 266–267

gerbils 232

gharials 157

ghost bats 247

giant clams 62–63

giardia lamblia 12–13

gibbons 236

gills 23, 105, 126, 136–137

giraffes 284–285, 286–287

gliding animals 133, 159, 206, 219

go-away birds 170, 171

goats 279

goldfishes 122

gophers 232

goliath beetles 93

goliath tarantulas 71

gorillas 236–237

gorses 38

goshawks 185

grasshoppers 86–87

greater flamingos 198–199

grebes 201

grivets 243

groups

colonies 192, 247, 248

flocks 161, 198, 211

herds 227, 275, 276, 277, 278, 283

hordes 243

mobs 268

packs 250, 251

prides 259

schools 118–119, 288

swarms 55, 78, 86

grouse 162, 163

growth rates 20, 27, 35, 71, 120

growth rings 61, 142

grubs *see* larvae

guanacos 285

guans 162, 163

guillemots 204

guinea pigs 232

guinea fowls 162

gulls 204–205

H

habitats 14, 122, 162, 233, 237

loss of 43, 126, 169, 187, 215, 239, 263, 281, 287

hammerkops 197

hamsters 231

hands 236

hares 228–229

harriers 185

harvestman spiders 70

hawks 182

heads 80, 101, 109, 140, 157, 185, 217

hearing 172, 216, 229, 272

hearts 132

hedgehogs 224, 225

height 33, 34, 51, 160, 190, 198

mammals 227, 239, 252, 255, 270, 281 284–285

herbivores (plant-eaters) 80, 217, 237

herds 227, 275, 276, 277, 278, 283

hermit crabs 76

herons 194, 195

herring 117

hibernation 153, 230, 246

sleep 177, 221, 223, 246, 278, 280

hinnies 273

hippopotamuses 280–281

hoatzins 171

hogs 282

holly trees 45

Honduran white bats 248–249

honey bees 102

honeybirds 180

honeyeaters 210

hoopoes 179

hooves 276, 277, 279, 283

hordes 243

hornbills 178–179

horntails 103

horns 147, 270, 271, 276, 277, 278, 279

antlers 283

horseflies 101

horses 272, 273

horseshoe bats 245

horsetails 34

house centipedes 69

house flies 100

house mice 232, 233

hoverflies 101

howler monkeys 241

humans 237, 250

hummingbirds 176, 177

humpback whales 290, 292–293

humps 284

huntsman spiders 70

huskies 250

hyacinths 41

hybrid animals 273

hydroids 52

hyphae 22

I

ibexes 279

ibises 195

iguanas 145, 146–147

impalas 278

intelligence 217, 226, 237, 288

brains 126

intestines 15, 56

isopods 79

J

jacamars 181
jacanas 203
jackals 250
jackrabbits 229
jaguars 258, 259
jays 211
jellyfish 52, 54–55
John Dories 117
jungle nymphs 80–81

K

kakapos 166, 167
kangaroos 219
keas 167
kestrels 183
killer whales 289
king vultures 186–187
kingfishers 179
kinkajous 265
kites 184, 185
kiwis 160, 161
koalas 221

koels 170
komodo dragons 148–149
kookaburras 179
krill 78–79

L

laburnum trees 46
ladybugs 92, 93
langurs 243
lanternfish 121
larch trees 36–37
larks 211, 213
larvae
  fishes 118
  insects 92, 98, 103
  invertebrates 48, 55, 63, 75
  plankton 18
lavender 38
leaves 31, 42, 249
legs
  amphibians 127
  birds 160, 202–203
  insects 81, 86, 87, 90, 93, 101

invertebrates 48, 49, 64, 66–67, 78
  mammals 237, 286
  reptiles 139, 140
legspan 71
lemon sponges 50
lemon trees 45
lemurs 234–235
length 83, 91, 109, 119, 149, 155
  birds 169, 175, 187, 215
  invertebrates 55, 63, 75
  mammals 263, 269, 293
leopards 258–259
lichens 27
life stages 96
  see also eggs, larvae
life spans 43, 85, 91, 120, 135
  birds 169, 175, 199, 205, 207, 215
  invertebrates 51, 55, 77
  mammals 227, 239, 269, 275, 281, 287, 293
  reptiles 142, 149, 155
lilac 38
lilies 30–31, 39, 41
limpets 60
linsangs 267
lionfish 104–105, 113
lions 259, 262–263
liverworts 32–33
lizards 138, 144–147

llamas 285
loaches 122
lobsters 78, 79
locusts 86
lop-eared rabbits 228
lorikeets 166
loris 235
lovebirds 167
lungs 139 *see also* breathing
lynx 261

M

macaques 242–243
macaws 166, 167, 168–169
mackerel 116
maggots 100
magpie-geese 188
magpies 211
mallards 189
malleefowl 163
mammoth wasps 103
manakins 208
mandrills 243
maple trees 44
maras 232
markings 88–89, 95, 97, 114, 143, 258 *see also* camouflage, colors
marmosets 240–241
marmots 230
marsupials 218–221
martens 265
martins 212
mating
  calls 89, 130–131, 201, 213
  competing for 93, 101, 153, 161, 274, 278, 283
  displays 113, 137, 161, 163, 169, 203, 208, 209, 211
  and eating 91
  for life 167, 207
  see also birth, reproduction
meerkats 266, 268–269
membranes 13, 15, 23, 105
merlins 183
metamorphosis 48, 126

Mexican red-kneed tarantulas 48–49

mice 231, 232, 233

midges 100

migration

  birds 170, 176, 189, 200–201, 203, 204–205, 212

  fishes 108, 111, 123

  insects 86, 95

  mammals 277, 291

mildews 26

military macaws 168–169

millipedes 68–69

mimicry 39, 63, 65, 95, 101, 166, 213

mink 265

minnows 123

mites 73

mobs 268

mockingbirds 213

mole rats 232

moles 225

mollusks 58–61, 62–63, 64–65

mongooses 266

monkey puzzles 36, 37

monkeys 240–243

moonrats 225

moorhens 200

moose 282–283

mosquitoes 100–101

mosses 32–33

moths 94, 95, 96, 97

motmots 178

mourning doves 164

mouths 75, 80, 98, 100, 110, 121, 125

  fangs 70, 72, 150, 217

  see also teeth

mudskippers 115

mules 273

mullets 114

mushrooms 23, 24–25

muskrats 231

mussels 59, 61

mute swans 189

N

naked mole rats 232

narwhals 290

Natterer's bats 246

natterjack toads 129

nautiluses 63

needlefish 113

necks 143, 151, 189, 198, 278, 286

nests

  birds 163, 170, 180, 182–183, 190, 209, 211, 212

  insects 88, 102, 103

  mammals 248

  reptiles 141

newts 136–137

nocturnal animals

  birds 172, 173

  insects 89, 94

  invertebrates 59

  mammals 240, 247, 265, 280

northern cardinals 208

noses *see* smell

nucleus 12

numbats 220

nunbirds 180

nunlets 180

nymphs 80–81, 82, 85, 91

O

oak trees 47

ocelots 258–259

octopuses 62–63

okapis 284, 285

olms 137

onagers 272, 273

opossums 218, 219

  possums 218–219, 211

orangutans 237, 238–239

orb weaver spiders 70, 72–73

orcas 289

orchids 39

organs 12, 49, 74, 81, 104

  brains 126

  ears 216, 224, 226, 228, 229, 246, 251

  eyes 81, 101, 109, 116, 124, 147

  hearts 132

  intestines 15, 56

  lungs 139 *see also* breathing

  stomachs 121, 150, 276

  senses 13, 48, 81, 104 *see also* smell, sight, hearing

orioles 210–211

ospreys 183

ostriches 160

otters 264–265

owls 172–173, 174–175

oxygen 104–105 *see also* breathing

oystercatchers 202

oysters 59

P

Pacific sea nettle 54–55

packs 250, 251

pandas 253

pangolins 223

panther chameleons 138–139

Pantopoda 74

parakeets 167

parasites 56, 75, 89, 100–101, 120

parental care

  amphibians 132, 133

  birds 161, 187, 193, 207

fishes 113, 125

  mammals 216, 227, 238, 249, 250, 259, 262, 269

  reptiles 152, 155, 156

parrotbills 213

parrots 166–167, 168–169

partridges 163

peacocks 162, 163

peccaries 282

pelicans 196, 197

penguins 190–191, 192–193

perch 125

perching birds 208–213, 214–215

pests 61, 99, 129, 232–233, 267, 282

pets 146, 154, 168, 232, 250, 273, 282, 284, 285

pheasants 162, 163

pichi armadillos 222

piculets 181

pigeons 164–165

pigs 27, 282–283

pikas 229

pill millipedes 68, 69

pincers 73, 76 *see also* claws, talons

pine trees 36, 37
pipesnakes 150
pipistrelle bats 247
piranhas 123
pittas 208, 209
plaice 117
plankton 17, 18–19
plasterer bees 103
plovers 202
poison-dart frogs 130, 132
poisonous animals
  amphibians 126, 129,
    130, 136
  fishes 113
  fungi 22, 25, 26
  insects 86
  invertebrates 52, 54, 57, 59,
    66, 68, 73
  plants 35, 36, 40, 46
  reptiles 144, 148
  microscopic life 14, 17
  see also venomous animals
polar bears 253, 254–255
polecats 265
pollen 31, 38
pollinators 39, 40, 41, 100,
  101, 102, 103
pond skaters 89
ponies 273
poppies 40
populations 14, 86, 117, 237,
  247, 276–277
porcupines 232, 233
pores 50
porpoises 288–289
Portuguese men-of-war 52

possums 218–219, 221
  opossums 218, 219
potoroos 218
pottos 235
pouches
  for carrying young 132, 193,
    218, 219, 220
  for food storage 187,
    197, 242
prairie dogs 230
prawns 78
praying mantises 90–91
prides 259
primates 234–235, 236–237,
  240–241, 242–243
proboscis monkeys 242–243
protoctists 18
psammodromus 145
ptarmigans 163
puffballs 25
puffbirds 180
puffer fish 112
puffins 204
pumas 261
pupas 96 see also larvae
pythons 152, 153

Q
quail doves 164
quails 163
quolls 221

R
rabbits 228–229
raccoons 265
ragworms 57
rails 200
ratfish 106
rats 232–233
rattlesnakes 151
rays 106–107
recycling 22
red-backed shrikes 214–215
red-eyed tree frogs 134–135
red lionfish 104–105
reef lobsters 78
reproduction 12, 14, 16, 31
  see also birth,
    eggs, mating
rheas 161
rhinos 270–271
roadrunners 171
robins 211, 212
rodents 230–233
rollers 179
roses 40
roundworms 56
royal ferns 35
rufous horneros 209
ruffs 203
Rüppell's vultures 158–159

S
sac fungi 26–27, 28–29
saki monkeys 240
salamanders 136–137
salmon 116–117
salmonella 15
saltwater fish 112–117
sandpipers 203
sapsuckers 181
sawfish 107
sawflies 102
sawsharks 107
scales 94, 112, 139, 142,
  156, 223
scallops 59

scavengers 79, 87, 147,
  221, 251
  birds 165, 182, 185, 186,
    205, 207
schools 118–119, 288
scorpions 72, 73
screamers 189
scutes 139
sea anemones 53, 114
sea cucumbers 66, 67
sea lettuces 21
sea lions 256–257
sea mice 57
sea pens 52, 53
sea potatoes 67
sea slugs 60–61
sea spiders 74–75
sea urchins 66, 67
sea whips 53
sea bream 114
seadragons 113
seahorses 113
seakraits 151
seals 256–257
seaweeds 20–21
secretary birds 183
seeds 38, 40, 47

dispersal (spreading) 31, 41, 43, 45, 46, 165

pollen 31, 38

pollinators 39, 40, 41, 100, 101, 102, 103

see also spores

self-defense *see* defenses

senses 13, 48, 81, 104

hearing 172, 216, 229, 272

see also smell, sight

sequoia trees 36–37

seriemas 201

setts 265

shags 197

sharks 106–109, 110–111

sheep 279

shelducks 188

shells 49

cases 52, 80

invertebrates 48, 58–61, 62, 65, 76

mammals 222

reptiles 140, 142, 143

single-celled life 16, 17

shire horses 273

shoebills 196

shrews 224–225

shrikes 210, 214–215

shrimp 78, 79

siamangs 236

sifakas 234

sight

amphibians 137

birds 203

fishes 109, 124

mammals 234, 244, 270, 289

see also eyes

silk moths 95

silk producers 70, 72–73, 95

silky anteaters 223

simians (primates) 234–235, 236–237, 240–241, 242–243

single celled life 14–15, 16–17

plankton 17, 18–19

siphonophores 52

size 19, 29, 111, 135, 248 *see also* height, length, weight

skates 106–107

skeletons 51, 52–53, 106, 112

bones 137, 158, 216, 244, 286

see also exoskeleton

skimmers 82–83

skin 49, 69, 115, 126, 131, 139, 192

mammals 216, 219, 236, 244

skinks 144, 145, 146

skunks 264

skylarks 213

sleep 177, 221, 223, 246, 278, 280

hibernation 153, 230, 246

sliders 140, 141

sloths 223

slow worms 146

slug moth caterpillars 98–99

slugs 60–61

smell

as defense 69, 85, 96, 153, 264, 267

for reproduction 25, 31, 279

senses 137, 148, 226, 244, 252, 271

snails 58–59, 61

snakes 139, 150–153, 154–155, 183, 266

snapper 114–115

snapping turtles 141

snowy owls 173

soles 117

solenodons 225

sound waves 246, 288, 289

sounds *see* calls

sparrows 210, 213

speed

birds 160, 171, 176, 183, 203

fishes 113

insects 97

mammals 219, 223, 232, 243, 250–251, 256, 260, 289

reptiles 149

sperm whales 291

spider monkeys 240, 241

spiders 48–49, 70–72, 74–75

spines 39, 40, 67, 105, 107, 116, 224

sponges 50–51

spoonbills 194–195

spores

fungal 22, 23, 24, 25, 26, 28, 29

plant 32, 33, 34

springboks 278

spruce trees 37

squid 64–65

squirrel monkeys 240

squirrels 230

staphylococcus 14–15

starfish 66, 67

stargazer lilies 30–31

starlings 212

stems 23, 30

stick insects 84–85

stilts 202–203

stingrays 106, 107

stings 49, 52, 53, 73, 102, 103, 116

stinkhorns 25

stoats 265

stomachs 121, 150, 276

stonefish 113

storks 194–195

streptococcus 15

sugar gliders 218, 219

Sumatran orangutans 237, 238–239

sun bears 253

sunbirds 208

swallows 212

swan mussels 61

swans 188, 189

swarms 55, 78, 86

swifts 177

T

tadpoles 127, 128, 129, 131, 132

tails 104, 107, 109, 145, 230, 240

talons 174

see also claws, pincers

tamanduas 223

tamarins 241

tapeworms 56

tapirs 270–271

tarantulas 48, 49, 70, 71

tarsiers 235

Tasmanian devils 221

teeth 106, 110, 115, 157

mammals 217, 230, 232, 281, 291

see also fangs, mouth

tegus 147

tench 122

tentacles 52, 53, 55, 65, 114, 225

terns 204–205

terrapins 140

territory 94, 241, 263, 274

Thai boxer praying mantises 90–91

thistles 40

thoraxes 81

thorn bugs 88

threatened species

amphibians 125

birds 169, 206

mammals 232, 239, 241, 270, 271, 285

plants 43

reptiles 149, 157

thrushes 213

ticks 72

tigers 216–217, 259

timber flies 101

tinamous 161

tinkerbirds 181

tits 209, 212–213

toadfish 113

toads 126–127, 128–129, 130, 131, 132, 133

todies 179

tokay geckos 147

tokoekas 160

toothed wracks 16

tongues 148, 220, 223, 253, 287

tortoises 139, 140, 141, 142–143

toucans 180, 181

tragopans 162–163

tree dragons 147

tree frogs 128, 133, 134–135

tree kangaroos 219

treehoppers 88–89

trees 36–37, 44–47

tropicbirds 196

trout 125

true bugs 88–89

truffles 27

trunks, elephant 226

trunks, tree 30

tulips 38–39

tuna 115

turacos 170, 171

turbot 116

turkey vultures 184

turkeys 162

turtle doves 164

turtles 139, 140–142

tusks 226, 227, 256, 280, 282, 290

U

uakaris 240

ural owls 172

urchins 65

V

vampire bats 244, 245

vaquitas 288

vase sponges 51

velvet worms 55

venomous animals
    fishes 107, 113, 116
    invertebrates 52, 54, 70
    mammals 225
    reptiles 150, 151, 154
    see also poisonous animals

venus flytraps 42–43

vipers 150, 151, 154–155

viscachas 233

voles 230

vultures 158–159, 182, 184–185, 186–187

W

waders 202–205

wagtails 212

wallabies 218

walnut trees 45

walrus 256

wapitis (elks) 283

warblers 209, 212

warm-blooded animals 115, 137, 152, 159, 216

warrens 228

warthogs 282–283

wasps 102, 103

water intake 28, 39, 33, 51, 126, 227, 284

water monitors 144

waxwings 212

weasels 265

weather systems 119

weeds 35, 40
    see also seaweed

weever fish 116

weevils 93

weights 25, 37, 62, 149, 151
    birds 175, 177, 201, 207
    large mammals 227, 237, 255, 273, 281, 283, 287, 289, 291, 293
    small mammals 218–219, 240–241, 269

wentletraps 58

weta 87

whale sharks 110–111

whales 288, 290–291, 292–293

whelks 59

whiskers 116, 218

whydahs 210

wigeons 188

wild turkeys 162

wildebeest 277

wings
    birds 161, 171, 174, 190, 196, 206
    insects 80, 86–87, 88–89, 92, 94, 100
    mammals 244

wingspan 95, 97, 169, 175, 184, 187, 195, 199, 207, 215, 245

wolves 251

wolverines 264–265

wombats 220

wood ducks 188

wood frogs 130, 131

woodcocks 203

woodpeckers 181

wood pigeons 164

working animals see domesticated animals

worms 48, 56–57

wrens 209, 212

wrynecks 181

Y

yaks 276

yellow-kneed sea spiders 74–75

yew trees 36–37

ylang-ylang trees 45

young
    birds 171, 175, 177
    fishes 116, 123
    insects 82, 83, 88
    mammals 218, 219, 224, 231, 238, 249, 253, 262, 269, 275, 281, 287, 293
    reptiles 141, 149, 155

Z

zebras 272, 274–275, 277

zooplankton 18–19

ACKNOWLEDGMENTS

THE SMITHSONIAN INSTITUTION:

Project Coordinator: Kealy Wilson

Smithsonian Enterprises:
Kealy Wilson, Product Development Manager
Ellen Nanney, Licensing Manager
Brigid Ferraro, Director of Licensing
Carol LeBlanc, Senior Vice President

Reviewers for the National Zoo: Donald Moore III, Director, Animal Care Sciences, Scott R. Derrickson, Deputy Director, Smithsonian Conservation Biology Institute, Ed Bronikowski, Senior Curator, Tony Barthel, Curator, Elephant Trails, Asia Trail, and Cheetah Conservation Station, Alan Peters, Curator, Invertebrate Exhibit & Pollinarium, Bob King, Curator, Primates, Steven Sarro, Curator, Small Mammal House, Jim Murphy, Curator, Reptile Discovery Center, Craig Saffoe, Curator, Great Cats, Kids' Farm and Andean Bears, Frank Clements, Park Manager, Horticulture, Stacey Tabellario, Animal Keeper, Asia Trail, Juan Rodriguez, Animal Keeper, Asia Trail, Gil Myers, Animal Keeper, Cheetah Conservation Station, Kate Volz, Animal Keeper, Cheetah Conservation Station, Mike Henley, Biologist, Invertebrate Exhibit & Pollinarium, Donna Stockton, Biologist, Invertebrate Exhibit & Pollinarium, Michael Miller, Animal Keeper, Invertebrate Exhibit & Pollinarium, Erin Stromberg, Animal Keeper, Primates, Kenton Kerns, Animal Keeper, Small Mammal House, David Kessler, Animal Keeper, Small Mammal House, Rebecca Smithson, Animal Keeper, Small Mammal House, Sara Hallager, Animal Keeper, Bird House, Hillary Colton, Animal Keeper, Bird House, Lori Smith, Animal Keeper, Bird House, Debi Talbott, Animal Keeper, Bird House, Kathleen Brader, Animal Keeper, Bird House, Gwendolyn Cooper, Animal Keeper, Bird House, Warren Lynch, Animal Keeper, Smithsonian Conservation Biology Institute, Budhan Pukazhenthi, Reproductive Physiologist, Smithsonian Conservation Biology Institute, Peter Marra, Research Ecologist, Smithsonian Migratory Bird Center, Pamela Baker-Masson, Director, Communications, Jennifer Zoon, Communications Assistant, and special thanks to Susie Ellis.

Reviewers for the National Museum of Natural History: Dr Don W Wilson, Curator Emeritus, Department of Vertebrate Zoology, Dr Carole C Baldwin, Curator of Fishes, Lynne R Parenti, Curator of Fishes and Research Scientist, G David Johnson, Ichthyologist/Curator, Division of Fishes, Carla J Dove, PhD, Feather Identification Lab.

DK would like to thank:
Katie John for text assistance, Alison Gardner, Sunita Gahir, Konica Juneja, Kanika Mittal, Divya PR, and Upasana Sharma for design assistance, Hedi Hunter for design styling, Lili Bryant, Neha Chaudhary, Megha Gupta, Nandini Gupta, Suefa Lee, Vineetha Mokkil, Yamuna Matheswaran, and Rupa Rao for editorial assistance, Kealy Wilson and Ellen Nanney from the Smithsonian Institution, Angela Baynham for proofreading, Elizabeth Wise for the index.

The publisher would like to thank the following for their kind permission to reproduce their photographs:

(Key: a-above; b-below/bottom; c-center; f-far; l-left; r-right; t-top)

1 **Fotolia:** He2 (ca). 3 **Fotolia:** He2 (ca). 5 **Science Photo Library:** Pasieka (tc). 6 **Dorling Kindersley:** Jeremy Hunt - modelmaker (cra). **Getty Images:** Joel Sartore (br). 8 **Science Photo Library:** CNRI (tl). 9 **Dorling Kindersley:** Natural History Museum, London (tr); Weymouth Sealife Centre (tl). **Getty Images:** Mint Images / Frans Lanting (bc). 10 **Dreamstime.com:** Isselee (cr). Science Photo Library: Pasieka (br). 11 **Alamy Images:** cbimages (bc). **Dorling Kindersley:** Jerry Young (cla). **FLPA:** Minden Pictures (clb). 12-13 **Science Photo Library:** 3d4medical.com (c). 14 **Alamy Images:** BSIP SA (c). CDC: (cl). **Corbis:** Visuals Unlimited (fcl). **Getty Images:** J. L. Carson (cla). **Science Photo Library:** CNRI (tl); Pasieka (tr); Professor N. Russell (fcr); A.B. Dowsett (br); Dr. Kari Lounatmaa (bc, cra). 15 **CDC:** (cla, cra). **Corbis:** Dennis Kunkel Microscopy, Inc. / Visuals Unlimited (cb). **Dorling Kindersley:** Uniformed Services University, Bethesda, MD (tl). **Science Photo Library:** Eye Of Science (c); SCIMAT (cl); Dr. Kari Lounatmaa (br). **USDA Agricultural Research Service:** Courtesy of USDA_ARS / Eric Erbe (tr). 17 **Photo Biopix. dk:** Jens Schou (cr). 20-21 **Science Photo Library:** Laguna Design. 26-27 **Getty Images:** Michael & Patricia Fogden. 27 **Dorling Kindersley:** Stephen Hayward (cr). 32 **Photo**

Biopix.dk: Jens Schou (ca). 33 **Photo Biopix.dk:** Jens Schou (br). 34 **Photo Biopix.dk:** Niels Sloth (bl). **Corbis:** Visuals Unlimited / William Ormerod (ca). **Dorling Kindersley:** Natural History Museum, London (cla). 35 **Photo Biopix.dk:** Jens schou (bc, cb, cl, cra, tr). **Getty Images:** Ed Reschke (br). **Science Photo Library:** Scott Camazine (bl). 38 **Dreamstime.com:** Gabriela Insuratelu (clb). 39 **Dorling Kindersley:** Neil Fletcher (clb). **Dreamstime.com:** Markit (c); Voltan1 (crb). 41 **Dreamstime.com:** Liumangtiger (cl). 42-43 **Dreamstime. com:** Marcouliana. 44 **Dreamstime.com:** WoodyStock (crb). 45 **Dreamstime.com:** Pehttt (cl). 46 **Dorling Kindersley:** Natural History Museum, London (ca). 47 **Dorling Kindersley:** Courtesy of Harry Tomlinson (c). **Getty Images:** 50-51 **Photoshot:** Laurie Campbell (c). 50 **Alamy Images:** VWpics / Ricardo Fernandez (clb). **FLPA:** (fclb). **Getty Images:** Age Fotostock / Marevision (cb, cl); Wolfgang Poelzer (tr); De Agostini Picture Library / DEA / P. Donnini (crb). **naturepl.com:** Jose B. Ruiz (ca). 51 **Alaska Fisheries Science Center, NOAA Fisheries Service:** (ftr). **Corbis:** Minden Pictures / Norbert Wu (tl); Visuals Unlimited / David Wrobel (c). **Getty Images:** Age Fotostock / Marevision (tr); Fotosearch Value (cr). 52 **FLPA:** Panda Photo (c). **Getty Images:** Fotosearch (br); Axel Rosenberg (c); Nature / UIG (fcrb). **naturepl.com:** Solvin Zankl (cl). 53 **Dorling Kindersley:** Natural History Museum, London (cra, tl). imagequestmarine.com: (tc). 54 **Ardea:** Steve Hopkin (c). **Corbis:** Minden Pictures / Fred Bavendam (c); Visuals Unlimited / Dr.. Robert Calentine (cb). naturepl.com: Sinclair Stammers (bl). **Photoshot:** ANT (tc). **Science Photo Library:** James H. Robinson (cla). 54-55 **Corbis:** Kerrick James. **FLPA:** D P Wilson (c). 55 **Alamy Images:** blickwinkel (cl). **FLPA:** Nigel Cattlin (cla). **Science Photo Library:** Dr. Morley Read (ca, tl). 59 **Getty Images:** Age Fotostock / Marevision (c). 60 **Getty Images:** Age Fotostock / Mary Jonilonis (br). **Science Photo Library:** Alexander Semenov (crb). 61 **FLPA:** Minden Pictures / Kevin Schafer (c); Walter Rohdich (tr). 62-63 **Corbis:** Science Faction / Norbert Wu. 64 **Corbis:** Visuals Unlimited (clb). **Dorling Kindersley:** Weymouth Sealife Centre (cb). **naturepl.com:** Sue Daly (c). **Science Photo Library:** Dante Fenolio (tr). 65 **Alamy Images:** Mike Veitch (clb). **Getty Images:** Photographer's Choice / Steven Hunt (tr); WaterFrame / Reinhard Dirscherl (ca). **Richard Ling:** (cl). **naturepl.com:** David Shale (tc). 66 **Corbis:** Minden Pictures / Fred Bavendam (bl). **Getty Images:** Botanica / James Baigrie (cl). 67 **Corbis:** Brandon D. Cole (c). Minden Pictures / Fred Bavendam (tr). **Getty Images:** Oxford Scientific / Karen Gowlett-Holmes (cra); Workbook Stock / Frederic Pacorel (c). 68 **FLPA:** David Hosking (clb). **Getty Images:** Flickr Open / Alan Cressler (crb); Visuals Unlimited, Inc. / Gerry Bishop (cl); Peter Arnold / James Gerholdt (bl). **naturepl.com:** Kim Taylor (tr). 69 **Alamy Images:** Leslie Garland Picture Library / Doug McCutcheon (ca). **Ardea:** Steve Hopkin (tr). **Corbis:** Minden Pictures / Thomas Marent (crb). **Dreamstime. com:** Milosluz (cb). **Getty Images:** Flickr Open / Shailesh Makwana (tr). 70 **Dreamstime.com:** Scott Harms (tr). **FLPA:** Olivier Digoit (cl). **Getty Images:** James H Robinson (cra). 71 **Corbis:** Steve Parish Publishing / Patrick Honan (cl). **Dorling Kindersley:** Geoff Brightling / Chris Reynolds and the BBC Team - modelmakers (bc). **FLPA:** Minden Pictures / Pete Oxford (cra). **Science Photo Library:** Simon D. Pollard (br). 72 **Corbis:** Science Faction / Stefan Sollfors (cla). **FLPA:** Photo Researchers (tc). **Getty Images:** Kallista Images (clb); Visuals Unlimited, Inc. / Robert Pickett (tr). 73 **Corbis:** Minden Pictures / Albert Lleal (bl). 74-75 OceanwideImages.com. 76 **Corbis:** Foto Natura / Minden Pictures / Stephen Belcher (bl); Minden Pictures / Fred Bavendam (cl). **Getty Images:** Visuals Unlimited, Inc. / Fabio Pupin (cl). imagequestmarine. com: (crb). 77 **Corbis:** Ocean (c). **Getty Images:** Age Fotostock / Marevision (c); (tr). 78 **Corbis:** Gary Bell (cl); Photocuisine / J. Garcia (tl); Design Pics / Dave Fleetham (bl). **Getty Images:** Visuals Unlimited / Gerald & Buff Corsi (bc). 79 **Dreamstime.com:** Olga Demchishina (cla). **FLPA:** Gerard Lacz (bc). imagequestmarine.com: (crb, tl). 83 Fotolia: Roque141 (tr). 84-85 **Dorling Kindersley:** Thomas Marent. 86-87 **FLPA:** Ingrid Visser (tc). 86 **FLPA:** Dave Pressland (c). **Getty Images:** AWL Images / William Gray (cla). **naturepl.com:** MYN / John Tiddy (bl); Ann & Steve Toon (br). 87 **Corbis:** Ocean (b); Damon Wilder (cra). **Dorling Kindersley:** Natural History Museum, London (cr). 88 **Corbis:** Minden Pictures / Ingo Arndt (cl); Visuals Unlimited / Alex Wild (br). **Dorling Kindersley:** Natural History Museum, London (b). 90-91 **Getty Images:** Adegsm. 92 **Dorling Kindersley:** Natural History Museum, London (cl, br); Jerry Young (ca). 93 **Dorling Kindersley:** Natural History Museum, London (cr). 94 **Dorling Kindersley:** Andrew Mackay (fcrb); Natural History

Museum, London (ftr, tc, tl, ftl, ca, cl, c, cr, fcr, clb, cb, crb, fbl, bl, bc, br). 95 **Dorling Kindersley:** Natural History Museum, London (tl, tc, tr, fcla, cla, ca, cra, fcra, cl, c, crb, cr, clb, fbl, bc, br, fbr). 96 **Dorling Kindersley:** Natural History Museum, London (tl, tc, cla, ca, cra, cl, c, cr, fcr, clb, cb, crb, fbl, bl, br, fbr). 97 **Dorling Kindersley:** Natural History Museum, London (tl, tc, cla, cr, cl, fclb, clb, crb, fcrb, cb, fbl, bl, br, fbr). 98-99 **Dorling Kindersley:** Thomas Marent. 99 **Dorling Kindersley:** Booth Museum of Natural History, Brighton (br). 100 **Alamy Images:** Premaphotos (fbr). **Dorling Kindersley:** Natural History Museum, London (bc); Jerry Young (tl). **Getty Images:** First Light / Grambo Grambo (cl). 101 **Corbis:** Minden Pictures / Stephen Dalton (bl). **Dorling Kindersley:** Natural History Museum, London (cl, br). **The Natural History Museum, London:** (tr). 102 **Dreamstime.com:** Dbmz (bc); Ryszard Laskowski (c); Meoita (cr). 103 **Dreamstime.com:** Amskad (tr). 106 **Corbis:** Minden Pictures / Pete Oxford (bl). **FLPA:** Norbert Wu (clb). **Getty Images:** Visuals Unlimited, Inc. / Andy Murch (cla). **Photoshot:** (ca, cl). 106-107 **Ardea:** Kenneth W Fink (tl). 107 **Alamy Images:** Stephen Frink Collection (c). **Corbis:** Visuals Unlimited / Patrice Ceisel (crb). **Getty Images:** Dr. Peter M Forster (b). 108 **Alamy Images:** Roberto Nistri (cr). **Getty Images:** Visuals Unlimited, Inc. / Andy Murch (tl, cl). 108-109 **Corbis:** Science Faction / Norbert Wu (bc). **Dorling Kindersley:** Jeremy Hunt—modelmaker (ca). 109 **Corbis:** Dave Fleetham / Design Pics (tl). **Getty Images:** De Agostini Picture Library (cb). 110-111 **Corbis:** National Geographic Society / Colin Parker. 112 **Dorling Kindersley:** Weymouth Sea Life Centre (ca). **Dreamstime.com:** Isselee (tr). 112-113 **Dreamstime.com:** Asther Lau Choon Siew (c). 113 **Alamy Images:** cbimages (cra). **Dorling Kindersley:** Weymouth Sea Life Centre (cb, c). **Dreamstime.com:** Peter Leahy (c). **Getty Images:** Marevision (crb). imagequestmarine.com: (bc). 114-115 **Alamy Images:** Emilio Ereza (bc). 115 **Dreamstime.com:** Lunamarina (br, cra). 116 **Dreamstime.com:** Andylid (bl); Serg_dibrova (tc). 117 **Corbis:** Dpa / Hinrich Baesemann (cr). **Dreamstime.com:** Yordan Rusev (crb). 118-119 **FLPA:** Imagebroker / Norbert Probst. 120 **Alamy Images:** Diarmuid Toman (c). 120 **Jón Baldur Hlíðberg (www.fauna.is):** (crb). **Corbis:** Visuals Unlimited / David Wrobel (cla). **naturepl.com:** David Shale (br); Doc White (bl). 121 **Alamy Images:** Roberto Nistri (bl). **FLPA:** Norbert Wu (c). **Getty Images:** Dan Kitwood (ca). **naturepl.com:** David Shale (cla, cra). 122 **Alamy Images:** Blickwinkel (bl). **Dorling Kindersley:** Jerry Young (c, fbl). **Getty Images:** DEA / A. Calegari (cb). 122-123 **Alamy Images:** Stocktrek Images / Michael Wood (bc). **Corbis:** Minden Pictures / Norbert Wu (tc). 123 **Alamy Images:** Blickwinkel (cra). **Dorling Kindersley:** Natural History Museum, London (tc); Linda Pitkin (tr). **Fotolia:** poco_bw (c). 124 **Dreamstime.com:** Stephan Pietzko (cla). **FLPA:** (cr). **Getty Images:** Ken Lucas (cla). 124-125 **FLPA:** OceanPhoto (bc). **Science Photo Library:** Tom Mchugh (c). 126-127 **SuperStock:** Chris Mattison / age fotostock. 128 **Photoshot:** James Carmichael Jr. (ca, bl). **Science Photo Library:** Dr..Morley Read (cla). 130 **Getty Images:** Photodisc / Life On White (cl); Purestock (clb). 131 **Corbis:** All Canada Photos / Jared Hobbs (crb). 132 **Corbis:** Minden Pictures / Piotr Naskrecki (tc). **Dreamstime.com:** Mgkuijpers (cr). **FLPA:** Imagebroker / Winfried Schäfer (clb); Photo Researchers (cra). **naturepl.com:** Michael D. Kern (bc). 133 **Corbis:** Minden Pictures / Stephen Dalton (c); Reuters / Jose Luis Saavedra (tc). **FLPA:** Minden Pictures / Michael & Patricia Fogden (cr); Minden Pictures / Piotr Naskrecki (ca). 134-135 **Getty Images:** Gail Shumway. 136 **FLPA:** Photo Researchers (tr). **naturepl. com:** Nature Production (bl). **Science Photo Library:** Dante Fenolio (c). 137 **Alamy Images:** Ladi Kirn (tr); Vibe Images / Jack Goldfarb (cr). **Corbis:** Minden Pictures / Pete Oxford (tl). **Dreamstime.com:** Jason P. Ross (br). **Getty Images:** Visuals Unlimited, Inc. / Michael Redmer (crb). **naturepl.com:** Barry Mansell (cra). **Science Photo Library:** E.R.Degginger (tr). 140-141 **Dreamstime.com:** Lloyd Luecke (tc). 140 **Corbis:** Minden Pictures / SA Team / Foto Natura (bl); David A. Northcott (crb). **Dorling Kindersley:** Jerry Young (br). **Dreamstime.com:** Amwu (tc). 141 **Corbis:** Visuals Unlimited / Michael Redmer (cb). **Dreamstime.com:** Peter Leahy (crb). **Getty Images:** Visuals Unlimited, Inc. / Michael Redmer (ca). 142 **Dreamstime.com:** Checco (crb). 143 **Getty Images:** Imagemore Co., Ltd. (cb). **Dorling Kindersley:** Jerry Young (cr, cl, br). **Dreamstime.com:** Amwu (cra). 145 **Alamy Images:** Searagen (br). **Dorling Kindersley:** Jerry Young (crb). 146 **Getty Images:** Mint Images / Frans Lanting (c). **Photoshot:** A.N.T. Photo Library (tc); Ken Griffiths (ca). 148-149 **Getty Images:** Cordier Sylvain. 150 **Alamy Images:** Michal Cerny (crb). **Corbis:** Auscape / Minden

Acknowledgments

Pictures / Jean-Paul Ferrero (cr); David Northcott (cla). **Dorling Kindersley:** Diego Reggianti (cra). 151 **FLPA:** Minden Pictures / Mitsuhiko Imamori (clb); Minden Pictures / Michael & Patricia Fogden (crb). **Getty Images:** Joel Sartore (tl). 154-155 **Getty Images:** Mark Kostich. 156 **Alamy Images:** Jan Csernoch (cb). **Dorling Kindersley:** Jerry Young (ca). **Dreamstime.com:** Nico Smit (bl). **Getty Images:** Minden Pictures / Mike Parry (cl). 156-157 **Photoshot:** Andrea & Antonella Ferrari (bc). 157 **Alamy Images:** Prisma Bildagentur AG/ Dani Carlo (cla). **Corbis:** Minden Pictures / Pete Oxford (clb); Minden Pictures / Luciano Candisani (crb). **Dreamstime.com:** Lukas Blazek (c). **Getty Images:** Age Fotostock / Morales (br). 160 **Alamy Images:** Holger Ehlers (br). **Corbis:** Eurasia Press / Steven Vidler (cr). **FLPA:** Minden Pictures / Tui De Roy (cra, bl). 161 **Alamy Images:** Images of Africa Photobank / David Keith Jones (c). **Dreamstime. com:** Tomas Pavelka (tr). **Getty Images:** Nigel Pavitt (tl). 162 **Corbis:** (ca); Kevin Schafer (cra). 163 **Dorling Kindersley:** Mike Lane (cr); Ian Montgomery (bc); Markus Varesvuo (clb); Jari Peltomaki (cl); Judd Patterson (cb); Brian E. Small (cla). **FLPA:** John Hawkins. 164 **Dorling Kindersley:** Tom Grey (cl); Brian E. Small (ftr). 165 **Alamy Images:** Genevieve Vallee (cla). **Corbis:** Martin Harvey (ca). **Dorling Kindersley:** Bob Steele (cra). **Martin B. Withers (cb). **Science Photo Library:** Michael Mccoy (tl). 168-169 **Corbis:** Minden Pictures / Pete Oxford. 169 **Alamy Images:** paul abbitt rml (bc). 170 **Alamy Images:** Regis Martin (cla). **Dorling Kindersley:** Brian E. Small (bc). **FLPA:** John Watkins (tl); Ignacio Yufera (clb). **Getty Images:** Nigel Pavitt (crb). 171 **Alamy Images:** Peter Fakler (tc). **Dorling Kindersley:** Brian E. Small (c). **Getty Images:** Jared Hobbs (br); J & C Sohns (cla). 172 **Dorling Kindersley:** Brian E. Small (cra, ca). 173 **Dorling Kindersley:** E. J. Peiker (crb); Bob Steele (cla, cl); Brian E. Small (fbr). **FLPA:** Ignacio Yufera (bl). 174-175 **Corbis:** All Canada Photos / Glenn Bartley. 176 **Dorling Kindersley:** Mike Danzenbaker (br); Robert Royse (fcr); Garth McElroy (fcl); Bob Steele (cb); Brian E. Small (fcra, cl); Brian E. Small (fcrb). **Getty Images:** Visuals Unlimited, Inc. / Glenn Bartley (clb). 177 **Alamy Images:** George Reszeter (cl). **Corbis:** Kevin Schafer (br). **Dorling Kindersley:** Mike Danzenbaker (c). **Getty Images:** Jay B. Adlersberg (cla). 178 **Corbis:** Winfried Wisniewski (crb). **FLPA:** Rolf Nussbaumer (tr). **Getty Images:** Matti Suopajärvi (cla). 179 **Corbis:** Minden Pictures / Foto Natura / Grzegorz Lesniewski (tl). **Dorling Kindersley:** Alan Murphy (crb). **FLPA:** Mark Sisson (tr). 180 **Fotolia:** Eduardo Rivero (cr). **Getty Images:** Kevin Schafer (cl). 181 **Dorling Kindersley:** Brian E. Small (crb). **Fotolia:** Impala (clb). **Getty Images:** CR Courson (tr). 184 **Dorling Kindersley:** The National Birds of Prey Centre, Gloucestershire (cl). 185 **Dorling Kindersley:** Chris Gomersall Photography (bl); The National Birds of Prey Centre, Gloucestershire (ca, cr). 186 **Dorling Kindersley:** The National Birds of Prey Centre, Gloucestershire (tl, cra, bc); Pert S. Weber (c). 186-187 **Corbis:** Minden Pictures / Gerry Ellis. 188 **Dorling Kindersley:** E. J. Peiker (cl); South of England Rare Breeds Centre, Ashford, Kent (tr); Markus Varesvuo (tc); Brian E. Small (tl, cra). 189 **Corbis:** All Canada Photos / Glenn Bartley (tc, tl). **Dorling Kindersley:** Garth McElroy (cra); Steve Young (br). 190 **Corbis:** Nick Rains (c). **Dreamstime.com:** Lukas Blazek (cr); Inaras (fcr); Nico Smit (tr); Olga Khoroshunova (br). **Getty Images:** Photographer's Choice RF / Frank Krahmer (cl). 191 **Corbis:** Galen Rowell (bc). **Dreamstime.com:** Gentoomultimedia (crb); Pu Sulan (tl). **FLPA:** Minden Pictures / Tui De Roy (br); Darrell Gulin (tr); Nigel Pavitt (bl). **Photoshot:** John Shaw (cr). 192-193 **Getty Images:** Mint Images / Frans Lanting. 194 **Corbis:** Joe McDonald (cr); Robert Harding World Imagery / Peter Barritt (cr). **Dorling Kindersley:** Chris Gomersall Photography (bc); Roger Tidman (br); David Cottridge (bl). 195 **Dorling Kindersley:** Brian E. Small (tc); Roger Tidman (cr). **Getty Images:** Josh Manring - JourneymanGallery.com—Travel Photographer (bc). 196 **Dorling Kindersley:** Brian E. Small (bl). FLPA: Minden Pictures / Tui De Roy (br); Tui De Roy (tr). **Fotolia:** Imagevixen (cra); Petergyure (br). 197 **Dorling Kindersley:** Judd Patterson (cb); Brian E. Small (crb, cl). **Dreamstime.com:** Worakit Sirijinda (br). **FLPA:** John Holmes (tr). **Fotolia:** CPJ Photography (cr); Impala (fcrb). **Getty Images:** Mint Images / Frans Lanting (ca). 198-199 **Corbis:** Theo Allofs (c). 200 **Corbis:** Eric and David Hosking (fcra); Minden Pictures / Foto Natura / Jasper Doest (c). **Dorling Kindersley:** Mike Lane (cra); Brian E. Small (tr, cra); Bob Steele (br). **Dreamstime.com:** Mirceax (bc). 201 **Corbis:** Frank Lukasseck (bc). **Dorling Kindersley:** Melvin Grey (bl). **naturepl.com:** Jose B. Ruiz (tr). 202 **Alamy Images:** Craig Ingram (cra). **Dorling Kindersley:** Robert Royse (ca); Bob Steele (br). **Getty Images:** Glenn Bartley (tr). 203 **Alamy Images:** Keith J. Smith (bc). **Dorling Kindersley:** Chris Gomersall Photography (ftl); Kevin T. Karlson (tl); Garth McElroy (cra); George McCarthy (cb). **FLPA:** Steve Young (bl). **Getty Images:** Dieter Schaefer (br). 204 **Dorling Kindersley:** Mike Danzenbaker (tr); Hanne and Jens Eriksson (ftl); Melvin Grey (tl); Brian E. Small (ftr); E. J.

Peiker (fcl); Mike Lane (c); Bob Steele (fcr, clb); Tomi Muukonen; Robert Royse (bl). **Dreamstime.com:** David Steele (bc). **FLPA:** IMAGEBROKER / INGO SCHULZ (br). 204-205 **FLPA:** Yossi Eshbol (ca). 205 **Dorling Kindersley:** E. J. Peiker (bc); Brian E. Small (crb); Bob Steele (bc). **Dreamstime.com:** Edurivero (tr). **FLPA:** Mike Lane (tl); James Lowen. 206-207 Corbis: Naturbild / Lars-Olof Johansson. 208 **Dorling Kindersley:** Brian E. Small (cra, fcr). **Dreamstime.com:** Foxyjoshi (tr); Susan Robinson (ca). **FLPA:** Imagebroker / Rolf Nussbaumer (clb). 209 **Corbis:** Frans Lemmens (ca). **Dorling Kindersley:** Robert Royse (cla); Brian E. Small (br, fbr). **FLPA:** David Hosking (cb); (cr). 210 **Dorling Kindersley:** Alan Murphy (ca); Jari Peltomaki (tc); Brian E. Small (ftr). **Dreamstime.com:** Rossco (tl). **FLPA:** Hugh Lansdown (fcra). **Getty Images:** Nacivet (fcrb); Roberta Olenick (crb). 211 **Dorling Kindersley:** Brian E. Small (ca). **Getty Images:** Vishdesh photography (cra). **Photoshot:** Marie Read (tl). 212 **Dorling Kindersley:** Garth McElroy (cb); Brian E. Small (tr, fcrb). **FLPA:** David Tipling (tc). 213 **Corbis:** Joe McDonald (cra). **Dorling Kindersley:** Chris Gomersall Photography (fclb); Brian E. Small (clb, bc). **FLPA:** Imagebroker / Rolf Nussbaumer (cb). 214-215 **Photoshot:** Dave Watts (c). 218 **Corbis:** Steve Parish Publishing (ca). **Dreamstime.com:** Brian Lasenby (cr). **FLPA:** Jurgen & Christine Sohns (crb); Martin B. Withers (cr, cb). 219 **Dorling Kindersley:** Ian Montgomery (crb). **Dreamstime.com:** Eastmanphoto (c). **FLPA:** Photo Researchers (cb); Eric Woods (tr). 220 **Corbis:** EPA / Julian Smith (tl); Minden Pictures / Auscape / Glen Threlfo (cra). **Dreamstime.com:** Marco Tomasini (ca). **FLPA:** Martin B. Withers (br). 221 **Alamy Images:** Gerry Pearce (tl). **Corbis:** Steve Kaufman (br). **FLPA:** Gerry Ellis (bl); Martin B. Withers (c, cl). 222 **Dorling Kindersley:** Jerry Young (cl). **Dreamstime.com:** Eastmanphoto (cr). **FLPA:** Imagebroker / Nico Stengert (cr). **Fotolia:** Eric Isselée (b). **Getty Images:** Tom Brakefield (crb). **naturepl.com:** Luiz Claudio Marigo (clb). 223 **Dorling Kindersley:** Greg and Yvonne Dean (tr). **Dreamstime.com:** Isselee (clb). **FLPA:** ImageBroker (cl); Minden Pictures / Kevin Schafer (tc); Frans Lanting (crb). **Getty Images:** Nigel Dennis (c). **Photoshot:** Gerald Cubitt (br); Jany Sauvanet (cb). 224 **Dorling Kindersley:** Rollin Verlinde (cb); Jerry Young (bl). **Dreamstime.com:** Martinsevcik (c); Naasrautenbach (crb). **FLPA:** David Hosking (cb); Konrad Wothe (tr); Minden Pictures / ZSSD (cl); S & D & K Maslowski (br). 224-225 **Photoshot:** Photo Researchers (c). 225 **Dorling Kindersley:** Rollin Verlinde (clb, bl, br). **Dreamstime.com:** Melinda Fawver (bc). **FLPA:** Biosphoto / Daniel Heuclin / B (tl); Biosphoto / Gregory Guida (tr); Panda Photo (c); S & D & K Maslowski (crb); Chris & Tilde Stuart (cb). **naturepl.com:** Nature Production (cra). 226-227 **stevebloom.com.** 228 **Dreamstime.com:** Samfoto (br). **naturepl.com:** Barry Mansell (c). 229 **Corbis:** Minden Pictures / Donald M. Jones (cra). **Dreamstime.com:** Rafael Angel Irusta Machin (tc); Peter.wey (c); Derrick Neill (br). **FLPA:** Martin B. Withers (tl). **Getty Images:** Purestock (bc). **Science Photo Library:** C.K. Lorenz (crb). 230 **Corbis:** Joe McDonald (c); Minden Pictures / Ch'ien Lee (tr). **Dorling Kindersley:** Rollin Verlinde (cb). **Dreamstime.com:** Isselee (cl, fcr). 231 **Dorling Kindersley:** Josef Hlasek (clb). **Dreamstime.com:** Docbombay (tr); Sergey Uryadnikov (bl). **FLPA:** Frank W. Lane (cb); Minden Pictures / Michael & Patricia Fogden (cra); S & D & K Maslowski (cla). Fotolia: Mgkuijpers (tl). **Getty Images:** David Campbell (ca); Peter Schoen (crb). 232 **Corbis:** Ocean (fbr). **Dreamstime.com:** Errlrc (bc); Isselee (cr). **Getty Images:** Steve Allen (fbl). 233 **Dreamstime.com:** Jarous (tl). **FLPA:** ImageBroker (cra). 234 **FLPA:** Bernd Rohrschneider (cla). **naturepl.com:** Pete Oxford (ca). 235 **Dorling Kindersley:** Thomas Marent (br). **Dreamstime.com:** Davthy (cb). **FLPA:** ImageBroker (bl); Minden Pictures / Chien Lee (tr); R & M Van Nostrand (c); Minden Pictures / Pete Oxford (clb); Minden Pictures / Konrad Wothe (clb); Chien Lee (ca). **Getty Images:** Mint Images (cr). **naturepl.com:** Jabruson (cl). 236 **Dorling Kindersley:** Courtesy of Twycross Zoo, Atherstone, Leicestershire (bc); Ian Montgomery (tr); Jerry Young (fcr). **Dreamstime.com:** Eric Gevaert (bl). **FLPA:** Minden Pictures / Thomas Marent (fcl); Jurgen & Christine Sohns (fcl). **naturepl.com:** Eric Baccega (cr); Bernard Castelein (cra). 237 **Dorling Kindersley:** Courtesy of Twycross Zoo, Atherstone, Leicestershire (bl). **FLPA:** Minden Pictures / Thomas Marent (br). **Getty Images:** Tom Brakefield (cl). 238-239 **Dorling Kindersley:** Thomas Marent. 240 **Alamy Images:** Amazon-Images (cb). **Corbis:** Minden Pictures / Thomas Marent (cb). **Dorling Kindersley:** Jerry Young (fcrb, bc). **Dreamstime.com:** Laurent Renault (fcr); Wojphoto (crb). **FLPA:** Jurgen & Christine Sohns (cra). 241 **Dorling Kindersley:** Exmoor Zoo, Devon (c); Jerry Young (crb). **FLPA:** Frans Lanting (t). Fotolia: Eric Isselée (br). 242-243 **Dreamstime.com:** Benjamin Schalkwijk (c). 242 **Corbis:** Minden Pictures / Thomas Marent (bl); Visuals Unlimited / Thomas Marent, (tr). **Dorling Kindersley:** Jerry Young (cl, br). **naturepl.com:** Suzi Eszterhas (bc). 243 **Alamy Images:** The Africa Image Library (bc). **Getty Images:** Comstock (ca). 244

Dorling Kindersley: Jerry Young (cr, cb, bc). **Science Photo Library:** Merlin Tuttle (bl). 245 **Dorling Kindersley:** Greg and Yvonne Dean (cla); Natural History Museum, London (cr). 246-247 **Dorling Kindersley:** Rollin Verlinde (c). 246 **FLPA:** Minden Pictures / Michael Durham (bl). 247 **Dorling Kindersley:** Rollin Verlinde (t, cl, bl); Jerry Young (tc). **Dreamstime.com:** Stevenrussellsmithphotos (cra). **Getty Images:** Kelley Miller (cr). **Science Photo Library:** B. G. Thomson (cb). 248-249 **Corbis:** Minden Pictures / Konrad Wothe. 250 **Dorling Kindersley:** Jerry Young (cl, crb, bc). **FLPA:** David Hosking (br); ImageBroker (bl). **Getty Images:** Tom Brakefield (cr). 251 **Dorling Kindersley:** Jerry Young (tc, cla, ca, cb, br, bl). 252-253 **Dreamstime.com:** Jens Klingebiel (c). 252 **Corbis:** Design Pics / Deb Garside (br). 253 **Dreamstime.com:** Mikhail Blajenov (bl); Petr Mašek (t). Fotolia: Wusuowei (br). 254-255 **Dreamstime.com:** Mirage3. 254 **Dreamstime.com:** Perseomedusa (c); Vladimir Seliverstov (bl). **FLPA:** Pete Oxford (tc). 256-257 **FLPA:** Gerard Lacz (tc). 257 **Dreamstime.com:** Africapics (bc); Brendan Van Son (br); Pablo Caridad (tr); Vladimir Melnik (cb); Ongm (c). 258 **Dreamstime.com:** Tom Brakefield (ca); Daniel J. Cox (t). **Dorling Kindersley:** Philip Dowell (bl). **Dreamstime.com:** Jeff Grabert (crb). 259 **Corbis:** Frank Lane Picture Agency / Terry Whittaker (c). **Dreamstime. com:** Lukas Blazek (ca); Isselee (bc). 260 **Dorling Kindersley:** Berlin Zoo (cr). **Dreamstime.com:** Lukas Blazek (bl). **Fotolia:** Sarah Cheriton-Jones (ca). 261 **Alamy Images:** Terry Whittaker (cr). **Corbis:** Ocean (c); Kevin Schafer (tc). **Dreamstime.com:** Rafael Angel Irusta Machin (cra); Outdoorsman (ca). 262-263 **FLPA:** Bernd Zoller / Imagebroker. 264-265 **Dreamstime.com:** Lukas Blazek (c). 264 **Dorling Kindersley:** Rollin Verlinde (clb). **Dreamstime.com:** Jeanninebryan (ca). **FLPA:** Mike Lane (br); L. Lee Rue (c). 265 **Dreamstime.com:** Meoita (c). **FLPA:** Silvestris Fotoservice (br); Minden Pictures (cra); W T Miller (ca). 266-267 **Getty Images:** Peter Chadwick (cb). 266 **Dorling Kindersley:** Marwell Zoological Park, Winchester (c). **FLPA:** Biosphoto / Patrice Correia (bl); Minden Pictures / Suzi Eszterhas (c); Martin B. Withers (cb); Philip Perry (bc). 267 **Alamy Images:** Arco Images GmbH (cl). **Corbis:** Reuters / China Photo (cb). **Dorling Kindersley:** Berlin Zoo (bc). **Dreamstime.com:** Lukas Blazek (tr); Smellme (bl). **FLPA:** Cyril Ruoso (cla). **naturepl.com:** Jabruson (cr). **Photoshot:** Gerald Cubitt (br); Nick Garbutt (c). 268-269 **Getty Images:** Thomas Dressler. 270-271 **Alamy Images:** Jeremy Cozannet (tc). **Dreamstime.com:** Susan Pettitt (bc). 270 **Dreamstime. com:** Pavel Cheiko (br); Judy Whitton (bl). 271 **Dreamstime.com:** Lukas Blazek (tc). 272 **Corbis:** Minden Pictures / Theo Allofs (cb). **Dreamstime.com:** Bahadir Yeniceri (cl). 273 **Dorling Kindersley:** Persimmon(Horse) belongs to Pat and Joanne Maxwell, Lodge Farm Arabian Stud, Oxon (br). **Dreamstime.com:** Tracie Grant (cr). 274-275 **Getty Images:** Ingram Publishing. 276 **Dreamstime.com:** F9photos (tr); Michael Flippo (cl); Isselee (c). 277 **Dreamstime.com:** Anankkml (tr); Isselee (bc); Efesan (fbr). **FLPA:** Michael Gore (cb); Martin B. Withers (clb); Ariadne Van Zandbergen (tc). 278 **Alamy Images:** Bill Gozansky (bl). **Corbis:** Visuals Unlimited / Adam Jones (cl). **FLPA:** David Hosking (br). **Getty Images:** Digital Vision (cla). **Photoshot:** Paul Brough (fcl). 279 **Dreamstime.com:** Mikhail Blajenov (tc); Frameangel (bc); Prillfoto (c); Robin Winkelman (fcl); Dragoneye (tr); Lukas Blazek (bl). **FLPA:** ImageBroker (bl). 280-281 **Corbis:** Reuters / HO / San Diego Zoo / Ken Bohn. 282 **Dorling Kindersley:** Rough Guides (c). **Dreamstime. com:** Scattoselvaggio (c). **Fotolia:** Anankkml (bl). 282-283 **Dreamstime.com:** Stephenmeese (c). 283 **Corbis:** Minden Pictures / Claus Meyer (tl); Minden Pictures / Thomas Marent (cr). **Dorling Kindersley:** Marwell Zoological Park, Winchester (cr). **Dreamstime. com:** Handsomepictures (tc); Tony Northrup (bc); Helen Panphiluva (br); Smellme (cb); Paul Schneider (tr). 284 **Corbis:** DLILLC (br). **Getty Images:** Fotosearch (bc). 285 **Alamy Images:** Paul Springett C. (tc). **Dreamstime.com:** Hasanugurlu (cla). **Fotolia:** StarJumper (bl). **Getty Images:** LatitudeStock / Patrick Ford (bc). 286-287 **FLPA:** Frans Lanting. 292-293 **Getty Images:** Watt Jim. 294-294 **Dorling Kindersley:** Philip Dowell (bl). 296 **Corbis:** Dennis Kunkel Microscopy, Inc. / Visuals Unlimited (tr). 300 **Dorling Kindersley:** Natural History Museum, London (tl). 302 **Dorling Kindersley:** Staab Studios / Geoff Brightling—modelmakers (tl)

Jacket images: *Front:* **Corbis:** The Food Passionates (crb); **Dorling Kindersley:** Natural History Museum, London (fclb); **Dreamstime.com:** Isselee (cra, cla); **Getty Images:** Mint Images / Frans Lanting (tr); *Back:* **Alamy Images:** Juniors Bildarchiv GmbH (clb), Life on white (cra); **Corbis:** Visuals Unlimited / Alex Wild (tc); **Dorling Kindersley:** Natural History Museum, London (ftl), Markus Varesvuo (ca), Weymouth Sea Life Centre (tl); **Dreamstime.com:** Isselee (tr, br); **Getty Images:** Tom Brakefield (cr); *Spine:* **Dreamstime.com:** Isselee (t)

All other images © Dorling Kindersley
For further information see: www.dkimages.com